Psychopathology and Differential Diagnosis
Volume One: History of Psychopathology

Personality, Psychopathology, and Psychotherapy:
Theoretical and Clinical Perspectives
Henry Kellerman, *Series Editor*

Psychopathology and Differential Diagnosis: A Primer

VOLUME ONE
History of Psychopathology

Henry Kellerman and *Anthony Burry*

COLUMBIA UNIVERSITY PRESS
NEW YORK

COLUMBIA UNIVERSITY PRESS
NEW YORK   GUILDFORD, SURREY

Copyright © 1988 Columbia University Press

LIBRARY OF CONGRESS
Library of Congress Cataloging-in-Publication Data

Kellerman, Henry.
  Psychopathology and differential diagnosis:
  a primer/Henry Kellerman and Anthony Burry.
    p.   cm.—(Personality, psychopathology, and psychotherapy:
  theoretical and clinical perspectives)
    Bibliography: v. 1, p.
    Includes index.
    Contents: v. 1. History of psychopathology.
    ISBN 0-231-06096-3 (set).
    ISBN 0-231-06702-X (v. 1).
    ISBN 0-231-06704-6 (v. 2)
    1. Psychology, Pathological—History.   I. Burry, Anthony.
  II. T   III. Series: Personality, psychopathology,
  and psychotherapy (New York, N.Y.)
    [DNLM: 1. Diagnosis, Differential.   2. Mental Disorders—
  diagnosis.   3. Psychopathology—history.   WM 100 K286p]
RC438.K44 1988   88-6120
616.89′09—dc19   CIP

Printed in the United States of America

Casebound editions of Columbia University Press books are Smyth-sewn
and are printed on permanent and durable acid-free paper

To the memory of my mother, Esther Kellerman

To my wife, Veena Burry

CONTENTS

PREFACE

This two-volume work, *Psychopathology and Differential Diagnosis: A Primer,* consists of an examination of salient themes of psychopathology and diagnosis as these themes evolved from the pre-Hippocratic era through the present. This presentation is followed in volume 2 by an examination of the diagnostic system currently utilized in *Diagnostic and Statistical Manual of Mental Disorders,* third edition *(DSM-III)* and revised third edition *(DSM-III-R),** as well as by consideration of diagnoses used clinically outside of the *DSM* nomenclature.

In this first volume, *History of Psychopathology,* two competing themes emerge regarding psychopathology and reverberate throughout history, shifting emphasis from one to the other, from era to era. The first conceptualization attributes causality in the development of psychopathology to both intrapersonal phenomena and interpersonal dynamics. The second major view, emerging as the central counterpoint to the first with respect to the causation of psychopathology, is the organic position. The organic or biological perspective holds that psychopathology in all its manifestations including treatment technologies is better informed by an understanding of heredity, psychopharmacological applications, and neurobiological events.

This debate regarding the etiology and genesis of psychopathology, and the gradual consolidation of the philosophical underpinnings of each of these positions as they developed throughout history, is the organizing framework of this first volume. In addition, the appearance, evolution, and usage of familiar diagnostic states such as anxiety, depression, hysteria, and psychosis are also traced in this first volume. Thus *History of Psychopathology* is not cast as a history of psychiatry. Rather, it is a dis-

---

DSM-III was published in 1980, *DSM-III-R* in 1987, by the American Psychiatric Association, Washington, D.C.

tillation of the history of psychopathology and diagnosis—in a sense sculpted from the overall history of psychiatry. It is intended that the analysis and presentation of the specific focus on psychopathology and classification that is considered in the first volume will secure a fuller appreciation of current classification systems such as those of *DSM-III* and *DSM-III-R* leading to *DSM-IV*, considered in volume 2.

The clinical material on psychopathology presented in volume 2 emphasizes not only symptom behavior but also etiology and underlying psychodynamics of aberrant functioning as well. In contrast, conventional manuals and texts on differential diagnosis emphasize categorization of diagnosis and are organized with reference to a few discriminating variables, such as reality testing, management of anxiety, and mood appropriateness. After reading such books, students in the mental health disciplines of psychology, psychiatry, social work, psychiatric nursing, rehabilitation psychiatry, and allied professions often develop a sense that psychopathology and differential diagnosis are separate aspects of the clinical field of abnormal psychology. The fact is, however, that differential diagnosis is actually a reflection of psychopathology; more specifically, differential diagnosis is an abstracted version of differential psychopathology.

This two-volume work proposes to maintain a single aim: to help students and professionals alike understand the point of congruence between diagnosis and psychopathology, and thus to see how psychopathological data are translated into diagnostic formulations. In addition, the two volumes taken together, and particularly this first volume, offer the reader an opportunity to appreciate how these diagnostic formulations have evolved from the broad philosophical and historical trends that have shaped clinical psychopathology. Such trends continue to influence the shifts in diagnostic conceptualization that emerge from contemporary debate, conflict, dissatisfaction with the state of the art, and desire to refine further the accuracy and effectiveness of clinical definitions.

In this volume, *History of Psychopathology*, the evolution of the understanding of psychopathology is traced from the rudimentary beginnings from which the concepts of personality, psychopathology, and diagnosis gradually developed. This progression is viewed through various eras up to the more contemporary conceptualizations involving complex theoretical formulations. These contemporary theories attempt to synthesize the essence of diagnosis as a fundamental condensation of a variety of psychopathologies within the broadly based template of personality.

Each of the six parts of this volume examines a particular era and tradition in the history of psychopathology. Some of these eras comprise several centuries, while others span considerably less time. Individual chapters are designed to assess a particular development in terms of its impact on the understanding and conceptualization of psychopathology. To that end, each chapter presents a distillation of an accomplishment within a given period regarding the development of knowledge that deepens awareness of psychopathology, its philosophical underpinnings, and psychological and/or biological assumptions. The volume offers convenient summaries and tables at the end of each chapter covering material regarding conceptions of psychopathology that correspond to the time period of the chapter. In addition, the text of the book is followed by a suggested reading list of source material.

In contrast to a typical history of psychiatry that presents the biographies of major contributors, *History of Psychopathology* attempts to create the history of the development of formulations of psychopathology through tracing the historical understanding of personality, diagnosis, and conceptions of psychopathology. Yet persons and theories intersect in the conceptual evolution of abnormal development, and historical figures are therefore presented throughout this book as well, although clearly within the context of the development of formulations of disturbances in personality functioning. The ideas of major investigators are selectively covered based upon their influence, both with respect to their cumulative effect on the broad field of research into the person and their lasting impact.

In Part 1, "Antiquity," the three-thousand-year-old roots of psychopathology and diagnosis are traced from the earliest literary and philosophic speculations through the ideas of the Greeks and Romans. During this period of antiquity, investigators were largely concerned with the locus of causative agents in mental distress. References to depression, suicide, and anxiety—to cite just a few states that were of clinical concern—were related to religion, demonology, and magic, and the causative theories of early investigators were focused on bodily humors and other mostly physical or external epicenters of possible etiology.

During the later stages of this overall period of antiquity, investigators shifted their focus toward the arena of personality and away from mere diagnostic labeling. This shift toward concern with personality implied that syndromes and aberrant phenomena were inextricably embedded within an individual's overall functioning. This emerging concept of overall personality would, in contemporary language, be called *character*.

Part 1 also examines the later stages of antiquity—the end of the Roman period—when investigators began to suggest that a particular configuration of personality or character depended upon the unique interface of a number of qualities, including the operation of emotions, the management of anxiety, intellectual functions, and behavior. Thus, in this first part of the book it becomes clear that by the advent of the Middle Ages, a vague yet discernible consensus was emerging that began, however tentatively, to draw connections between discrete phenomena of behavior and corresponding abstractions defining psychopathological diagnostic states. In addition, these seemingly separate domains of psychopathology and diagnosis were becoming understood in relation to the broader underlying tissue of personality—ultimately a unifying basis upon which to understand psychopathology.

Part 2, "The Middle Ages and the Renaissance," covers a long and complex period, from the fourth to the sixteenth century. During the early phase of this period, diagnostic trends effectively redirected the understanding of the causality of psychopathology toward the influence of external agents. Thus, a direct conflict arose between the medieval perspective and the focus during the Renaissance on the appreciation of existential phenomena. This conflict between belief in external causes—the power of demons, for example—and the idea that inner experience can be causative for psychopathology produced a variety of treatment methodologies for various forms of emotional distress; even in the absence of design, the conflict of ideas regarding causative factors created a great ferment in thinking.

Part 3, "The Modern World," analyzes the philosophical underpinnings of psychopathology from the seventeenth to the nineteenth century. During this era, the understanding of a host of aberrant behaviors referred to as psychopathological, and the diagnostic references to such behavior, became increasingly liberated from superstition. The use of observation in formulating diagnosis also became commonplace. Considerable consolidation was accomplished in the understanding of hysteria and in the formulation of psychosomatic phenomena. Thus, somatic phenomena were infused with psychological meaning. During this period, the triple axes of emotions, thoughts, and desires or needs were considered vital for any true understanding of personality.

But the Age of Enlightenment—the eighteenth century—also brought a resurgence of interest in the biological basis for mental distress. Therefore, what emerges historically in that period is a continual shift from one era to another regarding the causes of psychopathology, with a belief in biologically based causes alternating with an opposing belief—that the origin of aberrant behavior lies within the psychological realm. Contrasting treatment orientations—some involving concrete manipulations, versus others utilizing the influence of interpersonal behavior—corresponded with these theoretical shifts between biological and psychological etiology. It was also during this period of the seventeenth and eighteenth centuries that the range of disorders comprising neuroses and psychoses was considerably expanded.

This third part of the book also presents nineteenth-century orientations which reflected both widespread modern developments and another swing of the pendulum, back to a psychogenic explanation as central to psychopathology. At this time, even the role of sexuality in psychopathology became an arena of study, though a disputed one. Yet ultimately it was an era in which psychobiology prevailed, albeit with a healthy emphasis on the psychology of personality—especially with respect to understanding the emotions generally, and particularly the emotion of anger, specifically as this emotion applied to the deterioration of mental functioning.

Up to the nineteenth century, then, the arena consisting of diagnosis, psychopathology, and personality shared a trust in biological imperatives, but considered psychological approaches to understanding and treatment as perhaps more relevant to issues of psychopathology and especially to personality change. The psychological orientation surfaced as the one that investigators approached with compelling and even inexorable interest. In addition to producing a broad range of diagnostic constructs based on behavioral manifestations, the understanding of psychopathology was developing strong prerequisites regarding knowing the person more thoroughly. These prerequisites included some understanding of the person's emotions, some sense of the individual's defenses, a general appreciation of states of anxiety, measures of reality orientation relating to psychosis, and the integration of cognitive functions with emotional life.

The wide array of concepts that had developed by the late nineteenth century concerning diagnosis, psychopathology, and personality called for systems of parsimony to organize the accumulating plethora of data into understandable categories. Part 4 of *History of Psychopathology*, "Nosological Systems and the Appearance of Sigmund Freud," describes the organization of personality and psychopathology data in the form of nosological diagnostic systems. Of course, with the advent of Freudian and neo-Freudian systems, these diagnostic formulations became embedded in primary personality configurations from which psychopathology could be comprehended.

From the nosological system of Kraepelin and his systematization of psychosis, to the explication of neurotic states, the diagnostic systems proliferated along with knowledge of psychopathology and personality. It became clear that although Freudian theory created epigenetic imperatives, nevertheless psychoanalytic metapsychology steered the study of psychopathology, diagnosis, and personality away from a narrow biological and descriptive orientation and toward a psychological one. According to this approach, quite simply, the person could help himself. This psychological orientation also led investigators to the conclusion that despite the endless array of behaviors exhibited by people, there were perhaps only a few overall personality types.

This was a period during which typologies were developed and which an implicit biological substructure was assumed, which in turn generated particular personality classifications. Yet within this constraint of a given personality program, investigators were struggling to show that cultural adaptation and therapeutic experiences could triumph over biology and that people could change.

With the development of the typologies that are presented in part 5, "Typologies and Followers of Freud," a flowering of diagnostic concepts took place, and it became gradually clearer that diagnosis was essentially a shorthand synthesis of psychopathology. Freud's typology, especially with its focus on the development of psychosexual stages, related psychopathology and its differential diagnostic component to the crucial signal of anxiety. The state and nature of a person's anxiety clearly emerged at this point in the history of psychopathology as one of the single most telling diagnostic indicators of the vicissitudes of psychopathology. In fact, the typological systems within the theories of Horney and Fromm, as well as the work of Adler and Sullivan, considered an important component in the formation of personality to be the way in which anxiety was managed. This was also true for Erikson in his elaboration of the eight sequential stages of life, and later in the formulation of object relations theory and ego psychology.

Along with a focus on the vicissitudes of anxiety, the continuing debate as to whether personality is fundamentally biologically determined or is an adaptational and developmental phenomenon ushered in the era of ego psychology and object relations. With the construct of anxiety as a bridge, part 5, which describes how Freud and the followers of Freud developed theories and even ideologies around the issue of personality types, leads to the last part of the volume.

In part 6, "Contemporary Views: Ego Psychology and Object Relations," the ego psychologists are considered in their augmentation of the role of the ego in the formation of personality. Twentieth-century concepts of psychopathology, diagnosis, and personality are traced in the work of Freud, and following Freud, from the ego psychologists Hartmann, Mahler, Spitz, and Jacobson. Although the ego psychology developed by these authors is anchored in biology, nevertheless the failure of adaptation and consequent anxiety remains for them the key diagnostic indicator of psychopathology. The work of the ego psychologists has led to clearer explication of borderline and narcissistic states as well as depression, and the world of inner representations has also become profoundly central throughout the entire theoretical literature.

In addition, this last part of the book reviews the object relations school largely influenced by Melanie Klein. In this school, the management of anxiety is juxtaposed with the inner life of the infant, and a resulting kaleidescope reveals a complex of inner representations and relational issues developed further by the Kleinian followers Fairbairn, Guntrip, and Winnicott. New diagnostic considerations of paranoid, schizoid, and depressive orientations are reviewed. Finally, the work of Kohut and Kernberg is examined, showing how newer theories seem to help integrate developments in ego psychology—with its roots in biology and drives—with developments in object relations—with its focus on inner representations and early experiences between caretakers and infant. Object relations theory has already had a practical impact and has more or less permeated most treatment approaches.

Coexisting with the powerful effect that ego psychology, object relations theory, and self psychology have had on the understanding of diagnosis, psychopathology, and personality is the work involving bio/neuro/chemical effects of brain organization on behavior, thought, and feelings. This research into brain functions and pharmacology, racing ahead with investigations into the strictly biological bases of behavior, has its roots in the biological approach to understanding psychopathology also pointed out throughout this book. The newer work on brain function has not been incorporated into this volume, mostly because results are still being tested and will not be integrated into the understanding of psychopathological processes and diagnostic formulations for some time. Suffice it to say, however, that the brain/biology foundation that addresses the entire domain of personality seems to keep pace with the proliferation and considerable impact of psychological theories of personality.

The final chapter of *History of Psychopathology,* "Conclusion," reiterates the major theses heard throughout the volume, especially the philosophical counterpoint underlying the understanding of personality and its vicissitudes during the three-thousand-year history of psychopathology research.

It remains to be seen whether the most recent developments in the theory of personality will ultimately affect the diagnostic understanding of clinical syndromes. If the latest theoretical developments have a persistent influence, then diagnosis will continue to be the abstract, synthesized product of the variety of psychopathologies that it should be. With such integration between diagnosis and the theory of personality, psychopathology itself can be clearly understood to reflect the broader fabric of personality.

In volume 2, *The Diagnostic Primer,* this issue of closely tying diagnosis to personality theory—in contrast to treating diagnosis in a discrete, descriptive fashion—will be seen as the central issue in the grand design of keeping personality, psychopathology, and diagnosis thoroughly integrated.

ACKNOWLEDGMENTS

The authors take this opportunity to thank Theodore Halpern and Florence Eisenman for their careful and diligent typing of the manuscript. In addition, and as always, the library of the Postgraduate Center for Mental Health under the direction of Leona Mackler was an especially useful resource facility throughout the preparation of this book. We express our sincerest thanks to Ms. Mackler for her accessibility and her help in locating important citations as well as actual source material. We also extend our sincere appreciation to Elizabeth Sutton, Ann Miller, and Louise Waller of Columbia University Press, who were also always helpful throughout the production of this volume.

PART I
Antiquity

CHAPTER 1

Historical Roots of Psychopathology and Diagnosis

The earliest references to aberrant behavior are for the most part limited to its recognition and the attribution of its occurrence to supernatural interventions of a divine or demonic sort. Such references appear among numerous ancient peoples, including the Egyptians, Mesopotamians, Asian Indians, Chinese, and Hebrews. The Old Testament frequently alludes to madness, epilepsy, suicide, and depression among the many types of diagnostic entities recorded.

One of the problems that contributed to the difficulty the ancients had in analyzing and understanding psychopathology was the absence of the more contemporary proposition that the source of the aberrant behavior to be clarified resides within the individual. It has taken many efforts over centuries to be able to focus on the personal, rather than regarding an external phenomenon that inappropriately gets inside as the source of psychopathology. Yet, even in antiquity, some thinkers and philosophers found the idea of an intrinsic relation between psychopathology and personality compelling. For example, the Hebrews actually considered a "talking cure" for aberrant behavior, and they understood the essence of suggestibility and hypnosis in terms of misdirected attention. Of course, a dramatic precursor to twentieth-century psychodynamic understanding was the use of dream meaning by the Hebrews to clarify the forces of inner conflict. In addition, other ancient peoples such as the Egyptians recognized hysteria, and in the Far East—in China and India—personality characteristics were related to the influence of various parts of the anatomy. It was as though an irresistible urge to see the person as whole in mind and body compelled investigators to postulate that a correct balance between various elements, qualities, and anatomical parts was absolutely necessary for normal functioning and mental health. In spite of some views that psychopathological conflicts might be internal, by far the major means of accounting for mental disorder and aberrant behavior during antiquity was through the influence of external agents. These external agents, identified with deities or demons, were viewed as intruding on an individual's functioning; thus, supernatural forces were considered the cause of aberrant and inappropriate behavior.

While ancient references to psychopathology and expressions of concern about it surface in a variety of sources, it is the development by ancient Greek philosophers of an organized conception outside of the supernatural and the attempts by later Greeks at scientific study that generated the first realistic, nonmagical approaches to the understanding of psychopathology. This concern with mental health led to the first attempts to clarify the nature of psychopathology and to differentiate its varied types, as part of the development of a rational approach to the understanding of emotional disorders. Such concern with a rational approach to understanding psychopathology also led to subsequent efforts to formulate a diagnostic system—that is, a code or shorthand for presenting this psychopathology. Since dramatic progress toward such codification was made by the ancient Greeks, the transition from Greek supernatural thought to a rational understanding of psychopathology will be traced.

EARLY GREEK SUPERNATURAL VIEWS OF PSYCHOPATHOLOGY

The earliest Greek references to madness related its advent to gods or demons who caused unusual behavior and were identified as the source of irrationality. Divine intervention as the basis for disordered behavior and thinking is alluded to frequently in the epic poems of Homer. For example, in Homer's *Odyssey*, when Penelope is first told of the return of Odysseus by her faithful nurse, she responds:

Dear nurse, the gods have made thee mad, they who can make fool-
ish even one who is full wise, and set the simple-minded in the paths
of understanding; it is they that have marred thy wits, though here-
tofore thou wast sound of mind.*

Another instance in which the gods are cited as the external source
of madness occurs in Homer's *Iliad,* when conflict divides Agamemnon and Achilles. Agamemnon's account of his actions spec-
ifies the influence of the gods; he externalizes the source of his
irrationality, an explanation that is not questioned, though Agamemnon is still required to make up for the damage he has done.
Throughout Homer's work, external agents are shown as acting
on people in all sorts of ways to affect mental changes. These influences are passively received by the characters, but they bring
about such results as madness, expansiveness, despair, and even
blindness. A considerable range of experience is accounted for in
such a supernatural manner.

This conceptualization of madness with respect to the supernatural constitutes a primitive diagnostic statement. Even today,
extremely disoriented persons tend to view their own irrationality
in much the same manner in which it is portrayed in Homer's works
and in other prescientific representations of archaic mental construction. This tendency to attribute inner states to supernatural
explanations can be seen in contemporary paranoid subjects who
justify their irrationality with the disclaimer that "God told me to
do it," or "the devil made me do it." As an explanation of an
irrational act, the modern expression "I don't know what got into
me" also attributes motivation to an external agent. Such conceptualizations, ancient and modern, implying supernatural or unknown forces at work, represent an effort to localize psychopathology and irrationality as well as personal discomfort in a source
external to the individual.

The discovery of psychological principles that would permit
greater understanding of irrational behavior involved continuous
efforts to eclipse more irrational explanations. Ultimately, the appearance of delusions, hallucinations, and overall irrationality was
no longer attributed to external agents. In contemporary understanding, the mechanisms of repression, displacement, introjec-

Homer, *The Odyssey*. A. T. Murray, tr. (Cambridge, Mass.: Harvard University Press,
1946), 2: 375.

tion, acting-out, depersonalization, suppression of anger, and projection are some of the psychological phenomena brought to bear
in explaining irrationality. These are the kinds of concepts—hypothetical constructs as it were—that are utilized in modern psychology to analyze irrationality.

In addition, contemporary understanding of psychopathology is
also concerned with precipitating events; that is, with what hap-
pened to set off irrational behavior. For early, prescientific people,
it was sufficient that some external agent insinuated itself into and
pervaded the personality. In contemporary understanding, the relationship to another person, repressed anger at some incident, or
even the inability to face an event are some of the probable causes
that precipitate the process ultimately leading to an irrational act.
According to contemporary psychological understanding, "the devil
who made me do it" of the early, prerational Greeks would simply
be an unknown or unacknowledged aspect of the self, such as one's
repressed anger.

In the psychology of Homer's age, just as psychological disturbance was traced to external sources, the therapy for mental distress was similarly identified with an external substance. The external agents might include food, wine, or special drugs ingested
to reduce anxiety and mental discomfort. Prayers or the communication of well-chosen myths might also be used as external curative agents, presented so as to help the suffering person recover.
In other prescientific societies, the treatments for emotional distress also utilized efforts to expel the supposed supernatural visitation through prayer or magic. In ancient Greece, this approach
of relying on external sources for cure formed the basis for the
cult of Asclepius, the Greek god of healing, in which cures for both
physical and emotional disturbances were effected through magical and divine interventions.

A good example of such an irrational tradition is seen in this
cult of Asclepius, in which priests utilized their influence to induce
temple dreams. In these dreams, divine visitations were supposed
to occur, allowing for a curative experience for suffering patients.
While more purely physical ailments were of central concern to
the Asclepiads, problems of infertility, impotence, impaired sexual
fulfillment, and other conditions with sexual implications frequently appeared. The beauty of the temple settings, the encour-
agement and suggestive messages given to patients, the curative

reputation of the priests, and the testimonials of former patients must have all played a part in inspiring physical cures and psychological readjustment.

Within the prerational tradition, there nevertheless existed the rudiments of more advanced conceptual consistencies involving psychopathology and even treatment. Furthermore, the early supernatural orientation itself implied that abnormality, whether psychological or physical, is fundamentally acquired rather than genetic or inherited. The Homeric and early Greek representations of psychopathology and treatment reveal that even though the emphasis was magical and supernatural, efforts were nevertheless being made to go beyond merely describing or labeling psychopathology; these early Greeks implicitly introduced a point of view that offered a way in which aberrant behavior could be understood, dealt with, and treated. Their efforts included hypothesizing the incorporation of external agents as the cause of abnormal functioning, and utilizing particular external substances and influences—words, prayers, drugs, wine, induced dreams, and so forth—as curative countermeasures.

The major point that emerges from the early Greek views about the formation of emotional disturbance is that their conceptualizations required speculation about the connection of diagnosis to treatment, and this diagnosis-treatment linkage embodied a loosely defined metatheoretical system. Thus, the early Greeks considered mere description of disease manifestation insufficient for the purposes of understanding the nature of the disease and how best to modify it. What was needed to accomplish this higher-order goal—to diagnose in order to treat—were concepts that would deal with what was beneath the manifest, visible surface. These concepts relating to processes beneath the surface encompassed the invisible factors that involved the etiology itself. In this respect, subtle relationship features were largely unwittingly incorporated within treatment efforts. These relationship elements corresponded to the care, suggestion, and reputation associated with therapeutic procedures and substances, and to the healers recommending and administering these regimens. The prescientific, loosely defined, and vaguely conceived etiological diagnostic speculations set the stage for the activity of early Greek philosophers who sought to determine the components of pathology in more rational, material, and testable forms.

THE TRANSITION TO NATURAL
PERSPECTIVES TOWARD
PSYCHOPATHOLOGY

A major precursor to the development of a science of psychopathology and its diagnosis was Pythagoras, a pivotal Greek philosopher of the sixth century B.C. Pythagoras presented the idea
that the brain is the essential organ of man's intellect and the site
of mental illness. Some of his contemporaries actually experi-
mented with the brains of animals and related the brain to sensory
experiences. At this time the idea of humors was brought to bear
on overall questions of the appearance of aberrant behavior and
diseases. Humors were regarded as internal substances that were
associated with specific qualities. The conception of the manner
in which these internal substances influenced behavior and even
caused psychopathology involved an emphasis on a balance of
qualities necessary for health. Conversely, an imbalance of these
qualities was associated with disease. The equation used concerned
qualities such as moisture, dryness, hot and cold, and so on. Illness
comes about directly, it was conjectured, through an imbalance of
this equation, while health, on the other hand, reflects the pro-
portionate mixture of all the qualities.

Among the diseases considered during this period were disturbances of temperament. It was this idea, however faint, of a disturbance in temperament that first brought attention to the concept of differential psychopathology and differential diagnosis.
Furthermore, the consideration given to powers or qualities associated with externals (heat, cold, moisture, dryness) as well as
the localization within blood and brain, reveals the beginning of
a transformation from the idea of external causality to an internal
localization of disturbance; the cause of pathology was now on
the inside. In addition, the idea that equilibrium is needed among
different internal humors and their associated qualities which correspond to external manifestations in temperament and well-being
suggests a theoretical outlook regarding balanced functioning, as
well as the idea that aberrant behavior is associated with a shift
toward some imbalance.

Enlarging on the equation of substances, Empedocles, a fifth
century B.C. Greek philosopher, elaborated a theory of the cosmos

as composed of four elements. These four fundamental elements of nature were fire, earth, water, and air, and the attraction and separation of elements were attributed to principles of *love* and *strife,* in a remarkable early foreshadowing of Freud's instinctual polarities. It remained for the Greek physician Hippocrates to apply all of these early concepts regarding disease, basic elements, and qualities to the rigorous study of bodily and mental functioning and to the understanding, diagnosis, and treatment of disease, including psychopathology.

These early Greek philosophers and pre-Hippocratics made progress toward localizing disorder and disturbance within the individual instead of viewing it as an external visitation or influence. In keeping with this increasingly prominent view of internal factors as affecting mental and emotional functioning was a developing notion of the importance of psychological factors, related to the Hebrew focus on the meaning of dreams. These pre-Hippocratics asserted that dreams reflected internal, individual phenomena and were not the product of visitations or activities outside the individual. This step toward a rational view of psychological functioning is again a remarkable forshadowing, by 2,400 years, of Freud's demonstration of the proposition that the dream reflects only the individual dreamer.

The following chapter will examine the progress in thinking about psychopathology made by Hippocrates, who brought further order to the evolving conceptions of personality, psychopathology, and diagnosis.

SUMMARY OF DIAGNOSTIC FORMULATIONS

During antiquity, and especially during the period designated as pre-Hippocratic, the salient theme with which philosophers struggled was the locus and nature of causative variables in mental distress. Gradually, the localization of cause began to shift from external sources to internal ones. Table 1.1 shows some of the diagnostic formulations used during this period.

TABLE 1.1: Diagnostic Formulations of the Pre-Hippocratics

Diagnostic References

madness	hysteria
epilepsy	impotence
suicide	infertility
depression	anxiety

Curative agents

prayer	mythology
storytelling	wine
magic	drugs
suggestion	

*Shift from Supernatural to Natural and Internal Causes
of Psychopathology*

- Balance and imbalance of elements—fire, earth, air, and water—attributed to forces of love and strife.
- Balance and imbalance of qualities—moist-dry, hot-cold, bitter-sweet—regarded as etiological factors affecting blood and brain.
- Humors seen as basis for disease and psychopathology.
- Brain seen as essential organ of intellect and site of mental illness.

CHAPTER 2

Hippocrates: The First Classifier

As the father of a largely rational approach to medicine which included considerations of psychopathology and mental functioning, Hippocrates amalgamated the trends described in chapter 1 during the fifth and fourth centuries B.C. He and his followers utilized a model based on humors and organs to account for diseases and personality dispositions and to make treatment recommendations. In this model, causes for health and disorder were clearly localized within the individual. In the sphere of mental functioning, alterations in the qualities of the body were related, through their influence on the brain, to effects on behavior and mood.

The theory developed by Hippocrates encompassed four humors of the body—blood, phlegm, yellow bile, and black bile—as the basis for disease. Each humor was associated with a quality—blood with heat, phlegm with dryness, yellow bile with moisture, and black bile with cold. Disease resulted from an imbalance in the humors, and implicit in the theory was the idea that disease could be cured by the administration of the quality opposite to that of the deficient humor. In addition, other regimens and substances could be introduced to restore balance by altering blockages in the operation of humors or their qualities.

This formulation of a correlation between internal states and corresponding external properties represented an attempt to understand aberrant behavior on the basis of underlying inferential constructs; this was the major focus of attempts at diagnosis. Clearly, it was believed that the pursuit of diagnostic findings only became a relevant endeavor when the underlying nature of the disease could be understood. Thus, the singular purpose of diagnosis was treatment. Mere description of a disturbance was considered insufficient and incomplete in the Hippocratic approach to diagnosis. Rather, what emerged as central was the clarification of underlying disease phenomena that could presumably enable a corrective treatment design.

In understanding bodily phenomena associated with abnormality and disease, the Hippocratics considered the activity of various organs of the body and their connecting channels, as well as the activity of the brain, to be crucial. Any imbalance in a quality associated with a humor affected the head or brain. Disturbance resulted either because an excess of one of the qualities was directly influencing the brain, or because a humor had entered an inappropriate channel, blocking the flow of air to the brain. Air was considered necessary as a conveyer of intelligence to the brain; phlegm could cool and interfere with its flow, while blood could warm and promote its passage. As can be seen, the brain was regarded as highly significant in mental illnesses by the Hippocratics and was considered pivotal for mental phenomena in general.

The pre-Hippocratic philosophers had established a tendency to focus on internal states in their final formulations of diagnosis and treatment, an approach which Hippocrates then elaborated. But Hippocrates also stressed the vast importance of careful and systematic observation of behavior in understanding disease processes, relying heavily upon description of phenomena that could be scrutinized. The development of this technique of focusing on observables minimized interpretation of disease as a function of demonic or divine etiology; it undermined the magical and primitive ideas—including treatment regimens administered by priestly cults—adhered to in rival medical and supernatural orientations. Hippocrates' approach formed the basis instead for a rational, realistic, scientific evaluation of psychologically aberrant behavior as well as of medical diseases.

Thus, the early Greek philosophers transformed the study of pathological processes, moving from a preoccupation with the irrational toward a rational understanding consistent with modern scientific endeavor. The great legacy of the pre-Hippocratic Greek philosophers, with their internal focus, and of the Hippocratics, with their medical model, was to shift the conception of pathology and treatment from the primitive toward the scientific. Obviously, the delineation of humors and other somatic constructs as the basis for psychopathology is itself transitional between what is excessively inferential and based upon limited knowledge, and the metapsychological constructs utilized in modern psychology.

It can be argued that there is a degree of continuity between the ancient concerns with humors and modern conceptions such as id, ego, and superego as hypothetical constructs. Today, however, efforts are made to link theoretical constructs with observables such as specific environmental pressures, characteristic patterns of parent-child relationships, and developmental events, and to relate the theoretical constructs linked to observables with specific aberrant behaviors. These newer conceptions of causation should be considered scientific refinements that advance contemporary use of constructs and metatheory beyond what was possible for the early philosophers and prescientists, who nevertheless paved the way for a more rigorous approach to theory through a more refined observational emphasis.

Whatever bias may exist today, over two thousand years later, toward accepting descriptive nosology and rejecting metapsychological interpretation in the diagnostic codification may perhaps be traced back to the Hippocratic emphasis on description. But in contemporary metatheorizing, the underlying constructs comprise such factors as object relations, environmental influences on development, the organization of emotions, character trait formation, and the entire psychological impact of such events on the person. To continue to minimize metainterpretation as though humors were still the underlying reference events places a solely descriptive constraint on diagnostic nosology. In contemporary methodology, unfortunately, etiological richness is perhaps all too often sacrificed to an over-adherence to pure description in differential diagnosis.

Interestingly enough, in contemporary psychiatry an emphasis is developing on the exclusive role of somatic entities in psychopathology such as neural synapse phenomena, hormonal activity, and other chemical and physiological substrates of behavior and emotion. Similarly, in contemporary psychology, an emphasis has grown in recent years on the behavioral approach to the diagnosis of psychopathology and its treatment. In both cases, metapsychological interpretation is effectively bypassed and considered rather irrelevant. Examination of currently accepted diagnostic nosologies, such as those of *DSM-III* and *DSM-III-R*, leading to *DSM-IV*, will show the influence of these contemporary trends. Yet whether metapsychological interpretation should in fact be ignored in diagnostic formulations is a serious issue which has by no means been settled. The need to go beyond a descriptive nosology and its usefulness in differential diagnosis and treatment planning will be addressed in volume 2, *The Diagnostic Primer.*

EARLY FORMULATIONS
OF PSYCHOPATHOLOGY

Although Hippocrates also advocated description as part of the fabric of diagnosis, he certainly was not opposed to metainterpretation and in fact simultaneously emphasized it. Nevertheless, his focus remained on the bodily and the material. Hippocrates accomplished an amalgamation of the fragmented theories of earlier philosophers; in addition, he emphasized bedside observation in his determination to explain diseases on a natural basis. For example, he believed that those who viewed epilepsy as connected to a deity revealed a lack of interest in rational causation; they avoided responsibility for their inability to cure by basing their approach on religion instead of on empirical scientific principles. In contrast, Hippocrates stressed that epilepsy was caused by a specific disease of the brain.

With regard to psychological functioning, Hippocrates emphasized the brain as the central source of emotion, thoughts, and intelligence. A powerful statement of his indicates how closely he associated the brain with a wide range of psychological phenomena:

> Men ought to know that from the brain, and from the brain only, arise our pleasures, joys, laughter and jests, as well as our sorrows, pains, griefs and tears. Through it, in particular, we think, see, hear, and distinguish the ugly from the beautiful, the bad from the good, the pleasant from the unpleasant. . . . It is the same thing which makes us mad or delirious, inspires us with dread and fear, whether by night or by day, brings sleeplesness, inopportune mistakes, aimless anxieties, absentmindedness, and acts that are contrary to habit. These things that we suffer all come from the brain, when it is not healthy, but becomes abnormally hot, cold, moist, or dry.*

The Hippocratics provided the first descriptions of delirium as deriving from toxic reactions and also offered a cogent description of depression or melancholia as a symptom. For example, one de-

---

*Hippocrates, *On the Sacred Disease* (London: Loeb Classical Library, 1932), p. 175.

scription of delirium elaborates its underlying cause as being bile settling in the head, from which the observable impairment of acute hearing and vision and reports of pain in the temples are derived. The patient is further described as picking at his clothing, imagining that lice are crawling on them, thinking that he sees other creeping animals, that he sees armed men fighting, and as imagining himself fighting among them. The patient is additionally said to shout about battles and wars and to get up and threaten anyone who does not allow him to continue. Last, it is noted that the patient awakens from sleep in a startled way; he is terrified and is clearly reacting to frightening dreams.

This report describes sensory impairments, disorientation, hallucinations, and sleep terrors—a cluster of disturbances consistent with the syndrome associated with delirium tremens arising from withdrawal from alcohol. Systematic observations, detailed description of abnormalities, and specification of the underlying bodily cause are presented, including the implication of liver involvement, and treatment and preventative regimens are later offered. Other mental disturbances delineated by the Hippocratics include postpartum psychoses, phobias, and hysteria, all carefully described and differentiated. In fact, the Hippocratic recommendation of marriage and intercourse in the treatment of hysterical symptoms such as shortness of breath and unusual body pains in sexual areas implies an inclination toward regarding sexuality as a factor in the underlying etiology of this diagnosis. However, the Hippocratic belief in the sexual component of hysteria was dogmatic in its reference to a physical basis for the disorder. Hysteria was actually held to be the result of the womb having moved from its normal position. Thus, hysteria was regarded as virtually exclusive to women, and further, it was considered most prevalent in virgins or widows, women deprived of sexual intercourse. Consequently, the recommendation of intercourse as a treatment modality was based on the physiological conception of psychopathology.

Several implications can be noted concerning the differentiations introduced into psychopathology by Hippocrates. On the one hand, the emphasis on a physical basis for psychological phenomena limited the achievement of both diagnostic and treatment sophistication. On the other hand, however, the development of discriminations between psychopathological states such as phobia, hysteria, psychosis, organicity, and toxicity reveals that the respective domains of psychopathology and differential diagnosis were originally a unitary field within the study of abnormal psychology, and that diagnosis gradually emerged as a code for various types of aberrant behavior. This code contained a deep structure that included aspects of pathological process, considerations for treatment, etiology, and indications for outcome. At this early point in the history of diagnosis, its deep structure was composed of an attempt to interpret as well as to describe.

THE FIRST DIAGNOSTIC CLASSIFICATION OF PSYCHOPATHOLOGY

The first formal classification of aberrant behavior was offered by the Hippocratics. This classification included differentiation between mania, epilepsy, melancholia, and paranoia. Efforts to construe temperaments or personality types in terms of the theory of humors led to differentiated characterizations of individuals based on which humor predominated. A phlegmatic disposition, that characterizing lethargic and apathetic individuals, was originally believed to be based on the predominance of the phlegm humor; the melancholic propensity for sadness, sorrow, and depression, on an excess of black bile; the sanguine temperament, in which cheerfulness and optimism were outstanding, on an excess of blood humor; and the choleric or angry temperament, on an excess of yellow bile. It is interesting to note that the ancient Chinese also believed that there were four basic emotions—anger, happiness, sorrow, and fear—which they related to stimulation of the liver, heart, lungs, and kidneys respectively. Of course, contemporary usage has dropped these humor and organ underpinnings, but not the importance of temperament. The term *phlegmatic,* for example, still describes a person with a lethargic demeanor, as the Hippocratic tradition is now encoded in language.

In reviewing this history of Hippocratic contributions it is apparent that Hippocrates and the early Greek philosophers sought to utilize their era's ideas about basic elements and qualities associated with bodily functioning in their efforts to develop a rational approach to the study of psychopathology and its differential diagnosis. Developments in early Greek medicine, psychopathology, prephysics, and philosophy had close connections; the view of the cosmos as composed of four basic elements had many derivatives, including psychological temperaments. Table 2.1 is a synthesis and distillation of the contributions of early investigators in a variety of fields. The four basic elements of matter proposed by cosmological philosophers were related to the four qualities that the medical practitioners connected to the four humors of the body. Furthermore, each humor was not only associated with a characteristic quality, but also with a specific bodily organ. Finally, a personality temperament was identified with a predominance of each one of the humors.

This idea of basic elements is also the first representation of the understanding of personality differences based upon typologies. At this stage, the typological view of personality was an absolutist view of the personality of the subject; it did not consider the effect of the observer or interactive object on the subject. The following chapter will describe the introduction of the consideration of interpersonal phenomena and interactive influences between subject and object into analysis of personality, psychopathology, and diagnosis by examining the contributions of the later Greek philosophers.

SUMMARY OF DIAGNOSTIC FORMULATIONS

Taken together, the pre-Hippocratics and Hippocrates and his students had already formulated a small diagnostic grouping. Their formulations included references to and a focus on:

depression	delirium	postpartum psychosis
suicide	melancholia	paranoia (mental deterioration)
madness	phobia	phlegmatic, melancholic,
epilepsy	hysteria	sanguine, and choleric
impotence	mania	dispositions
	(excitement)	

From a contemporary perspective, these diagnostic formulations break down roughly into two clusters. The first centers on *depression;* it is represented by conditions variably labeled depression, suicide, impotence, melancholia, and postpartum psychosis, and by the melancholic and phlegmatic dispositions. The second grouping focuses on *excitement,* and is represented by conditions labeled madness, delirium, phobia, hysteria, mania, excitement, and paranoia, and by the choleric and sanguine dispositions. Table 2.2 shows these groupings.

TABLE 2.1: Basic Elements of Nature and Man as Conceived by the Early Greeks

Elements of Nature	Fire	Earth	Water	Air
Quality of element	heat	dryness	moisture	cold
Associated humor	blood	phlegm	yellow bile	black bile
Organ location	heart	brain	liver	spleen
Associated temperament	sanguine	phlegmatic	choleric	melancholic

TABLE 2.2: Basic Diagnostic Groupings Implied by the Pre-Hippocratics and Hippocrats

Depression	*Excitement*
depression	excitement
suicide	"madness"
impotence	delirium
melancholia	phobia
postpartum psychosis	hysteria
phlegmatic temperament	mania
melancholic temperament	paranoia
	choleric temperament
	sanguine temperament

CHAPTER 3

The Later Greek Philosophers

The early Greek philosophers and Hippocratic medical specialists emphasized efforts to comprehend and focus on the nature of things and on mechanical and rational explanations for physical phenomena and mental functioning, and for the manifestations, basis, and treatment of psychopathology. The crucial questions omitted from the advances of these early but quite rational investigators involved the personal life of people, their intrinsic nature, and their unique and characteristic mental processes. The mental processes the Greeks had not yet considered included reasoning, observation, the acquisition of knowledge, and the existence of logical and psychological problems. Neither had they yet studied social and ethical problems affecting both the individual and the particular human context within which the individual grows and develops in terms of personality, character structure, and ethical orientation.

Thus, a psychological dimension of man, his nature as one who observes and reasons about physical realities, was missing from the work of the philosophers who made the first scientific and rational advances toward initial clarifications of psychopathology and its diagnosis, understanding, and treatment. However, this more psychological, more subjective, less materialistic dimension was the concern of subsequent Greek philosophers known as the Sophists.

THE SOPHISTS

The Sophists were Greek philosophers who placed particular emphasis on the ways in which people came to know about the external world and to develop a body of knowledge and a system of values based on this learning. The particular orientation developed by the Sophists concerned the way in which the subjective viewer invariably influenced what was perceived, what was heard, and what was known, so that an interaction necessarily contributed to the interpretation of reality. Stimuli emanating from the object studied, along with the individualized responses of the investigator, together resulted in the understanding of the characteristics of the subject matter being considered. This philosophic approach not only emphasized the importance of the investigator, but introduced the necessity for separating what is contributed by the observer from the material studied. In the field of psychopathology, the point of view developed by the Sophists had several implications regarding the importance of the individual's personal values and of interpersonal interactions as a subject for psychological study.

The Sophists' emphasis on the importance of the observer transformed psychopathological study into a field that also reflected the subjective interests and proclivities of the individual as psychological phenomena to be considered. The values of each person were now seen as having inevitable weight in how he or she viewed circumstances, evaluated them, and made choices. Thus, the role of value judgments, and by implication, the role of family and even social forces, could be evaluated as influences on individual psychological functioning. In a broader sense, the physiological focus on the brain and on other bodily organs and processes was replaced by an emphasis on the mind and the thoughts, values, and personal referents of the individual. In terms of philosophy as well as of psychology and psychopathology, the teachings of the Sophists introduced a shift in concern from external and presumed internal material entities to human concerns and individual behavior—from man's physical being and the world external to him to his inner, psychological self. This focus on the individual's personal world as part of his psychological functioning was foreshadowed by earlier philosophical teachings such as those of Empedocles. Empedocles emphasized the importance of man's character and the hidden or internal connections that were more crucial than the obvious and overt connections in understanding the nature of personal functioning. Yet, the philosopher who most persuasively examined individual experience in terms of knowledge, observation, ethics, and social circumstances in order to arrive at an essential, true understanding of reality and personal existence was Socrates. Some of the contributions of Socrates to the development of psychological and psychopathological precepts will be presented in the next section.

SOCRATES

Taking a stand against the subjective view of experience held by the Sophists, Socrates (470–399 B.C.) still focused strongly on human values. Like Pythagoras and Empedocles before him, he promoted the view that the world can only be known and understood in a restricted sense and that studies devoted to the clarification of these external areas cannot provide crucial and necessary knowledge regarding man and living.

Socrates added a focus on reasoning and logic, however, as a means of uncovering and elucidating the values and principles essential for sound functioning. This Socratic precept regarding the uncovering process bears on the development of a psychological orientation in devising a way of living that strives for the fullest development of individual potential. In the Socratic method, a leader questioned and responded to participants, using dialogue to uncover the principles underlying thought and behavior. Through the inquisitive conversation comprising this dialogue, what was true, rational, and ethical could be identified and contrasted with the false and irrational. In obvious respects, this approach, of revealing through dialogue actual and ideal principles underlying thought and behavior, is remarkably consistent with interview techniques utilized by modern diagnosticians to identify the principles underlying patients' behavior. On the basis of delineating these underlying dimensions, psychopathology is assessed and its differentiations evaluated.

Thus, with the advent of the Sophists and Socrates, the earlier emphasis on aberrant behavior, abnormal psychology, and psychopathology became simply one aspect of the personality of the individual to be studied. This new focus implied two major principles. The first was that each person had a broad and consistent personality, different from what was reflected in symptomatic behavior. The second was that individuals could learn and could thereby change their basic personality orientations over time.

This optimistic view of human nature meant that aberrant behavior could be changed by reeducation, a point emphasized for example by Plato, so that psychopathology could be considered an impermanent state. This notion of the possibility of a shift in psychopathology—that is, the idea that psychological disturbance is a variable state—has profoundly influenced the history of ideas in the broad area of the psychology of the person. In contemporary abnormal psychology, for example, the concept of the modification of dysfunction is expressed in the view that a diagnosis of an individual's condition may shift over time, depending on the positive or negative progression of a disorder, while the central personality profile or essential character structure remains the same. In modern diagnostic usage, an example would be the description of a paranoid symptomatic process emerging in an individual who is typically a compulsive personality. Although the paranoid symptomatology may, in fact, become severe enough to pervade the individual's mental life and behavior, the optimistic view—which has its roots in the Socratic orientation toward the nature of personality and its development—implies that the basic personality can ultimately be brought into the foreground again.

As indicated above, Socrates' method centered on a dialogue between a leader and a participant, in which logical analysis was utilized to pursue ideas to their logical conclusions and to expose their contradictions in order to determine the truth. The leader's role was to draw out of the other person what needed to be known in order for that person to change. There are two additional significant points to be made about the Socratic method. First, it clearly assumed that gaining insight and information could help a person improve and understand himself as well as his relationship to the world in which he lives. Second, it assumed that acquiring this necessary increment in knowledge is part of a specific relating and interactional process that takes place through dialogue. Socrates could be said to have inferentially distinguished between character and symptom and even suggested a method of facilitating modifications in both. Character meant more enduring aspects of personality, while symptoms meant aberrant reactions. In addition, such a philosophical underpinning reveals a major theme throughout the history of the study of psychopathology; that is, the Socratic and Platonic assumption that interpersonal intervention can profoundly affect the personality strikes the theme of the psychological and nonphysical approach to change. In contemporary understanding, this theme continues to resound against its principle antagonist—namely, the material, pharmacological approach to psychological and personality change.

THE CONTRIBUTIONS
OF PLATONIC PHILOSOPHY

Plato (427–348 B.C.) continued Socrates' development of rational exploration as a means of determining the essential nature of what lay beneath surface appearance. Plato was also interested in connecting the deeper aspects of people to their functioning in the social world. In this development of rational exploration lies the fundamental idea that something of basic importance may not immediately be seen, because of the distinction between descriptive, manifest appearance and the unknown quality of underlying factors. In contemporary diagnostic conceptualizations, this difference between manifest and latent forces corresponds roughly to the difference between a symptomatic picture and what it covers, a deeper characterological system producing forces that are not directly appreciated. Plato also addressed the psychological concept that there remains something constant in each individual in spite of transient shifts that may be exhibited superficially.

The entire question of normal and aberrant behavior was compelling to Plato, and he evaluated the issue of irrational behavior extensively. He conceptualized irrational components of a person's functioning, such as impulses and appetites, as being distinct from the higher orders of reason, abstraction, and logic that struggle to direct the person. He focused on rationality and irrationality partly in order to clarify and understand the specific nature of that aspect of human functioning that comprises rational forces, as well as to understand the qualities involved in the rational elements that were in dynamic relation to one another. But his concern with rationality was also part of an overall effort to master and overcome irrational as well as disordered dimensions of individual functioning and social participation. The aspects of functioning that Plato considered irrational and "lower" he associated with falseness, self-deceit, fantasy, and instability, while he considered constancy based on ideas and knowledge associated with the truth to involve the "higher," rational mental activities. This division between irrational and rational functioning was a striking anticipation of Freud's distinction between an irrational primary process and a rational secondary process.

Plato's use of the term *eros* was related to his dynamic psychological conception of functioning and, in fact, the term was later utilized by Freud. Since for Plato, parts of human functioning such as reason, emotions (or impulses), and appetites were separated from one another, there was a conflict between these psychological components as well as a need for cooperation among them. Eros was proposed as the energy or force that constructively relates these divergent elements, allowing the individual to be directed toward still more encompassing goals. Freud used *Eros* as the overall term for the life forces—those constructively aimed at amalgamation— in contrast with the destructive instincts.

The approach utilized by Socrates and Plato in investigating reality and the functioning of behavior allows for categorization with diagnostic implications. These diagnostic implications pertain to the concept of reality testing, domination by irrational emotional forces, and inadequate behavior due to ignorance or insufficient education. With the emphasis and approach of Socrates and Plato, it became feasible to consider inner sources of ideas, values, and functioning, and then to explore the relationship between psychological constructs and adjustive and maladaptive personal states. Although this beginning attempt at diagnostic parsimony would be followed by long years of tangents, missteps, and refinements, one root of the essential urge to classify and diagnose is this Platonic vision. A connection to more contemporary developments can be seen in the parallel between Plato's postulate of lower functions such as appetites, desires, and drives that ought to be controlled by man's higher functions, man's reason, courage, and ambition, and Freud's view of an avaricious id that needs to be increasingly persuaded and controlled by the developing ego.

In Plato's formulation of a psychological biography in *The Republic,* he crystallizes the notion of character structure by proposing that early family and educational influences set the stage for the development of permanently etched behavior styles. Two important points emerge from this view: that personality functioning develops gradually and is influenced by external circumstances; and that changes in environmental structures can affect alterations in an individual's development. These points not only relate to modern findings about stages of development, but also to therapeutic efforts to limit psychopathology by enhancing positive external influences, whether family, school, or therapist. In fact, Plato's idea of rational development and living involved an educational process, a dispelling of ignorance and discovery of truth through careful, unemotional, and systematic analysis of concepts. Understanding, and especially knowledge about one's actual self, were for Plato the goal of thoughtful, rational living. The Socratic admonition popularized by Plato, "know thyself," suggests the ideal of a rational person guided by an aspiration to understand the self and the enduring aspects of what is true, independent of social conditions or personal desire.

GREEK PLAYWRIGHTS AND THE EXPLORATION OF CONFLICT

At this point in the history of understanding psychopathology, a distinct evolution away from physical explanations of aberrant behavior became possible. Now, alternative explanations avoided presumed biological and physiological entities such as humors and bodily organs in favor of concentrating on psychological constructs involving conflict, anxiety, and personal responsibility. For example, although the tragedians who wrote during the period of Plato's intellectual dominance still referred to supernatural forces such as Furies attacking individuals, they nevertheless began to depict troubled people whose suffering derived from anxiety, remorse, and inner conflict. Their tragedies dealt with intense personal and interpersonal conflicts, conflicts between the individual and the family, and between the individual and the state. These conflicts, with their resulting tension or guilt, were shown to impair capacity for evaluating reality and to severely strain social and personal functioning. These strains and tensions could evoke such anguish and distortions in protagonists that they would resort to homicide and suicide.

The Greek tragedians increasingly revealed the sources of personal suffering to be derived from internal conflict between psychological components of personality, rather than supernatural visitations or possession from the outside. In addition, the Greek playwrights showed the serious tensions within families in relation to the etiology of individual suffering, implying increasing recognition that family disturbances are a determinant of the conflict within individuals.

In keeping with the emphasis that Socrates and Plato placed on knowledge and especially on self-knowledge, in Sophocles' tragedy *Oedipus Rex* the title character struggles with several issues still relevant to contemporary metapsychology and psychopathology. One such issue is the degree of self-knowledge—what is too little? what is too much?—that will allow the individual to maintain a sense of equilibrium, to function effectively in the social world. Another issue is the way in which the pursuit of insight can be enlightening but also tragic, since one may learn unpleasant truths that make it difficult and uncomfortable to live with oneself. Still another issue relevant to the history of psychopathological diagnosis is the role of free will versus determinism in our everyday functioning. Here, Sophocles' play emphasized an idea that remains a contemporary concern—that individuals seek to change even though substantial parts of themselves have been determined by past experience. The importance of the issues of conflict and tension and of their regulation to the audience observing Greek tragedy was emphasized by Aristotle, who made many contributions to the appreciation of psychological functioning and the understanding of psychopathology.

ARISTOTLE'S CONTRIBUTION TO PSYCHOLOGY

The work of Aristotle (384–322 B.C.) recognized that masses of individuals could be reached collectively on an emotional-therapeutic level by the strong rendering of emotions in the tragic figures presented by the Greek playwrights. Aristotle emphasized the cathartic value to the audience of observing intense emotion. In current psychoanalytic terminology the concept of identification would be utilized to account for the audience's experience of powerful emotions corresponding with those enacted in the play. This identification process enabled cleansing and resolution through catharsis and abreaction in the observers. It also allowed the audience to achieve a more active mastery of the upsetting feelings that were both cultural and individual concerns, so that they could live more comfortably. In modern psychological terms, a major implication of this Aristotelian idea of the psychological value of catharsis is that groups of people are troubled with highly similar and specific conflicts involving emotions such as guilt, remorse, terror, and pity. Another implication of the Aristotelian view of catharsis was that a wide variety of specific aberrations are perhaps actually related to a very few core conflicts, and that these basic conflicts are shared and resonate in many people.

As can be seen, the fundamental point of view regarding the nature of madness and implications about mental functioning in general shifted in an essential manner from the time of the early Greeks, as reflected in Homer, to the time in which Plato and the tragedians investigated human conflict. Table 3.1 shows these contrasts.

Aristotle's scientific work, based on careful methodology and an effort to objectively detail natural phenomena, established much more rigorous standards for observation and for skillful classification of the various structures he analyzed. The precision he employed in his psychological investigations led to especially clear and detailed descriptions of the five senses. Another psychological area of interest for Aristotle was the analysis of consciousness. For example, he elaborated distinctions between sensation, motivation, and emotion. In his analysis of sensation, he considered the central categories to be the pleasant and the unpleasant, a view anticipating Freud's pleasure principle, in that the individual acted to avoid pain and secure pleasure. With regard to affects, Aristotle detailed a spectrum of basic emotions—hatred, anger, joy, desire,

TABLE 3.1: Sources of Psychopathology: The Ideas of Early versus
Later Greek Philosophers

	Early Greeks	Later Greeks
Source of disturbance	external	internal
treatment	magic	philosophical
theory	religious	scientific
metatheory	irrational	rational

fear, envy, courage, and pity—that he differentiated and described
so clearly that they are still meaningful in contemporary terms and
psychological functioning. Filling in the range of his psychological
study, Aristotle also considered imagery, memory, and fantasy in
substantial detail.

Thus, Aristotle consolidated a broad area of human functioning
as the subject matter of psychological investigation. In the various
areas that he explored and analyzed he both presented principles
and addressed problems that continue to interest modern psychologists and psychodiagnosticians. In contrast, during the Roman period, the next major stage in the evolution of psychopathological and diagnostic concerns, many of the attempts to clarify
mental functioning leaned in an extremely pragmatic or moralistic
direction. Principles taken from Greek investigators were frequently utilized by the Romans in a rigid, dogmatic manner, without retaining the Greek emphasis on inquiry itself along with the
Greek proclivity to refine hypotheses continually.

By the close of Greek civilization, two trends had been established concerning psychopathology, its diagnosis, differentiation,
and treatment, creating a polarity in the field that has persisted
and exists to the present time. This polarity arose at the start of
rational efforts to develop psychology, has existed simultaneously
or alternatively through every period of the development of understanding and treatment of emotional disorders, and continues
in contemporary investigations. On the one hand, the investigations of Hippocrates and his followers focused on concrete, material entities, bodily factors, and qualities of substances and organs believed necessary to restore the equilibrium of a
psychologically unbalanced body on a physiological level. On the
other hand, the work of investigators influenced by the Socratic
tradition began with a philosophical, metatheoretical perspective
embedded in a relationship; insight and dialogue were used to clarify the concerns that were affecting the suffering person's way of
life. The individual's suffering was emphasized and seen as the result of a particular, rigidly developed belief system. The investigators using the Socratic tradition of uncovering basic beliefs through
dialogues and analysis invariably focused on disturbances or conflicts within the individual, on conflicts between people, or on
problems in the way in which life is lived. The disturbances they
investigated and the diagnoses they developed derived from understanding the conflicts and the feelings associated with devia-

tions from values to be clarified, values that were regarded as central in human conduct.

The polarization between these two general points of view—the concrete, material view versus the introspective—has divided researchers, but has also promoted substantial developments, strengthening diagnostic and treatment issues from both sides. Aside from the conflict and animosity that frequently occurs between adherents of these two opposing views, the interplay between them has enriched overall insight into the diagnosis of psychopathology and its treatment.

In this book, the points of view of each side and the contributions and biases of each will be noted through different periods of history. At the same time, the implications for diagnostic efforts will be discussed through a consideration of the long and convoluted development of the understanding of emotional and psychological disturbances as they have historically unfolded.

The following chapter reviews the contributions of Roman investigators in the next significant phase of exploration of psychopathological and diagnostic phenomena and associated treatment concerns.

SUMMARY OF DIAGNOSTIC FORMULATIONS

The early diagnostic entities formulated by the pre-Hippocratic philosophers and by Hippocrates and his students were extended by the later Greeks, notably Socrates, Plato, the tragedians, and Aristotle. These diagnostic formulations explored the components of personality and their vicissitudes in contrast to focusing precisely on diagnostic labels. Table 3.2 presents some of the salient discoveries of personality mechanisms that were developed by these later Greeks.

TABLE 3.2: Contributions to the Understanding of Personality
by the Later Greeks

- Distinguished between the intellect and the drives, thus between inner controls versus drives and impulses; recognized the fateful conflict between higher, rational elements and lower, irrational ones.

TABLE 3.2, *continued*

• Defined sensation, motivation, and emotion among separate contents of consciousness.
• Advanced the concept of character structure.
• Formalized and identified the importance and universality of the psychological mechanism later referred to as identification.
• Understood the importance of the role of emotion in mental disturbance; began to focus on specific emotions, including guilt, anxiety, remorse, terror, pity, desire, fear, anger, envy, courage, joy, hatred, pleasure, and pain.
• Considered the importance of imagination and memory, a prelude to the understanding of cognitive constructions.
• Emphasized subtle, gradual social and educational influences leading to distortions in thinking and thus contributing to the etiology of psychopathology.
• Utilized the dialogue format to analyze beliefs systematically, to illuminate the essential structure of reality and the adaptions to reality necessary for the best way of living.

CHAPTER 4

The Roman Period

As the influence of Greek civilization was disseminated throughout the ancient Western world, the political leadership of Rome assumed increasing power and Roman civilization became the next major organizing force of antiquity. Roman thinking about psychological phenomena, about the nature of mental illness, and about its causes and cures gradually assimilated Greek accomplishments. In addition to unifying the Greek approaches, the Roman orientation usually emphasized pragmatic and moralistic factors. Nevertheless, elements within this Roman context do represent advances. In addition, a few individual Roman investigators are noteworthy for ideas and theories that furthered the rational framework for assessing mental illness, the framework necessary for developing meaningful differential diagnosis.

THE EMPHASIS ON A PHYSICAL BASIS FOR PSYCHOPATHOLOGY

Asclepiades, an early first-century B.C. Roman physician, overcame early Roman opposition to Greek thinking. He prescribed humane and dignified treatments not only for patients with physical diseases, but also for the mentally ill, about whom he made significant advances in diagnostics. He drew formal distinctions between the acute appearance and the chronic process of diseases, as well as between the more severe and the milder mental illnesses. He also delineated the differences between hallucinations, as marked perceptual-sensory distortions, and delusions, as fixed cognitive distortions, both of which are associated with more serious disturbances. Through his sympathetic approach to mental illness, he presented a conception of emotional disturbance as a condition requiring therapy.

The basis for Asclepiades' careful diagnostic refinements regarding psychopathology and his humanitarian treatment principles was a view of pathology derived from materialistic philosophy, which held that atoms were the components of matter. Essentially, the atomistic theory of health and pathology proposed that the blockage of the atoms that comprise man caused the manifestation of illness. The treatment that Asclepiades devised was intended to affect the atoms in a therapeutic way. One procedure, for example, involved exposing patients to pleasurable physical stimuli to improve their spirits. Another of his procedures was based on the principle of *contraria contrariis curantur,* that is, opposites are cured by opposites—a treatment opposite in effect to a symptom can alleviate the symptom. In accordance with this principle, a mute patient might for example be asked to cause an object to crash, thus making a loud sound.

The work of Asclepiades strikes the chord of the presumed material-biological basis of mental distress. While his approach avoided the Hippocratic idea of humors, its reference to underlying physical constructs called for the introduction of physical agents in the treatment program. Consequently, while Asclepiades can be considered an innovator in the humane treatment of patients, he was also one of the early investigators who set the stage for the biologically and chemically based treatment orientation that would have its greatest influence in the field of psychiatry nearly 2,000 years later.

Another Roman contributing to the development of a humane approach in treating manifestations of aberrant behavior was Aretaeus (A.D. 50–130). Emphasizing the importance of the careful clinical observation of patients based on the approach of Hippocrates, whom he sought to emulate, Aretaeus introduced long-term, longitudinal investigations of patients. These longitudinal studies brought a new dimension to the evaluation of psychopathology—the importance of the course of disease and its prognosis, an area that had received minimal attention until then. The relevance of this particular component in the development of diagnosis appeared again eighteen centuries later, in the work of Kraepelin. In Kraepelin's longitudinal observations, the course of psychopathology and its outcome were crucial determinants in making a differential diagnosis between various psychoses.

Several original discoveries and contributions were made through Aretaeus' longitudinal investigations and his attention to prognosis. He characterized the mood swing in manic and depressive states, citing the interval between moods as well. In addition, the longitudinal method allowed him to study seriously and give detailed descriptions of the personality of the individual before any breakdown occurred. In this way, he delineated and established the premorbid condition of patients with respect to overall personality functioning. He also evaluated intellectual functioning by discerning the way in which intellectual impairments appeared in some forms of psychopathology but not in others. In modern psychological work, the assessment of patients with respect to intellectual deterioration or intactness is carefully pursued both through psychological testing and psychiatric interview techniques; it is part of the evaluation of the nature of the underlying pathology. Aretaeus therefore provided a model of the psychologist at work, seeking to understand normative data in order to understand psychopathology, and evaluating areas of deterioration and intactness in order to formulate the diagnostic framework.

Although largely known for his medical contributions, the physician Galen (A.D. 129–199) also underscored biological approaches to assessing psychopathology. Among his contributions were investigations of brain lesions in animals, which he sought to correlate to functional disturbance. Investigations of nerve tissue throughout the body led him to theorize that the nervous system conducts impulses from the brain and the spinal cord to other parts of the body. Particularly relevant to the biological approach to psychology was his theory that some manifestations of psychopathology correlated with brain damage. This theoretical position eventually became a unifying supposition in modern neurologically and anatomically based investigations. Specific physical deficiencies were sought for each diagnosis evaluated in the network of psychopathology that was elaborated in pre-Freudian psychology.

THE EMPHASIS ON A PSYCHOLOGICAL BASIS FOR PSYCHOPATHOLOGY

In contrast with Galen's emphasis on physical and biological causality in pathological processes, the Roman politician and philosopher Cicero (106–43 B.C.) was concerned with physical and psychological interactions in the development, understanding, and treatment of a wide range of mental illness. Cicero stressed the special value of studying psychopathology. He considered its study essential because of his belief that physical illness could emanate from the effects of emotions. This point of view, never before so persistently emphasized, delineated the psychosomatic conception of psychopathology and the psychosomatic sector of aberrant behavior. The psychosomatic approach that Cicero developed considered the Hippocratic emphasis on humors—as causative of temperament, emotions, and psychopathology—to be an organ-based psychosomatic misconception. Instead, he proposed that even when there was somatic involvement, the more fruitful theoretical perspective was to seek psychological causation for psychopathology. On this basis, he introduced the idea that various intense emotions such as anger, apprehension, and sorrow could even cause somatic symptoms. Further, he added that rather than psychopathology being caused by the action of presumed bodily substances such as the humors, the intense emotions themselves could affect the ability to reason logically, and that an inability to manage such emotions could contribute to the etiology of striking psychopathology.

Cicero's psychosomatic conceptualization included the further ideas that the body can be affected by external variables, but that in the final analysis the mind can only become morbid from an impairment of reason. He supported this view that impairment in reasoning function was the basis for psychological disturbance with the observation that psychopathology is confined to humans, that it does not appear in animals because animals lack sophisticated forms of reason.

Insight regarding the role of impaired reason in psychological disturbance and the potential for the body to be involved when judgment is impaired helped to develop a deeper appreciation of the individual's responsibility for his functioning. Cicero's perspective implies the need for the individual to accept and understand the psychological source of his disturbance, and then to relate this understanding to change and care. Consequently, the essential contribution Cicero made was the idea that psychological functioning can be distinct from physical etiological elements and that individual responsibility is central, that responsibility cannot be displaced onto bodily processes that are not under individual control.

In connection with therapy, Cicero's emphasis on the importance of the management of emotion and the significance of reasoning led him to formulate treatment principles based on instruction and reason. Cure was sought through eradicating errors in thinking, through instruction that would minimize misguided thoughts and encourage more accurate thinking.

In his efforts to emphasize the need to study mental functioning as essentially psychological and therefore as needing to be evaluated from the psychological point of view, Cicero discriminated between and analyzed the important passions that humans experience. He classified these major emotions as fear, joy, discomfort, and intense desire. The term he used for passionate desire was *libido*—the first psychological use of this term, which enriched the vocabulary of emotions. This early reference to libido provides evidence that theorizing during antiquity about emotional and psychological variables found its way into modern dynamic and diagnostic considerations. The importance of *eros* to Plato, and the later use of the term in Freudian thinking, is a similar example.

In addition to analyzing the human passions, Cicero differentiated between two forms of psychopathology in his efforts to refine diagnostic precision. He termed *insania* a condition distinguished by the lack of sound or sensible judgment and by behavior involving qualities of character structure. A more serious condition, including the possibility of delusions, he categorized as *furor*. Cicero's careful description of delusions and hallucinations emphasized the recognition that in psychopathology, internal ideas could be dramatically discordant with external reality.

Like Cicero, Soranus (A.D. 93–138) also introduced innovations in the treatment of psychopathological conditions. On a theoretical level, however, Soranus adhered to the more conventional tradition of his era, which viewed mental illness as caused by organic aberrations. Within the range of treatments he stipulated for mentally disordered persons, some were nevertheless based on psychological interventions involving talking and relaxation, in contrast with typical physiological interventions. It is noteworthy that these psychological curative measures were advocated in spite of the physical elements emphasized in theory. The inclusion of such interpersonal influences in treatment, even when the psychological was disavowed at the level of theoretical conceptions regarding psychopathology, reveals the emerging importance of the domain of psychology.

In the period of antiquity dominated by the Romans, this increasing psychological emphasis—continuing to develop even when denied by theory—contributed to an important trend toward the humanization of treatment and encouraged the development of nonsomatic therapies. Even this brief review of the history of Roman influences on the delineation of psychopathology reveals the overall ferment in early investigators' thinking about emotional disorders, mental illnesses, and problems of living. The intellectual analysis of psychopathology was already, apparently, a compelling pursuit.

EPICURIANISM AND STOICISM

From a different field altogether, that of philosophy, came other important trends toward conceptualizing distress and various psychological mechanisms that might be utilized to avoid it. Greek in origin, the philosophical and ethical traditions of Epicurianism and Stoicism became popular and influential in Roman civilization. These philosophies addressed the need for individuals in a complicated and changing world to find a means to achieve a sense of well-being and psychological equilibrium in the conduct of their lives. The focus on acquiring balance and a sense of well-being in spite of turbulent surroundings links these philosophical and ethical approaches to the psychological concept of adjustment. The concern in these philosophies with distress, discomfort, and tension in the individual connects Epicurianism and Stoicism to the immensely important issue of the experience of anxiety as a vital component in the study of psychopathology.

Epicurianism and Stoicism both offered a means toward achieving happiness or peace through ethical principles that regulated how people lived. Tranquillity and happiness were essentially linked to securing a state characterized by lack of tension. For the Stoics, peace and happiness could be gained through becoming unaffected by circumstance. For the Epicurians, peace and happiness were to be attained through obtaining a sense of personal security. Thus, an emphasis on inner changes in temperament and attitude in order to cope with life's problems and turmoil was regarded as the key to achieving a state of well-being, an absence of anxiety, and a position of adjustment.

The Stoics considered the most sensible posture in living to be conformity to physical laws; they advocated the individual's unquestioning acceptance of the inexorable structure of reality. The Epicurians also recognized the inexorable nature of reality, but urged that the most sensible posture in living was to generate and experience the most enjoyment possible.

The principle of avoiding tension led both the Epicurians and the Stoics to focus on *ataraxia,* a desire to eliminate anxiety, to be free of trouble and disturbing emotions and to thereby achieve serenity. The limiting of anxiety was related to achieving freedom or independence from the unalterable phenomena of life. Mental distress was identified with tension or anxiety, and its relief was identified with avoiding it, or *ataraxia.* The use of psychotropic drugs in modern psychiatry is consistent with this principle; the tranquilizers known as *ataractics* are employed to reduce the experience of distress or anxiety. The concern with tension and upset constitutes an early focus on the vicissitudes of anxiety, which later emerged as the pivotal concept in the study of symptom formation, repression, acting-out, and even the trauma of depersonalization. The nosologies that were developed in the twentieth century were diagnostically organized in a way that discriminated between neurosis and character disorders on the basis of whether or not, or to what extent, anxiety and tension were palpable experiences.

The Epicurians' emphasis on attaining prolonged security in the enjoyment of pleasures rather than merely immediate gratification has obvious implications for psychopathology. In contemporary terms, application to long-range gains can be identified with higher-level adjustive functioning, while inclinations toward short-term pleasure benefits are frequently seen as pathological behaviors designed to circumvent and avoid immediate tensions. From a metapsychological point of view, the issue is the importance of adhering to the reality principle, with its adaptive potency, as opposed to being governed by the short-term pleasure principle, with its tendency toward maladjustment. Correspondingly, the goal of the Stoics, to obtain freedom from anxiety through compliance with the physical world, was a precursor to the emphasis modern thinking places on coping with stress and on ultimate levels of adaptation.

The philosophies of Epicurianism and Stoicism had a moralistic

and judgmental quality, rather than a consistent objectivity in analyzing and understanding human nature. This preoccupation with
moralizing was an obstacle to the development of a clear understanding of the norms of human functioning and of pathological
forms of deviation from these norms as part of scientific study. At
the same time, the efforts embodied by these philosophies to devise
a guide to living based on beliefs about the essential structure of
reality, and their insistence on the need for internal changes to
enable a position of security or reduced anxiety, are progressive
elements.

The later Greek and Roman explorations of psychological functioning tended to be practical and ethical, forming a strong tendency away from scientific exploration of the nature and functioning of the mind. In addition, the Greek and Roman philosophers
were essentially interested in developing broad, abstract, general
principles about strivings, emotions, and goals for living. Such abstractions were limited in their capacity to explain and describe
individual personalities or the behavior and functioning of disturbed patients. Although preoccupation in the later stages of antiquity with defining desirable ways of living did not sharply contribute to scientific development, nevertheless such concern with
adjustment did relate to therapeutic approaches in an empirical
way and certainly emphasized the importance of anxiety, security,
conflict, and adaptation to reality.

In the following chapter, the decline during the Middle Ages in
the development of a sound understanding of psychopathology, its
diagnosis, and treatment is discussed in order to make more visible
how difficult it was to arrive at a rational, scientific, and useful
diagnostic methodology with implications for a psychology of
psychopathology.

SUMMARY OF DIAGNOSTIC FORMULATIONS

During the Roman period, substantial progress was made in understanding and treating psychopathology and in investigating and
clarifying the vicissitudes of the mind. More sophisticated conceptions regarding maladjustment or disordered behavior were for-

mulated, and there was a greater focus on the emotions, anxiety, intellectual functions, diagnosis, and treatment. Table 4.1 summarizes the concepts of psychopathology that were further developed during the Roman period.

TABLE 4.1: Conceptions of Psychopathology Developed
During the Roman Period

Broad Conceptions of Psychopathology

- Acute and chronic disorders differentiated.
- Hallucinations distinguished from delusions.
- The concept that emotional factors could play a part in the etiology of physical disease as well as in psychopathology introduced.
- The psychosomatic field augmented, as a derivative of the view that emotions influence bodily functioning.
- The concept of premorbid or prepsychotic personality introduced, contributing to the understanding of characterological formulations.
- The proposition advanced that emotional and mental disturbances could be caused by brain trauma.

Advances in Diagnosis

- Longitudinal studies established, enabling investigation of factors in the course and outcome of psychopathology; manic and depressive episodes identified as part of the same syndrome in an individual, clarifying the diagnosis.
- Nosological conceptions refined with the division of pathology into two basic classifications: *insania,* representing a focus on character traits such as impaired judgment, and *furor,* conditions involving delusions.

The Importance of Anxiety

- The importance of the vicissitudes of anxiety further emphasized through formulation of the ethical principle of *ataraxia*—avoidance of tension through successful coping with the necessities and fixed aspects of life.
- Ability to tolerate frustration—a precursor to the developmental concept of delay—considered essential to achieving happiness and security.

The Focus on Emotions

- In a conception foreshadowing psychosomatic psychology, emotional difficulties identified as the direct cause of bodily changes.
- Initial effort to formalize a system of normative data made in order to

TABLE 4.1, *continued*

better understand psychological and pathological functioning, with focus on the importance of comprehending the nature of basic emotions.
• Discomfort, fear, joy, and intense desire, defined as *libido*, named as primary emotions; rage and grief associated with the etiology of psychopathology.

Emotional Distress and Intellectual Functions

• Rage, fear, and grief considered powerful enough to impair intellectual functions.
• Determination made that reason and judgment also affected by psychopathological experiences.
• The proposition advanced that intellectual capacities can deteriorate in mental illness.

Treatment Considerations

• A tradition of humane treatment of the mentally distressed established.
• A verbal treatment technique developed and considered essential for improvement of psychopathologically impaired individuals.
• Psychological approaches to treatment employed even when physically oriented metatheory advocated.

PART II
The Middle Ages and the Renaissance

CHAPTER 5
The Middle Ages

The investigators belonging to the classical world of Greece and Rome who began to explore the foundations, manifestations, and diagnosis of psychopathology strove to use reason and logic in place of superstition and externalization. Philosophers and physicians formed theories and analyzed various dysfunctional processes in order to build up a systematic network that could join syndromes to a meaningful foundation. When the order inherent in the ancient civilizations of Greece and Rome declined and broke apart, the evolution of techniques for closely examining circumstances and phenomena through the logic of science also slowed. In fact, the process of understanding the forms of and differences among psychopathological manifestations and of developing a rational basis for mental functioning became substantially distorted and even regressed.

The dramatic social, political, and religious changes that transformed the ancient world of Europe into medieval civilization became organized around Christianity, as both a faith and a force providing social coherence. Not only was there a turning away from the technical, scientific, and philosophical development of knowledge, fact, and self understanding, but there was also a synthesizing emphasis on religion throughout the influential centers of Europe. The combination of the decline of the older spirit of inquiry and the introduction of intense emphasis on faith and religion encouraged a return to supernatural explanations of events.

In the fields of psychology and psychopathology, the quest for understanding and for healing naturally came to revolve around the power of Christ, to be enlisted through prayer and worship. Believers looked not only to Christ, but also to saints to prevent or cure disease and dysfunction. In some cases, saints were petitioned for very specific purposes; St. Sebastian was known as the protector against the plague, for example, and St. Job as the protector against leprosy. In other cases, general protection was sought from a particular saint, such as St. Anthony, who was believed to shield people from all types of disease. While no specific saint governed the prevention or amelioration of mental illness, the faithful did turn to priests for advice about the healing of souls when mental aberrations occurred, and some of the victims of psychopathology must surely have contributed to the increasing prayer for and attention to miracle cures.

The central role of faith and prayer, the religious focus on the soul, and the belief in miracle in medieval society led not only to stagnation in the understanding of pathology, but also to regression to nonrational thought. In everyday life in the Middle Ages, psychological applications to a great extent took the form of prescientific demonology. Beyond prayer, faith, and hope, treatment of mental illness was essentially exorcism. While Christian ideals at first fostered a charitable outlook that encouraged the offering of comfort and support to the mentally ill, charity gradually deteriorated as religiously inspired teachings augmented the role of the devil as a figure identified with social movements as well as with personal forces. The devil was then believed to have the power to possess bodies and souls, and the Church eventually developed dogma which considered the mentally ill to be witches to be persecuted, cruelly tested, and killed. Isolated examples of humane and rational care represented persistent intrusions of past traditions during this period. Innovations in rational ordering, diagnosis, and understanding of the phenomena of psychopathology were tenuous and, in fact, discouraged, except when they could be contained within the context of religious dogma. In spite of the antiscientific and antipsychological bias of the times, several individuals made noteworthy advances in thinking about psychopathology, the importance of emotions and the inner life, and the differentiation of the normal from the abnormal. Such thinking suggests that even during this period of regression, psychological phenomena were compelling enough to be recognized and comprehended in terms that were beyond dogma and the routine pseudo-explanations of the era.

INTROSPECTION AND PSYCHOLOGY

As a focus of attention and a synthesizing structure, medieval Christianity naturally diminished regard within social and scholarly spheres for the traditions of introspection and for the value and importance of interpersonal relationships. Considerations involving inner processes, emotions, and individual and interpersonal factors were replaced by reliance on dogma and superstition taken as knowledge. There were, however, exceptions to this exclusive reliance on dogma and the avoidance of scrutinizing inner processes to illuminate human functioning; St. Augustine (354–430) made a unique and significant departure from conventional thinking during this period. Following his conversion to Christianity, Augustine's writings were devoted to the clarification of religious issues, but nevertheless his method of inquiry, since it relied on self-study, formed a major contribution to psychology. In the tradition of Socrates and Freud, Augustine relied upon introspection, and the data relevant to psychological functioning that he thus obtained enabled him to describe subjective emotional experiences vividly. Much of his famous *Confessions,* though written for religious purposes, consists of extensive self-analysis.

As is so frequently the case for innovators in psychology and psychopathology, unhesitating truthfulness was required of Augustine in his assessment of his personal, emotional, and intellectual functioning. Centuries earlier, Plato and Socrates had taken such a stance as they sought to separate truth from the influence of custom and to clarify the irrational elements that obscure the analytic operation of rationality. A similar principle of full truthfulness in exploring psychological phenomena would be attempted centuries later by Freud. Especially in the application of introspection to the investigation of oneself as subject, Freud and Augustine share a long tradition.

Like Freud, Augustine sought to inspect himself honestly and systematically in order to learn about his personal motivations. He was at first unaware of his inner strivings because of their unflattering nature; knowing about this aspect of himself was therefore unacceptable to his conscious recognition. Through this process of self-exploration, Augustine became aware of the emotional and irrational forces that affect thinking and motivation. In this way he foreshadowed the modern emphasis on complete and overall knowledge of mental phenomena as prerequisites to accurate diagnosis of pathology and assessment of areas of strength. In addition, this noted theologian captured the development of wide-ranging personal insight as a means of determining one's choice of the most constructive direction to pursue in life. Finally, Augustine's example also provided an innovative model for generalizing from the single case study, a common technique in contemporary clinical work.

Augustine used his own self-analysis, his persistent personal probing, to understand individual functioning in highly specific terms. Within this introspective context, he emphasized the major role played by conflicts and emotions and the inner struggle that characterized not only himself, but all people as they are torn and preoccupied by opposing motivations. Augustine's religious objective prevented the technique that he delineated from being used to explore psychopathology in a general way. The pressure of religion also prevented steps toward elaborating a conceptual approach to diagnostics. Nevertheless, in contrast to the largely retrogressive tendencies that developed during the period, the thread was maintained that leads to the modern emphasis on a full understanding of the individual, including an emphasis on inner concerns and the management of emotions and motivations in connection with diagnosis.

INVESTIGATIONS OF ORGANICITY

In contrast to the early emphasis on introspection provided by Augustine at the time when Christianity was forming the foundation for the new era of the Middle Ages that followed antiquity, the focus on inner psychological processes was generally eschewed by medieval investigators. For example, the study of the brain that was accomplished during the medieval period represented rational procedures as well as a distinctly organic bias that countered psychological reflection about psychopathology. Brain investigations during this period generated anatomical and physiological speculations, but this study was embedded in an environment oriented toward the understanding of emotional and mental distress as exclusively organically determined.

The work of St. Thomas Aquinas (1225–1274) provides a prime example of the reactionary and regressive steps taken with regard to the understanding of natural phenomena during the Middle Ages. To rationalize and justify his religious faith, Aquinas turned to the ideas of Aristotle, ironically causing the works of this original thinker to be utilized for centuries afterwards to oppress further developments in thought.

In addition, Aquinas formalized in his teaching the separation between body and soul, and the contention that the soul, since it is of divine origin, cannot become sick. This teaching relegated psychological functioning and the entire range of mental disturbances exclusively to the domain of organic bodily factors. Such a step backward to Hippocratic thinking, in which physical entities and manipulations were central, naturally hindered the development of insight into psychological functioning as well as the emergence of interest in mental phenomena as a field for study. Although Aquinas was not literally involved in the persistent dichotomy between psychological, introspective, and interpersonal approaches to treatment on the one hand, and pharmacological or chemical approaches and interventions on the other, he nevertheless contributed to its evolution. The theoretical stance of relegating mental disease exclusively to organic bodily factors had inexorable practical implications. By looking upon the psychological and psychopathological as mere correspondents of the physical part of life, Aquinas became an instrumental contributor to the pharmacological, chemical approach to the understanding and treatment of emotional and mental distress.

The relationship that Aquinas drew between the human soul and the divine also served those who viewed psychopathological manifestations as corruptions of the spirit. Mental illnesses, when seen as distortions of the soul, could be attributed to external intrusions by demons—a large step backward—or to corruptability due to weakness of faith and/or motivation—again, an impediment to advancements in knowledge. In either case, the door was closed to observing the processes and phenomena of psychopathology and to postulating natural and rational explanations based on a scientific, empirical approach. Instead, deductive connections were made to preestablished religious dogma. It was this approach, divorced from observation either of the external nature of things or of the inner and emotional facts of personal existence, that encouraged the utilization of Aristotle, the advocate of empiricism, in the service of dogmatic blindness.

In contrast to Aquinas, in the thirteenth century Roger Bacon maintained a focus on rationality in his investigations of nature and human functioning. His empirical approach led him to conclude that mental diseases were not supernaturally induced but instead developed in ways dependent on ordinary, natural processes that could be rationally understood. Bacon's emphasis on the value of observation also tacitly implied the possibility of differential diagnostic assessments within the range of psychopathology and their separate treatment. Clearly, Bacon's procedure was consistent with the observation and investigation practiced by such contributors to the clarification of psychological functioning as Aristotle, Augustine, and Freud.

PRESERVATION OF EARLIER CONTRIBUTIONS TO PSYCHOLOGY

While religious views of what could be studied and how it was to be investigated dominated the limited exploration of psychopathology, emotions, and psychology in medieval Europe, a similar attitude—though with interesting differences—developed in the eastern part of Europe. Here, during the early years of the Christian era, the Byzantine empire retained Greek and Roman contributions by actively maintaining and preserving the scientific writings of the ancient world.

The compilers' efforts to preserve ancient writings and manuscripts unfortunately brought about a conversion to dogmatism of the more rational Greek approaches that were being codified. Therefore, the Byzantine contribution was largely a matter of keeping older ideas from disappearing, even though progressive use of them was limited. For example, Greek and Roman medical writings, and psychological works by Aristotle, Asclepiades, and Soranus were not only maintained but relied upon by one practitioner-compiler who preserved the older texts without introducing anything additional. In another Byzantine compilation, three types of mental disorders were discussed on the basis of classical sources and then related to presumed disturbances in different parts of the brain. The effort to develop a differential psychopathology on an organic basis was further correlated to differentiations involving impairments of memory and reason. Other compilers added their own efforts to localize emotional disturbances in the brain. This codification was essentially a deadening process that eliminated the very emphasis on inquiry and active investigation that had been maintained by the authors who were copied.

Arab civilization during the Middle Ages also contributed to the preservation of the past. The Arabs took manuscripts from the countries they conquered, and they preserved, and sometimes developed, the knowledge they contained. The advances made by the Arabs, however, were mainly in medicine; their contribution to psychopathology and psychology was primarily limited to their preservation of older ideas. It was through Arab sources that many of the investigators from antiquity were reintroduced to medieval Europe. In fact, it was through Greek manuscripts preserved by the Arabs that Aquinas "rediscovered" Aristotle—only to regressively align Aristotle's precepts with Christian teaching. Hippocrates' teachings were also translated from Arabic versions and reintroduced to Europe in the eleventh century, only to reinforce emphasis on a correlation between psychopathology and impairments of the nervous system and the brain.

In spite of the pursuit of organic theories of disturbances in behavior, the essential medieval explanation for mental disorder was that it was the effect of an external force. Whether this force was considered a matter of lunar influence or of the devil, it was later associated with witchcraft. Thus, demonology not only persisted but also expanded through the medieval period. By the latter part of the Middle Ages, however, the gradual rediscovery of the philosophers and the investigative approach of the ancient world increasingly challenged the rigid and dogmatic medieval explanations of abnormal behavior. In a larger sense, traditions of society were also challenged by the insights gained from study of ancient originals, and a struggle developed between religious understanding and emphasis and rational considerations. This growing conflict signaled the waning of medieval civilization. A rebirth of intellectual curiosity consistent with that of the ancient world, and a new focus on secular concerns, marked the approach of the Renaissance.

The most important point for the development of a modern appreciation of psychopathology and diagnosis was the Renaissance emphasis on an approach involving inquiry and objective evaluation of natural phenomena that is associated with the modern development of science. In this regard, the Renaissance represents the emergence of modern approaches to the description, classification, and understanding of psychopathology to be presented in the next chapter.

SUMMARY OF DIAGNOSTIC FORMULATIONS

Because of the rigidity of Church teachings, during the Middle Ages a regression took place with respect to the causes, treatment, and understanding of mental distress. On a theoretical level, the thrust of the Church was either to reject Aristotelian and other rational teachings, or in some way to co-opt them. While correspondences between brain impairments and aberrant behavior were sought, most psychopathology was accounted for by the regressive stance of attributing such behavior to external causes.

Table 5.1 presents the major philosophical views regarding the causes, treatment, and understanding of psychopathology during the Middle Ages.

TABLE 5.1: Approaches to Psychopathology During the Middle Ages

Etiology

- Causes considered external.
- Demonic possession theory resurfaced: the belief that the devil can possess body and soul.
- Various types of mental illness related to various areas of the brain.
- Body and soul held to be separate, and the soul considered not subject to disease because of its divine origin. Therefore, mental illness thought to have organic causes only.
- Conflict appeared between supernatural demonic explanations on the one hand, and introspection, self-analysis, and observations and deduction on the other.

TABLE 5.1, *continued*

Treatment

- Prayer, including supplication of specific saints thought capable of protecting individuals from untoward events.
- Persecution, following theory that the mentally ill were witches.
- Exorcism of demonic influences, when possession considered the etiology of the condition.

CHAPTER 6

The Renaissance

The transition from the medieval era to the Renaissance was characterized by a growing appreciation of the writers of antiquity, who leaned toward more humanistic, rational, and scientific considerations in examining natural phenomena, in comparison with the medieval emphasis on faith. Greek learning was revived, and medieval supernatural conceptualizations were deemphasized, even though superstition continued and classical writers were revered more in keeping with faith and authority than reason. However, the intellectual transformation of society achieved during the Renaissance gradually crystallized into a pointed interest in discovering the actual nature of the world itself. This rebirth of scientific inquiry resulted in an approach to investigation that involved the study and evaluation of experience itself, rather than the study and acceptance only of what the ancients wrote about experience. The examination of the empirical phenomena of nature and the struggle toward nonreligious theoretical explanations led to advances in the range and content of psychopathology, as well as to advances in diagnosis and treatment.

OBSERVATION OF NATURAL PHENOMENA

During the Renaissance, new translations of ancient writers along with the invention of printing accelerated the spread of knowledge and furthered curiosity and interest in investigations about natural phenomena. At the same time, major changes in European society introduced new ideas and new ways of considering experience. Such stimulation weakened the irrational influences emanating from the Church and medieval society.

New interests and activities involving all areas of life achieved substantial impact by focusing specifically on the human condition, human needs, and nature. The structure and functioning of man and society became the focus of more detailed study and understanding. Psychological and philosophical studies in the Renaissance could give greater consideration to inner experience, such as emotions, as data for investigation and as aspects of existence worthy of analysis. Individual experience became elevated in importance, taking on a new primacy. All of these burgeoning activities intensively stimulated scientific curiosity and research. The renewed activity in both organic and psychological study brought about advances in psychopathology as well as the detailing of normal functioning.

The Renaissance shift away from an emphasis on dogma and authority, toward a stress on the importance of the individual study of nature with a goal of achieving the most accurate representations possible, is exemplified by the archetypal Renaissance man, Leonardo da Vinci. In his investigations at the physiological level, Leonardo examined both living and dead tissue, producing highly accurate anatomical drawings and depictions of the structure of the human brain. His emphasis on careful, original observations as a means of learning about nature and the function of structures not only increased knowledge about a wide range of human structures, but also advanced the antiauthoritarian spirit of inquiry in general, emphasizing the value of what could be derived from original research. This type of interest in understanding nature directly and experimentally, in factually determining its operations, gave impetus to the scientific approach that is necessary to describe and categorize the norms and deviations of natural phenomena, including mental and psychological functioning.

In addition to his work in the spheres of physiology and anatomy, Leonardo contributed directly to psychological matters in ways that either foreshadowed contemporary interests or revived areas of psychology that had become dormant—areas with long histories and current importance. His original contributions to the field of psychology had implications for establishing a more relevant and precise assessment of psychopathology. Leonardo anticipated Hermann Rorschach, for example, by approximately four hundred years, by giving serious consideration to individual differences revealed by people's perceptual responses to the ambiguous forms presented by clouds—a solid precurser to the entire process of projection and to projective testing, as well as a valuable approach to appreciating the inner person. Leonardo's writings on auto-suggestion and dreams also broadened the development of concepts within the field that was to become clinical psychology. In terms of more traditional psychological interests, he undertook investigations of visual perception and its psychological aspects, and he also studied the influence of emotions on memory and on facial expressions.

The sixteenth-century Renaissance figure Vesalius further replaced authoritarian tradition with empirical investigations through his studies of anatomy. Not only did he utilize direct studies of the human body to provide comprehensive and detailed findings, but when his new work made it necessary to do so, he contradicted the ideas of the venerated second-century physician Galen. Thus instead of maintaining a regressive attitude, Vesalius encouraged forward movement in the study of natural phenomena. The achievements in anatomy and physiology by Renaissance scientific workers who risked themselves by challenging classical and religious authority brought all investigators closer to depending on actual data in forming conceptualizations about normative events and pathological deviations from the norm. Such conceptualizations could then become the basis for theories about the ordering of normative data and deviations from the norm, based on an assessment of the range of normal functioning and the degree of seriousness of various pathological deviations. The establishment of concepts of norm and deviation from the norm as major conceptual concerns in the scientific world deeply influenced the study of psychopathology and its diagnosis.

OBSERVATION OF NATURAL PHENOMENA IN PSYCHOPATHOLOGY

A great dedication to observation emerges from the anatomical and physiological work of the Renaissance. This observational approach paves the way for the formation of concepts and theories that are closely related to data and actual findings, that are therefore more powerful in explanatory and predictive capability than arguments based merely upon authority. This type of scientific exploration is a necessary precursor to gathering the facts of psychopathology, ordering them, and devising a conceptual theory accounting for the array of carefully gathered findings. Even in the present, diagnosis is largely based on observation of actual behavior, collection of carefully established historical truths in which the specific etiological events are clinically determined, and patients' responses to standard stimuli presented through interview questions or test material.

Students of mental illness during the sixteenth century also followed this procedure of carefully obtaining data by closely observing patients and recording what was seen, producing clinically realistic observations. Johann Weyer was one of several clinicians investigating and evaluating psychopathology whose accuracy of detail in noting both the verbalizations and the overt behavior of emotionally disturbed people made his work comparable to the highly realistic drawing of the scientists who studied anatomy. Specific clinical syndromes and diagnostic entities were formulated and clinically identified during this period, including descriptions of mood disturbances such as melancholia and mania; even the diagnosis of psychopathy was made, with subtypes differentiated within conditions in some of these cases.

As can be seen, careful descriptions with emphasis on accurate detail appeared in the foreground, as clinicians began to attempt to understand psychopathology and its various diagnostic forms on a carefully conducted observational level. Some of the resulting writings are exceedingly detailed in clinical description, foreshadowing the work of nineteenth-century classifiers of mental disease such as Kraepelin. Just as Kraepelin's contributions reflect a physical bias, the work of the sixteenth-century clinicians also reveals reliance on organic speculation, and there are even supernatural carryovers.

The clinical efforts of the sixteenth-century psychopathologists do, however, reveal an urgency to develop the spirit of intellectual inquisitiveness and to apply it to the investigation of emotional disturbance. In addition, an awakening of interest in the way people actually lived, in their personal strivings and individuality, gradually became a pronounced component of psychological inquiry. This concern for qualities related to the inner experience of people as individuals is, of course, an essential step in detailing character and personality. Also, important subjective elements contribute to the psychological understanding of a person and to the development of psychological and theoretical concepts about

the underlying differences between individuals and between psychopathologies. The reestablishment of these personal constructs
as central in evaluating psychopathological and normative functioning is an important achievement of Renaissance activity.

A NEW VIEW OF PERSONALITY

Up to this point, the major focus of investigators of mental illness
was generally limited to disturbances reflecting overt psychosis,
psychopathic behavior, and brain damage. The more subtle problems of living that arise as a result of idiosyncratic personality
expression, needs, and feelings were largely ignored and considered a domain quite apart from that of mental illness. What we
now call neuroses, interpersonal conflicts, character problems, and
personality disorders are precisely those more subtle problems that
these early researchers considered different from mental illness. Investigators up to this point rarely conceived of treating the problems in living related to character and personality styles through
the same organic approach that was utilized for those who were
considered mentally ill on the basis of striking, overt behavioral
disturbance.

The current medical model that stresses a continuum from brain
damage to psychosis to character and personality disorder to neurosis tends to conceptualize treatment as the application of chemicals to all elements on the continuum. However, the work of investigators from earlier periods implied a discontinuity between
serious mental illness and problems in living reflected by personality and neurotic styles. The basis for treatment for these problems in living, in contrast with the conceptualization of treatment
derived from the current medical model, would suggest different
approaches for each of the two domains. Actually, this chemical-
nonchemical treatment dichotomy helps suggest the advantage of
exploring problems of living as a new aspect of psychopathology
deserving of its own investigation, classification, conceptualization, and treatment. The implicit suggestion is that the treatment
for such problems of living may well need to be quite different for
the distinct domain of psychopathology that relates to character
disorders and neuroses.

The chemical treatment approach appropriate for severe, acute, florid, and chronic-intractable psychosis can now be evaluated as perhaps reflecting qualities intrinsic to the severe pathology itself as distinct from the pathological qualities involved in problems of living. Such a dichotomy between debilitating psychosis on the one hand and lesser disturbance on the other had already been accepted in the sixteenth century. In fact, the differential characteristics of the two traditionally separate domains of psychopathology—psychoses and nonpsychoses—can be aptly conceptualized through consideration of the nature of the interactional interpersonal functioning of which the individual is capable. The variable of interpersonal relatedness provides a way of viewing that difference. For example, it is usually the case that in severe mental illness, there is a breakdown in the integrity of interpersonal functioning. In contrast, in the neurotic and characterological conditions, there are distortions and difficulties in interpersonal relating, but in most cases the fundamental process of relating remains intact. A rather simple distinction can be made with respect to treatment, in which chemical interactional interventions may be especially helpful for one domain, while verbal interactional interventions may have particular effectiveness for the other.

A recognition of these different domains—mental illness on the one hand, and personality styles on the other—does not diminish the importance of the subjective experience of those with severe mental illness. However, the distinctive personality style of severely disturbed persons is usually fragmented by profound disorganizational forces that are sufficient to attenuate contact with reality, including the important interpersonal aspect of reality. The adequacy of this essential connection to reality is frequently considered to be the fundamental distinction between the domains.

Problems in living that derive from the patterns of personality and internal character traits that relate to people's individuality create an opportunity to investigate a new area of psychological and mental functioning. This new approach involves emphasis on understanding the inner experience of individuals, an understanding that played a particularly unique role in the Renaissance.

The period of the Renaissance brought to prominence an emphasis on personal uniqueness, individuality, and recognition of the enormous importance of inner emotional conflicts. In addition, the period also underscored the importance of the inner determinants of psychological functioning, of the forms of psychopathology, and of differentiating between normalcy, psychopathology,

and individuals themselves. In the context of historical development, the importance of considering in a serious way the uniqueness of people can be traced to a diverse group of late medieval
or early Renaissance philosophers. These humanistic philosophers
built on Augustine's focus on introspection to elaborate further the
inner life of people. Concentrating on subjective experience as a
major construct for investigation connected the serious study of
nature that emerged during the Renaissance with the study of human existence. The study of personalities, which became a major
element and contribution of the Renaissance, ties together the emphasis on experience and the use of introspection. This focus on
the inner person is a direct thread to Freud's accentuation of internal determinants of personality functioning and of an individual's behavior, and it clearly shows the inexorable historical imperatives that influence succeeding generations in conceptualizing
psychopathology.

During the Renaissance, several developing themes stemmed from
the increased acceptance of individuality and the value that correspondingly came to be placed on the process of inner experience.
The field of psychological study widened to include the beginning
of the analysis and description of variations among internal determinants as well as study of the scope of emotions and their
effect on behavior and thinking. As an extension of interest in the
empirical investigation of nature, the investigation of the nature
of people itself became a field for undogmatic and scientific exploration. The complexity of human functioning thus became recognized, and psychological interest matched this recognition, as
can be seen in the increasing amount of writing about character,
thinking, and feelings, and about how all of these faculties develop.

How character patterns and goals can be changed—strengthened through education, or modified by other interventions—also
became a topic of inquiry and theoretical development. In the fif-
teenth century, the philosopher Pico della Mirandola wrote about
the use of education to accomplish personal ideals, an idea further
developed in the sixteenth century by the Spanish educator Vives.
In the educational approach to character change described by Vives,
an appreciation of individuality, emotional functioning, and character formation were central areas that could now be approached
in a highly objective manner. Vives' approach was therefore scientific, but it was also pragmatic in its recognition of the importance of application. At this time in the sixteenth century, Ma-

chiavelli contributed what he considered to be an objective approach to investigation. This objective approach could be seen as reinforcing the stance of Vives, although Machiavelli's interest in the vicissitudes of power, manipulation, and leadership goals raises serious questions about his objectivity. The part of Machiavelli's work that could be considered objective concerned his ability to reveal the power and leadership strivings that appear in certain people. Yet, because his understanding of such dynamics was framed within a political context, whether he truly revealed innate and objective findings is highly questionable.

The development and refinement of an objective approach to viewing, describing, and classifying the variety of individuals in their social functioning, as well as maintaining objectivity in clinical terms when more serious psychopathology was involved, were major achivements of the Renaissance. The accomplishment of such careful descriptive psychology is a prerequisite of the formation of a theoretical conceptualization of psychopathology based on presenting numerous case studies that elaborately describe various mental illnesses.

These gradual advances toward objective evaluations of natural phenomena—evaluations that sought to restrict the influence of bias in the study of behavior—appeared throughout the period within a context that nevertheless included numerous superstitious, pseudoscientific, and demonic preoccupations persisting from the medieval period. Thus, tendencies toward magic continued, as well as interest in such subjects as astrology as explanations for character and achievement—or its limitations. The eclipse of such old ideas by the new was captured by the Renaissance playwright Shakespeare, in the powerful assertion: "The fault, dear Brutus, is not in our stars, / But in ourselves, that we are underlings."

Another figure important to the applied and clinical psychology of the sixteenth century was the Swiss physician Paracelsus. Despite the fact that Paracelsus practiced astrology, he contended that mental illnesses were caused by disturbances in the substances of the body, not by the stars he utilized in other contexts. Paracelsus made a further contribution to rationalism in his dedication to combating the witch-hunting that remained prevalent throughout the Renaissance. Another sixteenth-century physician, Johann Weyer, also opposed witch-hunting through an appeal to rationality that was related to the newer, scientific, nonsuperstitious approaches to explaining psychopathology. The data Weyer employed in forming his conclusions were marshalled through interview techniques, which he utilized to provide naturalistic explanations in evaluating psychopathology. The Renaissance investigators who advanced objectivity and rationality, questioning the irrational assumptions involved in belief in witchcraft, diminished the leftover power of demonic explanations for unusual behavior; thus they repeated the accomplishment of the ancient Greek rationalists.

Weyer's extensive use of interview techniques in gathering data from a range of sources highlights the importance, in evaluating psychopathology, of ascertaining and clarifying the essential. Attempting to apprehend reality involves identifying the distortions that are introduced by biases, which affect the reporting of events. When distortion was recognized, a true picture of the structure of reality, independent of people's subjective reports, could be developed. From numerous reports, an essence of the real situation could be derived, conveying the greatest descriptive accuracy. In many ways, this emphasis on accuracy of description exemplifies the thrust of the entire Renaissance period. Study of the actual nature of people and events was invaluable in the foundation of a more productive psychology. This more scientific approach provided a realistic underpinning that enabled the formulation of constructive and comprehensive conceptualizations about the causes, courses, classifications, and treatments for mental illness and individual problems in living.

The rediscovery of realistic assessment and explanation, which eventually undermined the persistence of superstitious and pseudoscientific ideas, was a major achievement of the Renaissance. The study of people from objective and individual perspectives also formed a basis for further refinement in the study of psychopathology. There is no doubt that in contemporary diagnostics, the crucial emphasis on reality testing as the *sine qua non* of diagnostic determination—at least with respect to differentiating psychosis from normalcy—has its essential genesis in the Renaissance. Furthermore, it was during the Renaissance that the focus on the treatment of distress, psychotic and nonpsychotic, became resoundingly supportive of the introspective tradition. The possibility of treating distress without the use of chemical agents of any kind was fortified in an enduring way.

In the next period of development, during the seventeenth century, scientific explanations themselves became a prominent focus in the understanding of the human mind and the realm of psychopathology. This seventeenth-century exploration shall be considered in the following chapter.

SUMMARY OF DIAGNOSTIC FORMULATIONS

During the Renaissance, reliance on supernatural and demonic explanations for disturbed behavior, such as that of so-called witches, was directly confronted by attempts to truly understand a person's life and experience. Existence was explored in terms of inner determinants such as emotions and character as well as in terms of ability for interpersonal relating. Case studies were carefully detailed so that "witches," for example, were shown to be in fact mentally ill. The realization that such people were not inherently demonic changed the direction of investigation from concern with external signs to exploration of internal experiences. The achievements of Renaissance investigators suggest a differential diagnostic matrix beginning to develop, reflecting the range of psychopathology and implying the possibility of different treatment methodologies. Table 6.1 lists some of the salient concepts advanced during the Renaissance with respect to understanding the individual and psychopathology generally.

TABLE 6.1: Formulations of Psychopathology and Assessment
Approaches Developed During the Renaissance

Diagnostic Entities

- Psychopathic personality
- Phobia
- Melancholia
- Mania and its different types
- Psychosis
- Brain damage
- Severe disturbance differentiated from problems of living

Approaches to Understanding the Person

- Emotion and experience described as a means of understanding personality.
- Observation preferred over reliance on authority.

TABLE 6.1, *continued*

- Objective data of character functioning, such as leadership styles, considered; moralizing judgments eliminated, so that actual personality was clearly depicted.
- Concept of the norm and of deviation from the norm developed.
- Data from interviews of mentally disturbed people examined.
- Inner experience emphasized, facilitating study of personality and character structure.
- Strivings, intellect, and especially feelings of the person accentuated.
- Interpersonal relations considered important.
- Individual differences and individuality noted and evaluated.
- Supernatural deemphasized.
- Brain-anatomical studies carefully pursued.

Treatment

- Building character through education, requiring knowledge of the emotions.
- Reducing distress through introspective self-examination.

PART III
The Modern World

CHAPTER 7

The Modern World and the Study of Psychopathology

As the Renaissance opened the way toward looking directly at nature and people and describing the ways they actually functioned, superstition and reliance on authority were gradually countered. This Renaissance accomplishment led to further examination of extremely varied phenomena. During the seventeenth century, the scientific orientation of the modern world was established through dramatic new developments in philosophical, empirical, and psychological areas. Together, advances in these approaches to attaining knowledge promoted the view that there is a logical, rational basis for all aspects of existence that can be uncovered by the work of science. This view of an understandable order stimulated the drive to investigate as much as possible and led to extensive refinements in the methods employed in scientific inquiry.

CONTRIBUTIONS TO CONCEPTUALIZING PSYCHOPATHOLOGY

The essential contribution of seventeenth-century scientific work to defining, conceptualizing, and treating psychopathology was its emphasis on reason in uncovering and understanding the inner life of people. Growing out of the Renaissance use of empirical observation and assessment to understand clinical phenomena and psychopathology, the work of the English physician Thomas Sydenham typifies the seventeenth-century emphasis on empiricism and rationality. His contributions were completely based on strict observation, which he used to uncover the nature of psychopathological disorders. In devising treatments appropriate for the disorders that he studied, he relied on clinical judgments based on understandings gained through observation and interaction with patients. The important point displayed is the spirit of discovery based on observing the particular psychopathology in question, which then formed the basis for definitions, diagnosis, and treatment.

Sydenham's original contributions to clinical description covered the pathology of hysteria. His observations of hysterical patients enabled him to relate the conversion symptoms occurring among hysterical syndromes—such as paralysis, headaches, and other such irregularities—to the operation of intense emotion. His work on hysteria led him to appreciate the psychological nature of this disorder and convinced him that hysteria was not a physical or organic disturbance. His contribution to the appreciation of hysteria was significant but still quite general, reflecting his era's very rudimentary understanding of this disorder. Yet, his focus on the important role of emotion in hysteria and on the possibility that physical symptoms and emotions were somehow equivalent represented a fertile insight.

This advance in the understanding of hysteria was developed in the twentieth century in more specific terms, to include dynamics involving oedipal issues and defenses involving denial and repression. During Sydenham's period, however, the understanding of hysteria was experiencing its first true metamorphosis, in coming to be viewed in more completely psychological and emotion terms. This would lead to the creation of a specific syndromal formulation that ultimately involved the family drama, emotions, defenses, personality dispositions, and even intrapsychic implications. In this way, Sydenham formed the basis for the modern use of exacting observation of clinical phenomena to determine an etiology based solely on psychological laws. The mysterious elements typically introduced in earlier eras—related to the bias of the investigators, or the pressures of those times—could now be removed from the study of aberrant functioning, making possible a modern psychological groundwork for the full spectrum of psychopathology.

Sydenham's highly objective and detailed descriptions of hysteria enabled him to diagnostically differentiate several kinds of hysterical reactions from one another while retaining the defining core of hysterical functioning as the important element throughout these distinct manifestations. Further, he was dedicated to decisively differentiating the psychologically based hysterical symptoms from the physiological disorders that the hysterias tended to mimic. Such work, emanating from the value Sydenham placed on clinical judgment based on comprehensive observation, forms the modern approach to investigating psychopathology and actually diagnosing it. His emphasis on the importance of antecedent emotional factors in the development of syndromes and the implication of a dynamic interplay between emotions and defense established a particular path that was then followed by succeeding scientific investigators of psychopathology.

EMOTION AND EARLY PSYCHOSOMATIC CONCEPTS

Thus, the seventeenth century saw a thrust toward psychological understanding both of emotional disorders and of disorders previously regarded as physical. The role of emotion in the etiology of psychopathology was advanced by several investigators, one of whom was the seventeenth-century physician William Harvey. Even though much of his contribution was in the biological realm, his discounting of the reports of others and his preference for his own observation enabled him to realize that the full range of people's emotional experiences strongly affected body functioning. Among the emotions that he considered were fear, hate, anxiety, grief, and pleasure. On the basis of his observations, he constructed a viable approach to the psychosomatic interplay of forces that contributed to a deeper understanding of numerous subtleties within the field of psychopathology.

Psychosomatic study was conceptually extended at this time by the clear recognition that psychological events can be expressed through the body itself. Examples of this emotion-psychological-physical amalgam are the phenomena of blushing, heart palpitations, and conversion symptoms. The emotion-psychological-physical equation was recognized in earlier eras, albeit obliquely, and without any appreciable foundation in clinical experience and evidence. In the seventeenth century, however, a genuine turning point was reached, in that the investigators observing psychosomatic phenomena were now in a position to accurately and systematically perceive the overwhelming importance of emotions, including anxiety, in the formation of diagnostic entities. Yet, it is clear that the full emergence of psychosomatic study had to wait for later times, when its implications could become more fully apparent and could be utilized in psychological diagnosis and treatment. New philosophical approaches to the study of sensation and to the understanding of knowledge itself enabled new discoveries regarding the etiology of psychopathology and its essential makeup. Of course, the ideas that were forming about psychosomatic or psychophysiological phenomena provided a bridge between the philosophical orientation of the time on the one hand, and a striving to uncover emotional and psychological mechanisms on the other.

Renewed refinements in analyzing psychopathology emanated from the philosophical tradition established by Thomas Hobbes and John Locke. These philosophers focused ultimately on the vicissitudes of mental life such as perception and motivation, and on the characteristics and qualities of what may be learned and known. For example, Hobbes reduced mental functioning to the joining of the building blocks of sensory perceptions through associations. He saw the sequence of perceptions as important to what was learned through this associationism, but equally important were the emotional qualities of pleasure and pain that became part of a physiologically based mechanism for actively seeking pleasure and avoiding pain. This conceptualization, relating learning to the association of sensations—physiologically guided by pleasure and pain responses—provided a significant impetus for the development of formal aspects of Freud's theories. It is directly relevant to psychopathology and its treatment, as well as to Freud's concept of the pleasure principle as a psychological link to self-preservative instincts.

The connection between the emergence of psychosomatic concepts, the philosophical orientation of Hobbes and Locke, and, ultimately, the theories of Freud, again reveals the inexorable imprint of history, reaching to contemporary times. For example, the technique of association developed by Freud, which in an important respect was built on the philosophical tradition of associationism, allowed modern psychologists to penetrate the unconscious and to construe it as a powerful organizer of experience. Through this penetration of the unconscious and better understanding of the issue of seeking pleasure and avoiding pain, modern investigators could establish that equilibrium and homeostasis, based on goals of preserving life, are principles of human functioning. This concept of a self-preservation principle became central in the work of both Darwin and Freud. It influenced thinking about human experience in general, and of course about psychopathology, in the most powerful way. An important implication of this emerging way of understanding human experience was that psychopathology arises out of a faulty or misguided attempt to preserve life during stressful times.

The new way of viewing physiological and psychological manifestations and disturbances as interactive is also consistent with ideas developed by the eminent seventeenth-century Dutch-Jewish philosopher Baruch Spinoza. He attempted to demonstrate the inseparability of the mind and the body and further emphasized the importance of the immaterial, making it possible to give significant weight to psychological factors. In addition to his important contributions toward minimizing dualism between physical and psychological factors—by seeing the two as merely different aspects of the same phenomenon—he elevated the methodological importance of reason as the key to understanding the entire functioning of nature. Many of the concepts that Spinoza addressed are central to the study of psychology, and thus created a direction for psychology whereby certain subject matter was invariably included. His thought pertained significantly to the role of emotion, the understanding of psychopathology, and the inner conflicts which are dilemmas for people, triggering stress and anxiety. In addition to the influence of emotions in human motivation, Spinoza also investigated determinism, strains in interpersonal relationships, and anxiety, which related etiologically to internal conflict. Focus on such themes obviously expanded the scope of material to be considered in the realm of psychopathology. At the same time such focus emphasized the importance of rationalism, insight, and overall cognitive qualities in encouraging the analysis of the seemingly irrational components of personality—especially emotional functioning.

In keeping with the general philosophical theme that developed during this century and which laid the groundwork for so much scientific investigation, Spinoza also related psychological functioning to self-preservative interests. This contribution was important because it elevated causality and the knowledge of antecedants to the level of the major factors in objective and scientific study. Spinoza's reliance on the idea of self-preservation had particular relevance to psychological events, and it had obvious connection to the later development of Freud's framework. Spinoza's emphasis on factors such as how events are perceived, how sensations are experienced, and the role played in such mental activities by personal motivation had the effect of widening the boundaries of psychology.

These contributions by Spinoza consequently deepened the sophistication and rationality with which psychopathology could be examined. Spinoza further utilized the concept of self-preservative inclinations in people to understand shifts in awareness; he also saw relinquishment of awareness as dependent on whether what is conscious enhances or diminishes the individual's view of himself. This use of a dimension of self-awareness by Spinoza reveals an emerging concept of a dynamic unconscious.

Along with many of the philosophical contributions developed during the seventeenth century, Spinoza also tended to foreshadow the intensification of the understanding of normative and pathological psychological functioning that would accrue through the twentieth century. Such contributions by Spinoza included his emphasis on the importance and fluctuation of awareness, his focus on emotions themselves as well as the range of their expression, and his theories about ambivalence and the integrative role of mental functioning in the individual's existence. Spinoza's emphasis on reason as a key element in adaption also bears on later concerns that emerged in the struggle between the rational and the irrational.

In the next century, further advances affected all areas of science, technology, and invention. Increasingly, psychology could also be, in principle, an area subject to comprehensive rational understanding. In the next chapter these advances in psychological understanding will be described.

SUMMARY OF DIAGNOSTIC FORMULATIONS

The emergence of the modern world in the seventeenth century and the introduction of a clear rationalism brought greater depth and consistency to the understanding of psychopathology. In general, the study of psychopathology became further liberated from a reliance on superstition during this period, and the bodily manifestations of psychopathology came to be seen more readily as revealing significant effects of emotions and personality functioning. Table 7.1 presents some of the salient features of this age that helped to give greater clarity and sophistication to the tenets and principles of psychopathology.

TABLE 7.1: Concepts of Psychopathology Developed During the Seventeenth Century

Philosophic Underpinnings

- Rational approach, focusing on the importance of observation and reasoning. The notion of self-preservation elucidated as the basis of a motivational system. Such a motivational system, relying on needs of protection and pleasure, an immediate precursor of the idea of the unconscious.
- Sensory perceptions seen as the source of mental activity and the mediator of knowledge of the external world. Because it is filtered through the sensations, this knowledge seen as subjective. Thus, a distinction made between the internal and external.

Formulations of Diagnoses, Emotions, and Psychopathology

- Bodily processes experienced as affects, thoughts, and desires.
- Focus placed on the control of internal forces, desires, and feelings.
- Careful delineation made of hysteria, in which intense emotion was associated with hysterical symptoms such as paralysis, headache, nausea, and palpitations.
- Psychosomatic concepts developed and related to pleasure, pain, fear, grief, envy, love, shame, hatred, spite, passion, and anxiety.
- Psychogenic causes of mental and physical illness differentiated from organic ones.
- Idea of ambivalence suggested, along with the importance of analyzing the interplay or dynamics of emotions as they interact.

Treatment Issues

- Importance of fully understanding the emotional circumstances surrounding the onset of a disorder stressed as a first step in any treatment approach.
- Treatments devised in relation to clinical observation and interaction with patients instead of theoretical preconceptions.

CHAPTER 8

The Age of Enlightenment: The Eighteenth Century

During the various periods of history when efforts have been made to advance rational conceptualizations of psychopathology, to identify and diagnose the psychological sources of the anxiety experienced by patients, and to devise appropriate therapies for these disturbances, contradictory trends have often arisen. Such periods reflect the conflict between efforts toward rationally inspired new discoveries by some groups, and intensifications of regressive reliance on magical methods by other groups. During the eighteenth century, such contradictions were especially apparent. On the one hand, greater enlightenment in the understanding of patients with severe mental illness brought about noteworthy and lasting reforms; more humane treatment was advocated, and advances were made in rational approaches to analyzing abnormal behavior and the transformation of these approaches into diagnostic nosologies. On the other hand, pseudoscientific theories were also abundant, postulating forces and physiology in the etiology and cure of psychopathology. Among the forces proposed were special invisible fluids, magnetic and electrical powers, and vital substances, all administered with suggestive promises of cure.

The orientation of many of these pseudoscientific theories was toward presumed organic bases for psychological functioning. Clearly, such an emphasis restricted the expansion of a psychological focus regarding normal and abnormal functioning. In some ways, however, the importance of factors pertaining to the interpersonal relationship of patient and helper became clearer precisely from evaluation of the more bizarre physical approaches. The role of interpersonal factors became more salient when the pseudoscientific trappings of therapies were changed and it became clear that the influence of personal factors of the healer and the willingness of sufferers to be healed were the crucial ingredients promoting therapeutic change. The power of suggestion and the predisposition of patients to be influenced by such power were major dimensions, then, in the expansion of the understanding of psychopathology during this period, even though this understanding of interpersonal factors derived from pseudoscientific, superstitious, and regressive approaches.

PSEUDOSCIENTIFIC FADS REVEALING INTERPERSONAL INFLUENCES

Among the more popular and well-known superstitions presented as rational was the phrenology developed by Franz Gall, a German physician working in Paris. While Gall's scholarly brain studies had acknowledged merit, he proposed a relation between the character traits of people and anatomical locations of the cerebral cortex, and in this he did not follow rational scientific procedures. Gall's idea that prominent cerebral bulges meant greater development of the associated character trait was still more farfetched. The added assertion of Spurzheim and other phrenologists that appropriate training regimens could affect the cranium and improve character was an example of the exploitation that such psuedscientific practices inspired. These exploitations acted to the detriment of advancing understanding of psychopathology and diagnosis on more rational levels.

The "animal magnetism" theory of Franz Mesmer was another popular superstition that did at least contribute indirectly to deepening the understanding of the importance of the power of suggestion. Mesmer's understanding of the suggestibility of patients, especially those who would be diagnosed as hysterical, and his skill in influencing people in groups ultimately contributed to the developing understanding of the influence a healer could have on symptoms when a disturbed patient maintained belief in that healer. This uncritical acceptance is another example of the lengths to which people were willing to go to achieve some comfort. The important point is the reliance on some sort of physical agent, such as the magnetism Mesmer ceremoniously purported to control, presented in a persuasive manner, often by a charismatic individual, usually a physician. In retrospect, it is apparent that while the emphasis was on the curative potential of the physical remedy, whatever improvement occurred was most likely due to the authority of the inventor or administering physician, as well as to the expectations, caring, appreciation, and other subtle relationship qualities that invested the personal interaction. Even in modern-day treatment, there remains a strong desire for physical agents that will rectify psychological and emotional distress. Yet, it has become increasingly evident that the relationship between prescriber and sufferer has a great deal of power in whatever amelioration is achieved, and that the subtle persuasiveness of the prescriber also enhances change.

The advent of charismatic figures such as Mesmer who utilized ceremony, suggestion, and authority to partially alleviate psychopathological disturbance first of all made it gradually clearer that interpersonal factors had to be understood as playing an instrumental part in the personality changes that occurred, even if these changes were temporary. Second, these figures laid the groundwork for the investigation of hypnosis and its scientific applications that links this age with the work of Charcot and Freud in the next century. Thus, as pointed out earlier, it can be seen that solid scientific advances arose from pseudoscientific adventures, especially in the arena of hysteria and anxiety management.

Other regressive therapeutic techniques, which reflected a confused conceptualization of psychopathology and of the severity of the personal anxiety involved in distressed psychological functioning, included the administration of various tonics and even bloodletting and water shock. All were rationalized on the basis of physical determinants postulated for psychological disturbances.

The enormous activity during this period involving fads and superstitions directed toward changes in psychopathology spread pseudoscientific traditions. Simultaneously, the period reflected the sense that psychopathology could be considered a separate domain of study containing its own infrastructure and subject to understanding, control, refinement, and the development of treatment strategies. Thus, a great leap occurred in exploring psychopathology and the individual elements of personality in its management. Because it became clearer that psychopathology was a bona fide arena of study and that a genuinely important frontier was marked by new developments in understanding psychopathology, many more investigators than ever before entered the field. The fervor associated with the rituals and promises of charismatic figures thus ultimately attracted more reasoned investigators to the field of psychopathology. These investigators then introduced careful definitions of psychopathological factors, ordered them in diagnostic nosologies, and learned about beneficial ways of regulating patient anxiety. This regulation of anxiety was accomplished in part through the relationship factor of trust, once the etiology of anxiety was clarified.

DIAGNOSTIC CLASSIFICATION SYSTEMS

As outlined above, then, the eighteenth century was largely a period in which regressive physiological constructs were utilized to explain psychopathology, and therapeutic efforts were related largely to the suggestive use of forces or physical interventions; in either case, these efforts were based on the view that concrete material entities were the basis for disturbance. During such a period, efforts to classify the psychological were inevitably encumbered by physiological underpinnings that restricted the value and fruitfulness of the classification schemes devised.

During this period of classification, some presumed neurotic behavior was attributed to physiological causes and categorized accordingly. One advance was made, however, in terms of the social implications of aberrant behavior; the view arose that aberration needed to be separated from issues of ego and self-esteem. Yet even here, disordered behavior was attributed to physiological substrates, and such behavior was organized into commonalities and labeled according to criteria of psychopathology in relation to these substrates.

Other attempts at classification actually utilized diagnoses that are familiar to this day. These included neurasthenia, hysteria, and hypochondriasis—precursors, of course, to a group of diagnoses that may be considered, broadly speaking, of a hysterical nature and that led in the next hundred years directly to the work of Charcot, Breuer, and Freud. It may be suggested that contemporary approaches to the understanding of psychopathology and treatment entered essentially through the door of hysteria during the eighteenth century. It should also be noted that in the early eighteenth century, in keeping with the strong physical-organic bias maintained in views of the causality of psychopathology and the rapid development of brain anatomy as a field of study, neurological causes were considered etiological factors in hysteria and hypochondriasis.

A relatively workable nosology of the period was proposed by the British physician William Cullen. His classification of mental illnesses was hampered by the idea that most psychological disturbances were of organic cause. Psychological conflicts and problems involved in patterns of living and psychological development were not generally considered to be of any real importance in the etiology of psychopathology. In Cullen's study of etiology, however, some disturbances were related to congenital pathogenic sources, while for others, the possibility of pathogenic factors exerting influence after birth was postulated; that is, he acknowledged the possibility of acquired psychopathology. The importance of this view is that acquired psychopathology implied character formation that is influenced by learning and that can therefore be modified.

In Cullen's nosological system, the group that comprised neuroses were based in part on acquired pathologies that were not exclusively attributed to organic causes. Three types of insanity that Cullen additionally categorized in his nosology were the following:

Melancholia, in which a few distorted ideas occur with the bulk of intellectual functioning intact.

Mania, in which there is extensive debilitation with the presence of violent and impulsive behavior.

Dementia, in which debilitation occurs with deficiencies in the functioning of the intellect and will and with constricted display of emotions.

For purposes of diagnosis, Cullen emphasized the importance of assessing external symptom manifestations and even cyclical patterns, indicating again the progress that can be made when a position other than that of physical determination is used, even partially, in connection with analyzing psychopathological entities. Cullen's focus on external syndrome manifestations and their course over time enabled him to assert that acute conditions had better prognostic possibilities than diagnoses involving chronic disturbances. This is a clinical observation that continues to be valid to the present day; it has become a cohesive piller of the understanding of psychopathological functioning, one that is especially relevant to prognosis and treatment.

In spite of Cullen's contributions to diagnosing psychopathology in meaningful terms, the underlying view in his nosological scheme was so weighted toward etiology based on biopathology that internal biological events were used as explanations in a way that paralleled the ancient, prerational use of external supernatural explanations as causative factors. Treatments that were recommended necessarily involved measures associated with physiological disturbances. These therapies included the usual primitive, physically oriented activities such as purges and bloodletting. Here again, the reliance on antiquated internal postulates can be seen to foster a sterile reliance on techniques that are ineffective for resolving psychological distress. This sort of treatment approach implied an underlying diagnostic philosophy that can be likened to such primitive physical entities as those that Hippocrates postulated in his theory of humors—physical substances that determined psychopathology and its treatment. In fact, during the period of the Enlightenment, some investigators extensively revived the Hippocratic theory of humors as the etiological basis for psychological disturbances, a perspective that reinforced the physiological treatment orientations that were widespread. Other investigators, promoting interest in and research on nervous system functioning, utilized neurological processes in much the same way that humors were relied upon to account for the presence of psychopathology. The reliance on physiology in a way parallel with the more primitive notion of humors was also apparent when considered from the point of view of psychotherapy recommendations: the necessary treatment choice was viewed as the one that would affect the presumed organic basis for the disturbance, and therefore centered on a physical approach.

The assumption of physiological underpinnings in psychopathology understandably stimulated some researchers to perform autopsies. Through numerous studies of brain pathology, the Italian anatomist Giovanni Battista Morgagni, for example, was influential in developing efforts to localize mental illness in specific brain areas. The ancient reliance on Hippocratic physiological speculation was now displaced by concern regarding areas of the brain, but through influences such as Morgagni's the same emphasis on reducing psychology to physiology was maintained.

THE PSYCHOLOGICAL-INTERPERSONAL
APPROACH TO DIAGNOSIS
AND TREATMENT

Among the enlightened and progressive investigators of the eighteenth century was Pinel, the French physician whose work augmented the currents of rationality. Pinel contributed to the study of psychopathology, its clarification, and efforts to relate curative psychological treatments to the diagnoses of psychopathology. Although sympathetic to the possibility that the central nervous system might form an ultimate basis for psychopathology, the understanding that guided Pinel's investigations was essentially based on psychological ideas. A psychological perspective was included in his orientation toward mental disturbances and their classification, because he attributed importance in etiology to life experiences. His clinical observations were the basis for a useful classification system. He separated psychotic disturbances into four categories that were obviously influenced by the work of Cullen: manias with delerium, manias without delerium, melancholia, and dementia.

Pinel's descriptions of mental disturbances included a main focus on symptoms, and he described the basic psychotic syndromes of hallucinatory experiences, excitements, mood aberrations, and depression. He also focused on the importance of emotions and studied cognitive properties as a valuable consideration in the understanding of psychopathology.

Although Pinel gave substantial weight to the role of heredity as a causative factor in mental illness, this did not bias the observation and classifying that he carefully undertook. He also attributed significant influence to interpersonal variables in the development of mental illness. Just as Pinel avoided confusing his observations with metaphysical speculations, physiological fads, and brain, blood, and nerve causation, he similarly eschewed treatment approaches based on those speculative causative hypotheses.

The humanization of the typically harsh treatment of the mentally ill was greatly furthered by Pinel and is one of the achievements that marks the eighteenth century as the Age of Enlightenment. Relying on the concept that psychopathological disturbance was a psychological problem requiring psychological understanding, and, therefore, psychological treatment, Pinal influenced the growing trend toward nonphysical treatment approaches. Followers of Pinel utilized concepts of interpersonal relating by the therapist, with the goal of improving the psychotic patient's reality testing. The overall trend in this eighteenth-century period was therefore clearly toward a deemphasis of institutional and hereditary factors; instead, interpersonal considerations began to determine the nature of diagnosis as well as treatment. Reality testing as a diagnostic construct gained more prominence, and a crystallization of psychotherapy, especially with respect to the role of therapist, became more apparent at this time. Further, the therapist's role became important in the development of the idea of therapeutic communities, which since then have continued to be seen as instrumental in restructuring the adjustment of patients who have been disturbed in the context of severe family conflict. Of course, the advent of group therapy, family therapy, and day hospital rehabilitation treatment modalities one hundred fifty years later has its roots in the emergent focus on the power of interpersonal relating that was part of the eighteenth-century humanitarian ferment.

The reformers who have been discussed, as well as other eighteenth-century investigators with similar ideas, provided several lasting contributions. Their insight into the importance of the psychological nature of emotional disturbance had prominent diagnostic implications and was also relevant to the treatment of patients, as well as to more humane regard for the disturbed. This psychological and humane orientation also helped in the application of reason and observation to people's behavior, because the actual behavior could thus be perceived more truthfully and realistically, uncontaminated by physical bias or treatment. This humanistic contribution further augmented the growing tendency toward a psychological approach to the study of human behavior, interpersonal conflict, personal conflict, and, consequently, to psychopathology and social functioning.

The contradictory developments of the eighteenth century were followed in the next century by a period of inner focus. The humanization of treatment by Pinel and his followers allowed the seriousness of psychopathology to surface. At the same time, the pseudoscientific approaches that sought suggestive means to make suffering vanish only brought about a deeper respect, ultimately, for the despair from which humans could suffer.

In the nineteenth century, reliance on both reason and suggestion was eclipsed by greater regard for emotions and the inner despair of living. This nineteenth-century focus often had ramifications that involved faith and mysticism. The nineteenth-century reaction brought a turning away from scientific appreciation of the external universe to a focusing inward, a concentration of attention on the inner life and personality. The individual's struggle within himself received attention, and the features of inner conflict became a major preoccupation. Thus, the disenchantment with science and rationality led to a deeper expression and appreciation of the importance of dynamic conflict within the individual, the need to actively repress fearful or forbidden feelings, and the psychological assessment and understanding of psychopathology. These trends of the nineteenth century will be presented in the next chapter.

SUMMARY OF DIAGNOSTIC FORMULATIONS

The Age of Enlightenment was actually a polarized age with respect to the understanding of psychopathology and its treatment. During this period a strong tendency to rely on magical and supernatural explanations persisted. Such explanations put faith in antiquated concepts of humors, faulty neurological postulates, and so-called physical-medical procedures. Yet there also developed a more progressive approach which relied on more precise data and on more sound psychological principles.

Table 8.1 lists some of these contradictory approaches and conceptualizations with respect to diagnostic understanding as well as treatment approaches during this period.

TABLE 8.1: Diagnostic and Treatment Paradoxes During the Age of Enlightment (Eighteenth Century)

Nosology

- Various classifications based on behavior, without informed underlying constructs. Biopathology took the place of external supernatural forces as causative agent in mental illness.
- Early nosology of proposed neurotic behavior range included hysteria, hypochondriasis, and nervous exhaustion or neurasthenia.

TABLE 8.1, *continued*

- Pinel's more informed nosology of psychosis included melancholias, manias with delerium, manias without delerium, and dementia—i.e., intellectual deterioration. Pinel described hallucinatory experiences, manics' flight of ideas, withdrawal, and mood swings; also stressed importance of emotions, and distinguished between attention, judgment, and memory. Recognized heredity, but also stressed importance of knowing the person and his motivations and of focusing on faulty education; recognized the importance of specifically analyzing a wide range of emotions.

Treatment

- Antiquated or uninformed regimens of treatment of mental illness continued or developed, including the phrenology of Gall, the "animal magnetism" of Mesmer, bloodletting, and purges.
- Treatment involving humane efforts at understanding mental distress emphasized by Pinel and those he influenced.

CHAPTER 9

Nineteenth-Century Interest in the Nature of Psychopathology

Following the advances of the Age of Enlightenment, which included the more humane understanding and treatment of patients, a period followed in which the emotional factors that are interwoven in psychopathology could be seriously evaluated and pursued. This study of human emotion and the postulation of different agencies within the person that regulated or were associated with these emotions provided a strong groundwork for the study of patients, and of all people, in a systematically psychological way. Further, the intense focus on delineating and clarifying the inner factors involved in emotional life and conflict within people also increased the persistent tendency to relate psychotherapeutic interventions to psychological factors. These factors were now emerging, as various aspects of psychopathology were differentiated in terms of their emotional and psychological foundations. Thus, during the nineteenth century the individual's struggle with himself—his inner life—for the most part replaced the previous urgency to know more about the external world.

THE THEME OF PSYCHOGENESIS

As the inner life and its emotions and passions emerged for investigation, interest in psychology was mobilized and noteworthy advances were made. In previous eras, the work of many investigators represented a continuing attempt to reduce psychology to the physical and the bodily; such, for example, was Gall's use of phrenology. However, another persistent historical tendency was the study of psychology in connection with inner ramifications, but without physical reference, as exemplified perhaps by Spinoza's unique view of the individual's psychological functioning in non-materialistic terms. This psychological aspect of the person's makeup became more sharply defined and explored in the nineteenth century. It became the time during which modern psychology came to birth, with the dynamic and motivational components that still provide the underpinnings for a meaningful diagnostic and therapeutic approach.

Early in this nineteenth-century period, this more psychological tradition was strengthened by the investigator Johann Reil, who clarified that psychotherapy was a new instrument for treatment that could even affect bodily illness. This conception implied the important recognition of the interaction that obtains between psychological and physical aspects of functioning. The development of psychotherapy as a system to be considered seriously was important not only in shifting focus to the psychological, but also in promoting an alternative in the treatment of psychopathology that would have the same status as the use of physiologically oriented interventions. Another innovative idea was Reil's belief that before psychopathology could be adequately understood, attention needed to be devoted to understanding personality generally—an important realization that psychopathology was embedded in personality.

The innovative features of Reil's perspective can be seen in the range of ideas he emphasized. He took the extreme position that even disturbances of the brain could be ameliorated by influences that affected the individual's ideas and feelings. This view was a parallel to his belief that the cure for mental disturbance had to derive from psychological influences.

In spite of the fact that many of Reil's psychotherapeutic ideas were naive, elements of his system link up with trends that later broadened to include noteworthy diagnostic principles. One such element is the role of sexuality, which he considered significant in the treatment of such psychopathology as the condition of hysteria and the appearance of delusions involving sexual ideation. Even though Reil also administered some primitive therapies, what is important about his psychotherapy was his effort to find logical connections between a symptom and an ameliorative therapy that would be independent of pharmacology and physiology. Thus, determination of what could be effective was based on Reil's regard for the nature of the symptom and his observations of what led to improvement, compared to what did not help. His approach was to change the patient's patterns of feeling and behavior. His basic rationale was the psychological premise, which made the patient's psychopathology distinct from any physiological presumptions.

DESCRIPTIVE CLINICAL SYNDROMES AND DIFFERENTIAL DIAGNOSIS

A further contribution to clarifying the physiological composition of psychopathology came from France, where descriptions of clinical syndromes were developed by Jean Esquirol. Esquirol advanced what would eventually be a tradition of the descriptive nature of diagnosis. In addition, he compiled the precipitating events involved with the appearance of clinical syndromes. Thus, the conception of etiology as consisting of a process including various domains of personality as well as external events emerged as an important consideration in the understanding of psychopathology.

Reflecting his emphasis on the inner functioning of individuals, Esquirol made a point of defining hallucinations in exacting clinical terms, so that as a phenomenon, hallucinations became relevant to differential diagnosis. Such use of concepts having to do with the mind revealed the increasing importance of the psychological point of view during this period.

Esquirol also clinically differentiated obsessive rumination, depression, and affective disturbances; interestingly enough, he attempted to classify these in the context of a diagnostic formulation related to his concept of monomania. In an explicit sense, monomania was a focus on a specific idea, which in contemporary psychology would be considered obsessional in nature. In an implicit sense, the use of the term *mania* suggests that Esquirol viewed psychopathology as a disruption of impulse and as a function of how this impulse is managed—for example, does the impulse generate obsessions, or create depression? Thus, because of his hypotheses regarding the domination of affects over thoughts, Esquirol can be considered one of the early investigators of psychic structure. Also during this period, a major effort by psychopathologists was to consider the nature of impulse versus control. Their theories in this area revealed what is today considered the vicissitudes of psychopathic behavior.

In another example of clarifying a psychopathological diagnosis, sustained and careful clinical observation led to the realization that psychotically depressed patients would frequently have moods of manic excitement alternating with their periods of depression. In the mid-nineteenth century this condition became known as *circular madness*, or *madness with double form*. These efforts at greater precision in the diagnostic nomenclature reflected the increasingly careful clinical observations that were associated with a deeper understanding of this double form or circular madness category.

In the late nineteenth century this condition was finally labeled *manic-depressive psychosis*. The understanding of the complex elements of this type of psychosis and the effort to clarify the components of it—even though their loose association had been noted thousands of years earlier—had now, in the early to mid-nineteenth century, created a sense of differential diagnosis as part of a classification system in the organization of psychopathology. This development in the understanding of diagnosis already reveals an inexorable momentum—a process of differentiating psychopathological conditions that continues to the present time. Along with a focus on the constructs of impulse and control and on psychopathic and manic-depressive syndromes, mental processes such as hallucinatory experiences and hypnagogic states were also joining the catalogue of symptoms that contributed to the classification of various syndromes.

A further indication of the growing refinement of diagnostic entities was in the newly coined term *hebephrenia* and the description of its associated behavior—silliness and inappropriate laughter. The categorization of this inappropriateness of affect as hebephrenic was a precursor to the establishment of various subtypes of schizophrenia.

At this time, the concept of *repression* was also introduced, adding to the overall ferment of thought regarding the psychological complexity of personality. Although elements of repression were foreshadowed by Hobbes and Spinoza, the full role of motivation in the dynamic mechanism of repression was not recognized until Freud's clarification. However, the groundwork was being laid by the nineteenth-century investigators who were concerned about understanding more deeply the psychological mechanisms connected to the increasingly sophisticated observations they were making. In addition, the development of a basis for clarifying symptoms of psychopathology, and the recognition that it was necessary to devote consideration to a range of elements in diagnosis, led to broader considerations of diagnosis and psychopathology.

In the nineteenth century, then, an enrichment of clinical language, an understanding of some unique syndromes, and a greater diagnostic range was applied to the overall appreciation of personality. In addition, beginning efforts were made to consider how psychological phenomena were involved in overall personality functioning. The ordering of personality variables and a greater sense of the underlying parsimony of personality remained issues to be more fully appreciated in the twentieth century.

METAPSYCHOLOGY
AND PSYCHODYNAMICS

The nineteenth-century concern with latent and emotional processes led toward a comprehension of overall personality functioning as well as of the psychological substrata of abnormality. Thus, investigators augmented the preceding descriptive level of abnormal psychology and brought to the understanding of psychopathology a more dynamic conceptualization in the formulation of personality theory. For example, introspection was utilized as a basis for developing a psychological understanding of dreams.

Jacques Moreau was among the first to offer important insights into personality, and he mobilized a new area for psychological research based on his study of dreams. He reasoned that dreams were similar to hallucinations and then proposed that dreams represented a common element appearing in both abnormal and normal functioning. His stress on psychological mechanisms and on what occurs in both normal and abnormal phenomena suggests an understanding of diagnosis and dynamics embedded in the area of personality functioning. The variables related to investigating personality, pathology, and diagnosis included conflict, impulses, and interpersonal tensions, rather than physiological and biochemical agents. Thus, for Moreau, a resemblance between the disturbed and the normal could be clarified in terms of the processes that emerge in the phenomenon of dreaming. This approach further consolidated the importance of one of the two central themes throughout the history of the study of mental illness; that is, the conviction that mental aberration is related to environmental, interpersonal, and intrapersonal events, rather than strictly to physical agents.

DIFFERENTIATING PSYCHOSIS FROM NORMALCY: THE EGO AND REALITY

Further elaborating upon dream life, Moreau explored subjective psychological phenomena and how they related in the dream experience and psychosis. He proposed that in the context of internal functioning, subjective and irrational elements have greater effect on psychological processes. Just as the dreamer is withdrawn, turned toward the internal, the psychotic is also inwardly focused. The domination by internal, irrational processes in both dream and psychosis led Moreau to establish an identity between these two phenomena. Further, he sharpened the approach to understanding personality functioning that made central the influence of irrational pressures on an individual's functioning and the psychological mechanisms by which these operated. He saw that in some individuals, irrational forces and wishes could be relatively restricted and contained, while in others, these emotional phenomena played a more dominant role. The degree of this difference would be instrumental in differentiating normal from abnormal functioning. In contrast, in seeking to understand mental illness the advocates of physical causation and treatment—representing the other of the two central tendencies in the history of psychopathology and treatment—would propose biochemical, physical factors as instrumental in the difference between irrational and normal behavior.

Other investigators, such as Johann Heinroth, also explored psychotic manifestations in order to understand personality. Based on his concept of a moralistic conscience, Heinroth focused on feelings of guilt as contributing to inner conflict and generating disturbance. In addition to the moralistic level, Heinroth also elaborated levels of mental functioning associated with pleasure-oriented instinctual feelings and with cognitive factors involving intelligence and the interpretation of reality. Thus, anticipating Freud's eventual distribution of mental functioning into a tripartite model of forces consisting of ego, superego, and id, Heinroth divided psychological process into three levels comparable to Freud's. In fact, Heinroth's work, in part, provides the foundation for some important psychoanalytic dynamic conceptions. His appreciation of the complexity of individual functioning led Heinroth to advise seeking the most advantageous relationship in matching patient to therapist and treatment. His conceptualization of conflict between internal forces and his theory of a sequence of stages in personality development reveals the period's advancing psychological sophistication.

Another quantum leap in the tradition of building a psychodynamic understanding of etiology and psychopathology came with the psychosomatic framework developed by Friedrich Benecke. Benecke simply proposed the staggering hypothesis that ideas or conflict might be expressed through physical symptoms—a prime example of the strength of psychological formulations in understanding etiology and psychopathology during this period.

THE COEXISTING FOCUS
ON PSYCHOBIOLOGY

Several of Heinroth's contemporaries regarded human functioning in terms of psychobiology. These investigators evaluated the influence of drives on reasoning and attempted to localize the parts of the brain that were associated with them. In addition, they concentrated on the psychobiological disturbance of emotion and proposed that such conflict can then appear in psychopathological form. For example, Friedrich Groos, both a philosopher and a psychiatrist in the psychobiological tradition, considered physiological and psychological influences as corresponding aspects of the human organism. He proposed that people can be affected by physical forces, and when expression of these influences are prevented, emotional disturbance can result. Thus, as Freud postulated in his early theoretical writings, instincts need to be understood in order to truly understand psychopathology.

At this point in the history of psychopathology, discoveries and theories seem to be racing directly toward the theories elaborated

by Sigmund Freud. At this time, during the early nineteenth century, it was also noted that anger and aggression were inextricably
related to psychopathology and could become especially prominent during psychotic breakdown. This finding regarding the nature of anger and aggression and the manner of its expression remains a frequently observed phenomenon during what are today
defined as depersonalization experiences within the psychotic
process.

While the psychological and psychodynamic concepts developed
during the earlier part of the nineteenth century were emphatic
and striking, after the middle of the century, organically based approaches emerged and completely overshadowed the dynamic direction. By the time Freud made his first contributions to psychodynamics at the end of the nineteenth century, his orientation
appeared innovative, and the psychobiological perspective practically had to be reinvented.

In the following chapter, a clear reaction to the ferment of psychological factors emphasized during this period is traced through
the work of scientists, physicians, and experimentors who focused
largely on the brain and nervous system as the central repository
source for all explanations of the causes of mental distress. This
discussion will be followed by the emergence of Freud, who then
needed to resurrect the psychobiological perspective.

SUMMARY OF DIAGNOSTIC FORMULATIONS

The theoretical and empirical ideas of early nineteenth-century investigators advanced the study of psychopathology toward a fuller
appreciation of several important elements. One was the internal
basis for emotional disturbance, its relation to personal conflict
and interpersonal stress caused by characterology. Another important element was the recognition of the crucial part played both
by psychological aspects of human functioning and by biological
components that relate to emotions. These developments indicate
the fertility of the psychobiological approach that became prominent. They also suggest the importance of regarding human beings
in terms of unified personality systems. The personalities of individuals would henceforth need to be understood in connection both
with subjective psychological features and with the physiological

side of these features. These nineteenth-century investigators gradually made it clearer that significant parts of this unity could be cut off from consciousness.

The psychobiological perspective advanced in the nineteenth century was so productive in augmenting the role of psychological and personality functioning in the understanding of psychopathology that advances also accrued to the psychosomatic area of study. In keeping with a view of the human being as a unity, increased investigation in the psychosomatic sphere would be expected, from both psychological and physiological perspectives.

In table 9.1, the philosophical, diagnostic, and psychopathology formulations as well as treatment orientations of this nineteenth-century period are presented.

TABLE 9.1: Summary of Philosophical, Diagnostic, and Treatment Orientations of the Nineteenth Century

Philosophical

- Internal experience stressed, in contrast to investigative focus on the external world.
- Modern psychology born, with emphasis on knowing the dynamic and motivational components of personality.
- Psychological understanding of psychopathology considered central.
- Role of sexuality in psychopathology considered important.
- Emphasis on psychobiological functioning of the person characterized the age, with the accent on the psychological aspect of this psychobiology.

Diagnosis and Psychopathology

- Models of the mind formulated. Three levels of psychological process proposed: (1) instinctual feelings, aiming toward pleasure; (2) the ego, guided by intellect and testing of reality; (3) conscience.
- Illusion distinguished from hallucination.
- *Monomania* named as a pathological manifestation, and defined as the possession of obsessive ideas.
- Manic-depressive psychosis viewed as a unified condition diagnosed as *circular madness* or *madness with double form*.
- Hypnagogic experiences defined.
- Hebephrenia characterized and defined.
- The interpretation of dreams emphasized, contributing to the understanding of conflict, psychopathology, and overlap between normal and pathological functioning.

TABLE 9.1, *continued*

- Repression defined and the idea of emotional blockage specified.
- Knowledge of the nature of emotions considered central to understanding psychopathology.
- Anger evaluated as a crucial emotion, appearing in intense form during mental breakdown.

Treatment

- Concept developed that treatment depended on an understanding of ideas and feelings and that even disturbances of the brain could be ameliorated by working on these ideas and feelings.
- A diverse array of therapies brought to bear in the treatment of mental disorders.
- Idea of matching patient and therapist reflected the sense that empathy and understanding was important.

PART IV
Nosological Systems and the Appearance of Sigmund Freud

CHAPTER 10

The Reemergence of the Physical Approach and Early Classification Schemes

In the latter part of the nineteenth century, there was a dramatic shift from a psychological orientation back to an organic approach in accounting for psychopathology. This shift once again reflects the two distinct outlooks that vie for explanatory power in determining the foundation of psychopathology, in treating it, and in forming the basis for a diagnostic scheme. The emphasis of early nineteenth-century investigators who began to illuminate a dynamic personality structure, as opposed to the focus on the organic approach that developed afterward, stemmed from their efforts to form a comprehensive and abstract view of the overall field of psychopathology.

The development of a global conception of psychopathology and its causes necessitated more limited devotion to the continued development of a careful observational basis. Because of this commitment to an overall view, phenomena such as inner conflict could be related to religious principles and goals. When such relationships were formed, however, the investigator's philosophic orientation tended to overshadow what was actually observed with patients. When Freud made internal conflict once again a central concern, he differed from early nineteenth-century investigators precisely by his exceptional care in maintaining a focus on the data. In keeping with his regard for the behavior he observed in his patients, he continually tested the theories he developed and readjusted them as contradictory observations emerged. Freud also went beyond those who had anticipated his theories by adding a methodology that he believed would generate data relevant to a thorough investigation of personality and psychopathology.

The nineteenth-century theorists who maintained a dynamic emphasis relied on conceptualizing the person as a psychobiological unity, implicitly suggesting interconnections between psychological and biological forces that mobilize conflict between people and within individuals. But this early nineteenth-century emphasis on psychobiological unity was followed around 1850 by investigations emphasizing descriptive classifications with only limited therapeutic connections. The scientists who conducted these investigations implicitly considered the nervous system the source of mental illness. Advances in such fields as physics and chemistry suggested this view of disturbed behavior as derivative of nervous system activity; in addition, the publication in 1859 of Charles Darwin's *On the Origin of Species by Means of Natural Selection* diminished the amount of attention given to concepts such as purpose and vital forces. Within such an intellectual context, ideas about internal psychological determinants appeared overly abstract and distinctly contrary to the scientific interests of the times. The certainty and concreteness of the new studies of the material aspects of organisms reduced the appeal of such nonmaterial ideas as that of psychological determinants in psychopathology. Therefore, a narrow approach, emphasizing scientific correctness, took the place of the study of psychological forces, emotional conflict, and personality development in efforts to account for psychopathology and to develop differential diagnosis.

Neurological considerations, especially brain pathology, emerged as the central concern in attempts to understand psychopathology. Interestingly, it was out of training in this approach that Freud's career as a neurologist began. His sensitivity to what he viewed as the shortcomings of efforts to understand disturbances in behavior through neurology stimulated his search for a more useful conception of psychopathology.

NEUROLOGICAL INTERPRETATIONS OF PSYCHOPATHOLOGY

The general growth in scientific study in many fields during the nineteenth century stimulated research oriented towards organic explanations for psychological phenomena. Several investigators had already sought material organic bases for psychopathology through postmortem examinations of the brains of patients who had been psychotic. One of the most important neurological findings that encouraged this approach to psychopathology was derived from examining patients with syphilis. Victims of this disease developed a psychopathological condition known as general pareseis, and autopsies of these patients later revealed brain lesions. Using such findings, a theoretical model was extrapolated that hypothesized pathology of the brain as the primary factor in particular mental illnesses. This hypothesis guided researchers before any direct correlation of data was available showing the connection between a brain event and overt psychopathology. However, the finding that brain damage was associated with general pareseis virtually dictated pursuit of corresponding findings with other conditions, and this investigative approach characterized developments during the later nineteenth century.

The field of neurology was thus dominated by the preconception that some cerebral damage or activity was connected with all mental disturbances. The demonstration that various dementias associated with brain deterioration through alcoholism and senility were correlated with lesions in the brain conformed to the theory that mental disturbance corresponded to neurological impairment. One of the leaders of the theory of essential cerebral damage in psychopathology was Wilhelm Griesinger, who was strongly committed to the organic point of view. In his investigations within this frame of reference, he uncovered and detailed personality alterations in patients with brain damage. In apparent recognition, however, that the organic position was incomplete, he also discussed in his writings the role of such nonorganic factors as the ego, repression, psychosis, and dreams. He acknowledged psychological aspects of emotional disorders, but considered them secondary to organic causality. In addition, he connected some of these personality configurations, such as poor self-esteem and feelings of depression, to the premorbid personality, as a prerequisite for fully assessing the patient's disorder. He considered assessment of the premorbid personality essential in strengthening and reestablishing the reality-oriented ego of the patient in a program of psychotherapy.

The connection between dreams and psychopathological symptoms was also noted by Griesinger, and he described wish fulfillment as essential to both. In this way he suggested an analogous relationship between dreaming and insanity. Tension, affect, internal strife, and guilt were also considered by this wide-ranging researcher, but his main interest was always the search for underlying cerebral pathology as the basis for the psychological correlates. This concentration on organic components also influenced his therapeutic recommendations, in which he utilized concepts relating affect and cognition to alterations in cerebral activity. He advocated both somatic and psychological treatment, ranging from medication to occupational training.

The organic approach to psychopathology, advancing along with admixtures of psychologically insightful contributions, was strengthened by laboratory investigations in the field of neurophysiology. This research explored, for example, the effects of electrical stimulation on cerebral functioning. The experiments were designed to localize brain functions by drawing correlations between portions of animals' brains that were systematically destroyed and behavioral alterations that followed. Applying the findings of these investigations to humans helped determine that functions such as speech and motor activity were connected to activity in specific lobes of the brain. Russian physiologists such as Pavlov elaborated findings and theories connecting psychological and physical reactions to neural processes.

Efforts to relate the findings of neuroanatomy and neurophysiology to neurotic functioning were unconvincing because of the inevitable compromises that had to be introduced in order to base psychopathology involving neurotic syndromes solely on organic foundations. Various therapies utilizing electrical devices and currents were advocated, but it became clear that the temporary modifications of symptomatology that they effected were related to the effects of suggestion.

During this period, Freud's use of physical methods in his neurological practice proved to be ineffective, and he began to explore the use of hypnosis. Basically, he was disenchanted with the electric therapies of the time. While numerous neurological findings of significant merit were being accumulated, assertions relating neurology to psychological and psychopathological phenomena were frequently unfortunate. For example, the neurologist Theodore Meynert argued that the psychological phenomena of excitement and depression in patients were caused by either excesses or inadequacies of blood in cerebral vessels, and he classified mental illnesses according to his studies of cell pathology in the nervous system. This theoretical approach led to treatment regimes for emotional disorders utilizing drugs intended to alter these cerebral vessels. The resemblance to the Hippocratic concepts and approach is strikingly apparent, showing the persistence of the comprehensively materialistic, physiological analysis of emotional and psychological functioning.

As advances in neurological theory were made and their implications experimentally tested, a consolidation involving physiology and neurology was developed, suggesting principles of classification for neurological phenomena. It was assumed that psychopathology would parallel neurological impairments in an all-embracing nosology.

EARLY CLASSIFICATION SYSTEMS OF PSYCHOPATHOLOGY AND NEUROLOGY

In the first classification systems developed during this period, psychopathological symptoms were formed into syndrome groups. These included *cyclothymia,* alternating moods of depression and elation, and *catatonia,* a psychosis involving bizarre postures, with mutism and potential excitement; a later addition was *hebephrenia,* in which inappropriate behavioral mannerisms, affect and communication disturbances occurred. Thus, the comprehensive description of the schizophrenic syndrome was emerging along with that of a psychotic mood disturbance. Efforts to link brain deterioration with the psychological deterioration apparent in schizophrenic functioning were complicated by the observations from case studies that the typical onset of schizophrenic dysfunction occurred during adolescence. The adolescent time of onset so frequently seen was the basis for calling the syndrome *dementia praecox* (pre-mature dementia) at that time.

The clinical studies conducted under the assumption of a neurological basis for mental illness produced distinct syndrome pictures that clinicians attempted to correlate with neurological and cerebral pathological findings or hypotheses. With this coincidence of data, and the coherent symptom clusters that were differentiated and studied, a more general classification of the data was called for; that is, an overall nosological framework.

Emil Kraepelin, a believer in the organic etiology of psychopathology, developed a descriptive classification that was focused
on patients' behavioral manifestations of their disturbances and
their presumed organic underpinnings. Kraepelin solidified the diagnosis of dementia praecox as the psychosis of delusions, hallucinations, and bizarre behavior with a relatively early onset in life
and gradual deterioration in the course of the syndrome. He described a catatonic type of dementia praecox, in which mutism
and/or excitement was present, a hebephrenic type in which inappropriate affect and communication occurred, and added the
paranoid type, which involved persecutory delusions.

In addition to organizing dementia praecox into various subtypes, Kraepelin sharply differentiated the nosological class of dementia praecox from manic-depressive psychosis. The basis for the
distinction between these two psychotic categories was the course
of the disturbance. Kraepelin observed that in the case of manic-
depressive psychosis, not only did depressive and excited mood
states frequently appear in alternate periods, but states of relatively nonpsychotic adjustment also alternated with the phases of
psychotic mood disturbance.

At this point in the history of the diagnosis of psychopathology,
the idea of the classification of disorders was so compelling to clinicians and researchers that the development of classificatory systems took on inexorable momentum. The advent of neat nosologies, presumably encompassing the entire range of disorders, created
a focus more on cure than on deeper and fuller conceptualization.
Therefore, although the rapid increase in the use of classification
helped to organize the clinician's thinking, it also created a rigid
framework that tended to exclude recognition of individual differences, and it fostered a sense of the immutability of diagnosis.

The greatest contribution of Kraepelin's diagnostic achievements was in bringing a degree of order into the random body of
clinical data that had been accumulated by the later nineteenth-
century investigators. Advances in the sciences had encouraged focused studies on a variety of syndromes, and Kraepelin's nosology
utilized a theoretical approach based on the neurological view of
mental illness. Within this framework, psychological manifestations had importance only as a means for establishing classifications. The nosological ordering that Kraepelin established has persisted in many respects. However, his descriptive approach, based
largely on manifest patient behavior, has restricted stimulation of

more possibilities to appreciate etiology and psychodynamics. Consequently, the development of a deeper understanding of inner cognitive and emotional experiences in the pathology of the psychoses and their relevance to etiology and treatment have not generally been supported by Kraepelin's diagnostic approach.

Kraepelin's nosological categories placed a limitation on the development of the psychological meanings and implications of the various disturbances he categorized. In addition, his theory of psychopathology, in its reflection of neurological etiologies, could not clarify such meanings by recognizing the effects of emotional experience on mental functioning. For these reasons, an antipsychological, even sterile quality was perpetuated by the nosological framework he bequeathed to the field of psychopathology. Only Freud's efforts, which were more similar to those of the precursors of dynamic psychology in the era before the one Kraepelin culminated, refocused attention on the patient as an individual with a unique personal history and conflicting motivations. The spirit of the neurological approach so overshadowed the emphasis of the earlier nineteenth century on the individual in conflict that Freud had to virtually reinvent the dynamic approach. Nevertheless, the long-range conflict between the two approaches in the development of theories, treatments, and nosology in mental illness seems always to continue. The conflict may be viewed in terms of which type of agent should be studied—whether neurological, physiological, and/or chemical analysis, or psychological insight, provides the best way to understand and treat the manifestations of psychopathology.

The work of several philosophers and scientific investigators who emphasized the importance of emotions, conflict, and neurotic functioning will be presented in the next chapter. These new ideas contributed to the renewed emergence of interest in a dynamic basis for psychological functioning.

SUMMARY OF DIAGNOSTIC FORMULATIONS

By the middle of the nineteenth century, a renewed emphasis on description, systematization, and classification of mental illnesses was generated by the growth of neurologically oriented investigations. Kraepelin's classification efforts established once and for all the utilization of nosological systems in psychopathology, though his system limited the understanding of psychodynamics. Pathology of the brain was seen as the major factor in mental illness during this time. It was thought that all mental illness was connected to some cerebral damage. Table 10.1 presents some of the major currents in the thinking of this period.

TABLE 10.1: Diagnostic Formulations of the Late Nineteenth Century

Etiology

• Investigations into a variety of neurotic psychopathologies made, in order to locate their organic bases.
• Excitement and depression physiologically related to cerebral vessels, in keeping with organic-physiological orientation.
• Study of syphilis established the hypothesis that psychosis caused by brain pathology.

Central Psychological Concepts Advanced

• Concept of repression further elaborated.
• Ego further recognized.
• Idea of premorbid personality and psychotic personality in same person acknowledged, implying a psychopathological process.
• Wish fulfillment theorized as a central construct both in the dream and in psychopathological symptoms.

Diagnostic Nomenclature

• Cyclothymia related to depression and elation.
• Dementia praecox identified, characterized by onset during adolescence and continuous pathological deterioration.
• Manic-depressive psychosis diagnostically differentiated from dementia praecox on basis of onset in maturity, alternation of disturbed moods with intermittant periods of normalcy, and lack of pathological deterioration.
• Catatonia defined in terms of mutism and/or excitement and classified as subtype of dementia praecox.
• Hebephrenia defined as subtype of dementia praecox with regressed and inappropriate behavior.
• Paranoid subtype of dementia praecox added on basis of persecutory delusions.

CHAPTER 11

Precursors to Freudian Psychology and the Dynamic Understanding of Psychopathology

In the early part of the nineteenth century, numerous ideas developed by philosophers and scientists contributed to the evolution of a psychological appreciation of emotional and perceptual functioning. The inner affective life of people was given greater consideration, and constructs bearing on a dynamic representation of psychological functioning were emphasized. Such developments not only clarified the realm of normal psychological functioning, but also permitted significant understanding of important formative aspects of the range of psychopathology that was observed, and of the attendant experience of anxiety.

Among those during the early nineteenth century who played a role in developing a dynamic framework for the general psychology of affective and ideational experience was the German philosopher Johann Herbart. His ideas played a part in penetrating the inner structure of psychopathological phenomena dynamically, and so contributed, ultimately, to Freud's theories. To Locke's emphasis on ideas, Herbart added the concept of force, which he held to be an inherent component of each idea. By emphasizing force, Herbart allowed the dynamic dimension to come to the forefront in the recognition and understanding of conflicts between ideas. Herbart also introduced concepts relevant to consciousness that were crucial for the emergence of dynamic psychology. As a result, ideas and psychological processes could be construed as acting in dynamic relation to one another on the unconscious level. Thus, Herbart concluded that individuals and consciousness are influenced without awareness, a key construct for a psychological understanding of psychopathology and of the experiences of anxiety and emotional confusion that accompany disordered psychological functioning.

The idea of force introduced by Herbart invested the association of ideas and experiences, and the resulting mental functioning, with a quantitative component. He thus established a basis for striving between ideas to assert their influence, and suggested a mechanism by which stronger ideas are more likely to register in consciousness. These philosophical conjectures relate to Freud's theory on several counts. Freud utilized the idea of a focus of attention that makes a particular element conscious, as well as the idea that a continual repressive force becomes necessary to expel thoughts from consciousness and to sustain repression of the complex of associations that interconnect such repressed thoughts. The concept of forces connected to ideas, that then serve as motivations that are not conscious but which are still capable of influencing behavior, also encouraged the use of hypnosis as a tool for exploring people's functioning and investigating psychopathological phenomena for scientific purposes.

FURTHER PHILOSOPHIC FOCUS ON THE IRRATIONAL

Another nineteenth-century philosopher who introduced concepts that anticipated Freud's recognition of the importance of the irrational aspects of man was Schopenhauer, who emphasized the significant role of feeling and striving. In Schopenhauer's thought, the intellect served dynamic and irrational forces connected to *will*, the persistent irrational striving that he regarded as having the greatest influence over people's functioning. This irrationality opposed reason and morality, and attention and dedication were necessary in striving toward freedom from irrationality and from the influence of the emotions.

The philosophical contributions of Friedrich Nietzsche also emanated from a view that irrational aspects of human functioning were major, relentless forces that could never be avoided. Nietzsche advocated the development of the "will to power" as a means to master the irrationality that dominated human life.

The philosophers who emphasized the influence of irrational elements in people and in nature not only revealed the power and significance of the emotions—the irrational passions—in motivating human activity, but they also raised an issue that would seem to be almost the antithesis to their argument: in what ways can the rational and logical investigations of scientists assess and analyze the apparent strength of the powerful passions, which seem to be outside the purview of rationality?

One extremely influential response to the thesis of the persistently dominating irrational side of man was made by Freud. Freud sought to bring the irrational component of man under greater rational control by facing and exploring the unconscious elements in mental functioning in the manner customary to scientific investigation. Freud's encapsulation of the goal of his treatment, "Where id was, ego shall be," signifies the achievement of conscious control over irrationality gained by securing greater understanding of one's irrational makeup, which would then result in more reasonable behavior. The theory and technique Freud developed was based on a logical analysis of the irrational and usually hidden forces that motivate people and which are, in his theory, central to psychological functioning, as well as to the development of psychopathology.

INVESTIGATIONS OF HYSTERIA: RATIONAL APPROACHES TO PATHOLOGY

The philosophers who brought focus to the irrational aspects of man saw emotional and irrational functioning as crucial psychological motivations in people. The relatively hidden elements in these powerful motivators suggest the concept of a dynamic—that is, an influential—unconscious. Several later nineteenth-century clinicians, who were scientific as opposed to philosophic precursors of Freud, became increasingly specific about the nature of unconscious functioning. In order to establish scientific and therefore rational foundations for such functioning, which was considered irrational, neurological constructs and theories were at first used extensively in investigators' efforts.

A leading late nineteenth-century French neurologist who strongly influenced Freud was Jean-Martin Charcot. He carefully and seriously studied patients presenting a range of unusual symptoms that did not seem at first to reflect diagnostic consistency. These psychopathological manifestations included loss of receptive responses to touch in localized body areas and paralysis of parts of limbs, as well as the full spectrum of other bodily and physiological disorders that would come to the attention of a neurologist. Charcot diagnostically considered all of these syndromes hysterical and neurotic. Although he was committed to a neurological explanation of etiology, his focus on unusual symptoms that did not follow traditional neurological pathways, and which could be dramatically affected through hypnosis, suggested the outstanding role that psychological influences have in hysterical reactions. Charcot's discussion of psychological trauma and sexuality in connection with hysterical symptomatology further stimulated psychological conjecture regarding etiology and diagnosis. By stimulating and modifying symptoms of hysteria through hypnotic influences, Charcot demonstrated the connection between a variety of hysterias and mental functioning.

The phenomenon of suggestibility as a component of hysterical functioning, along with Charcot's experimental induction and alteration of symptoms, increased the psychological appreciation of the neuroses. Thus, Charcot's major importance ultimately stemmed from the fact that his work created a bridge between observable physical conditions and intangible agents related to the induction, modification, and cure of these physical manifestations.

Others during this period maintained that organicity constituted a central etiological condition of hysterical reactions; this school of thought included Pierre Janet and Josef Breuer. Janet introduced the diagnosis of psychasthenia—a psychological weakness—and suggested the diagnosis of multiple personality as well. Emphasizing the importance of dissociation in the formation of symptoms, Janet did refer to processes outside of consciousness. Nevertheless, he relied on the rather primitive notion of basic neurological and organic deficits to explain all of the phenomena of hysteria and neurosis that he studied.

In his investigations, Janet also discovered what would prove to be exceedingly significant in the psychological view of dysfunction—the power of catharsis in relieving symptoms. Janet noted that often catharsis was effected through the retelling of historical or traumatic events. He nevertheless persisted in a neurological explanation even though his patient's symptoms improved through the emotionally pronounced and directed verbal expression of meaningful events that constitutes catharsis. Breuer also discovered the ameliorative effect of catharsis and recognized his patients' pressure to initiate and achieve cathartic reactions, but he also minimized their importance. The partially curative effects of these abreactions in which intense emotion forced the expression of painful experiences was not recognized in terms of the importance in treatment of encouraging emotional depth in the interview of patients. Thus, in a sense both Janet and Breuer had the opportunity to develop psychoanalysis, but they did not pursue the psychological implications, or even what was obviously psychological, in their own work. Yet, Freud did credit Breuer with discovering the germ that led to the broad psychoanalytic conception.

In contrast to Charcot, Janet, and Breuer, in the late nineteenth century the French investigators Ambrose-August Liebeault and Hyppolyte-Marie Bernheim decided that it was actually the psychological component of suggestibility, rather than organic weakness postulated by those adhering to neurological explanations, that accounted for hypnotic effects. Bernheim advanced the cause of the unconscious with the use of posthypnotic techniques and became a precursor to Freud by bringing hysteria into the realm of the psychological.

The approach shared by both Janet and Breuer, as well as by the other adherents of the organic point of view who investigated hysteria through hypnosis, can be stated quite simply. Since neurology was assumed to be the causative explanation, the psychological functioning of patients, in terms of personal history and the influence of unconscious phenomena, was regarded as unimportant and was therefore never incorporated into theories or concepts of psychopathology or psychotherapy.

THE STUDY OF SEXUALITY
IN PSYCHOPATHOLOGY

One of the central factors that influenced researchers such as Janet and Breuer to avoid the psychological implications and explorations of hysterical patients' symptomatology was the sexual ramifications arising in the behavior and verbal reports of their patients. During this Victorian period, pervasive sexual prohibitions affected not only the professional lives of scientists but also, more subtlely, their own personal reactions, which may in turn have influenced their scientific investigations. Limited study of sexuality was permissible in a scientific context, provided that deviance or perversion were investigated as abnormal. However, the sexual life, the feelings and fantasies of ordinary people, were studiously avoided. In fact, it is well known that Freud's uncompromising, scientific articulation of the sexual elements in the etiology of hysteria brought great discredit to his reputation. It was undoubtedly the anticipation of this sort of reaction that prevented earlier workers with the same data from drawing useful observations about the role played by sexual etiology in psychopathology.

The French researchers who investigated hysteria and evaluated neurotic phenomena instead of confining their research to psychosis did awaken a renewed interest in psychology toward the end of the nineteenth century. This renewal of interest included some appreciation of the sexual implications in etiology, although this was never directly confronted. The climate of the times discouraged consideration of sexual matters in normal and patient populations as well as in scientific circles, and the excitement about neurology made an organic etiology the prepotent explanation for virtually all researchers. However, renewed interest in psychology was widespread, as was increasing interest in sexual research. In the late nineteenth century, Richard von Krafft-Ebing and Havelock Ellis investigated a variety of sexual aberrations. More broadly, these scientists were involved in the investigations of emotional and instinctual life that reflected psychological and sociological components of human behavior.

The cumulative effect of these types of investigations into sexual functioning, along with the very active thinking devoted to the etiology of hysterias, was the beginning acknowledgment of the role of sex in human life. Sexuality could now be regarded more readily as connected with important activities and conflicts in all human beings. The consideration of aberrations paved the way for bringing normal sexual development into the scientific arena as an aspect of human study.

SYMPTOMS AND TREATMENT

In America, the psychiatrist Morton Prince reflected the spread of increased interest in psychological phenomena. He explored cases of multiple personalities, which he identified with hysteria. About this time, other phenomena associated with hysteria, such as automatic writing, were also described. In fact, by the beginning of the twentieth century, one of the major accomplishments in the study of psychopathology was the extent to which investigators of emotional disturbance focused more and more on neurotic as well as normal behavior, as opposed to the earlier focus mostly on psychotic, severely disturbed behavior. The increasing study of neurosis advanced the field of psychopathology, because neurotic conditions lent themselves more readily to explanations that related to psychological experience in the individual's history. By shifting to study of neurotic functioning, psychopathologists could more naturally raise considerations that had implications for the psychology of normal functioning.

Another stimulus that derived from the study of neurotic patients and their relation to the norm was the fact that the study of neurotic psychological functioning more clearly suggested treatment possibilities that would be helpful and make a difference. Controversy arose over how neurotic disturbance could be treated by psychotherapy. An approach was developed based on persuasion and reason, in contrast with psychotherapy that utilized an emotionally heightened relationship with the therapist to achieve symptomatic change. The latter approach, represented by the French psychiatrist Joseph Déjerine, emphasized the patient's emotional investment in the therapist, which allowed the patient to convey intimacies of his life and to develop what in contemporary psychoanalytic parlance would be called a positive transference. The patient's confidence in the therapist had to do with feelings rather than ideas, and feelings then emerged as the basis for successful treatment. Déjerine's essential view, then, was that reason and persuasion would have no effect unless they were used in the context of a meaningful interpersonal relationship that would make new ideas resonant to the patient.

The conflicting approaches to psychotherapy that arose at this time are interesting from the point of view of one of the modern debates in the field of psychotherapy. Many contemporary psychotherapists emphasize cognitive restructuring as a technique, as opposed to regarding as curative factors emotional insight and relationship qualities. The tendency to dichotomize reason and emotion is part of a long-term dispute in philosophy as well as in psychology and perhaps reflects man's struggle as a species to integrate these two forceful components of personal life. Even within the scope of psychoanalysis, where emphasis on emotional and relationship influences predominates, the question is often raised whether cure is achieved through insight or through emotional experience within treatment. Déjerine brought the importance of emotions into the foreground in both somatic and psychological disturbances. He also posited subconscious influences and traumatizing emotional stress in the etiology of hysteria. Thus, Déjerine emerges as one of the first clinicians to elaborate and deepen the search for psychological meaning.

The influence of Déjerine and of other significant psychiatrists, psychologists, and physiologists coincided in the Swiss psychiatrist Edouard Claparède, whose work had great impact on the later study of intelligence by the Swiss psychologist Jean Piaget. Claparède's contribution provided a channel for incorporating the dimension of intelligence and the enhancement of conscious thought into considerations of personality functioning and psychopathology.

Claparède anticipated Freud in his study of sleep and the protective functions it serves. He regarded the symptomatology of hysteria in similar terms of protection. The sum of his contributions broadened the domain explored by psychology and deepened the consideration of meaning attributable to psychological functioning.

This review of the work at the end of the nineteenth century of investigators of hysteria, sexual phenomena, sleep experience, and process issues involved in the psychotherapy of neurotic psychopathology reveals the extent of activity then being devoted to investigating psychological functioning in patients and to expanding the psychological perspective. A more inclusive focus on neurotic psychopathology than had previously appeared was also introduced. Complementing this emerging tendency to investigate neurosis from the psychological point of view, writers of novels, plays, and poetry during this period explored intrapsychic conflicts of people even before Freud, and did so with striking sophistication and thoroughness. Through the medium of fiction, writers could represent people fully and in depth. Scientists were approaching such representations, but could not yet allow themselves to understand certain aspects of man, either because of the sexual prohibitions of the period or because of the neurological bias that precluded appreciation of human and psychological conflict. But in the work of creative artists, this inner experience could now become accessible. In the next chapter, the theoretical developments of Freud that encompass the psychological functioning and inner conflicts that are central to the development of individuals will be presented.

SUMMARY OF DIAGNOSTIC FORMULATIONS

In the later part of the nineteenth century, a shift was taking place toward psychological explanations for psychopathology. The major, immediate precursors to the contemporary understanding of diagnostic distillations of psychopathological phenomena arose during this period. It was an era that for the most part reflected a greater focus on neurotic functioning and on normative data; there was reduced interest in solely psychotic manifestations. Table 11.1 presents some of the salient contributions of the period.

TABLE 11.1: Conceptual Issues of Psychopathology Representing
Late Nineteenth-Century Thinking

Diagnostic Advances

• Studies of hysteria and its symptoms undertaken.
• Hypnosis utilized experimentally to establish psychogenic paralysis.
• Multiple personality and dissociative manifestations identified and related to psychopathology of hysteria.
• *Psychasthenia* coined as a diagnosis, to encompass fatigue and shock.
• Automatic writing isolated as a symptom related to hysteria.
• Recognition of emotional factors as the cause of somatic problems, for example of the stomach and skin, further expanded the notion of psychosomatic symptomatology.
• Interest shifted away from psychosis toward neurosis, reflecting a corresponding shift from biological to psychological explanations of causation.

Dynamic Considerations

• Idea emerged of the dichotomous individual beset with irrational impulses on the one hand, and needing to utilize resources to control irrational forces on the other.
• Importance of the unconscious surfaced in a variety of contexts.
• Studies of sleep undertaken.

TABLE 11.1, *continued*

Treatment Issues

- Cathartic reactions in treatment situations revealed emotionally traumatic events of etiological significance previously inaccessible to memory or verbalization.
- The role of sexuality and its vicissitudes in relation to hysteria observed and broadly developed.
- Catharsis and abreaction recognized, reflecting focus on talking about conflict and distress as an apparent need of neurotic patients.
- Experiencing and reporting of feelings in a relationship of trust and personal investment became basis for successful treatment, in contrast with moral persuasion and educational, rational appeal.

CHAPTER 12

Sigmund Freud

In the 1890s Sigmund Freud was much impressed with the psychologically oriented researchers and eager to find applications of the neurological investigations he studied. Freud essentially consolidated and expanded these beginning investigations leading to the in-depth study of personality functioning and the range of psychopathology found in so-called normal and neurotic individuals. In his development of psychoanalysis, he brought into sharp focus the central roles of intrapsychic conflict, psychological stages of development, and the interplay of the individual, family, and society that forms character structure. In addition, his discoveries brought to light the importance of primary process material, personal fantasy, and the motivational role of inner, hidden personal strivings. To give all of these contributions a framework, he provided a structural analysis of the mental agents that organize intrapsychic functioning in the individual and that permit a rigorous detailing of various psychopathological configurations.

Attached to the insights and discoveries Freud made about the psychological apparatus that determines the inner functioning of man is a system of psychology from which is derived a unique system of psychotherapy—that of psychoanalysis. The importance of the psychoanalytic method that derives from Freudian theory is that it offers a totally psychological means of ameliorating intrapsychic and interpersonal conflict. Its focus on the central concept of transference introduces a purely psychological dimension which connects the past, through various developmental stages and interpersonal influences, with the present relationship between therapist and patient. Emphasis upon and analysis of this central psychological construct, the transference, is the medium through which cure and change are effected and the impediments to the individual's continued development are removed, allowing the pursuit of constructive future options.

The entire therapeutic process is geared to diminishing the repressive forces that have made the bulk of the patient's psychological functioning and areas of conflict unconscious, inaccessible, and rigidly unchanging. The weakening of repression encourages an expanded domain of conscious activity and a greater awareness of important aspects of self. The conquest of repression allows the individual to know himself more deeply, to acknowledge his own motivations more responsibly, and to be himself more fully. The achievements of this therapeutic approach, based as they are on essentially psychological constructs and verbal communication, eliminate the role of chemicals, neurons, and other material, physical agents except when they are employed for metaphorical purposes.

PROLOGUE TO THE DEVELOPMENT OF THE PSYCHOANALYTIC METHOD

Freud eventually blended a rigorous scientific attitude with his intuitive strength and his curiosity about human functioning. In spite of the many directions Freud's immense future growth would take, he maintained a scientific attitude. He accomplished substantial work on the nervous system in his apprenticeship with Ernst Brücke, but he maintained his humanistic and philosophical interests. He published research, for example, on a number of neurological subjects while also becoming informed about the psychological-psychodynamic concepts of Herbart, such as issues of the unconscious. He then studied the psychopathological aspects of hysteria and the use of hypnotism, and in his continuing quest to understand manifestations of psychopathology, especially of hysteria, he began an association with Charcot.

Freud was particularly influenced by Charcot's demonstration with hysterics that psychological potencies could be the salient variables in a host of what were called conversion reactions or hysterias, including various forms of paralysis and anesthesias. Freud next affiliated himself with Josef Breuer, who was then treating a patient referred to as "Anna O.," a woman with hysterical symptoms. Through treating Anna O., Breuer and Freud formulated several important concepts based on discoveries derived from their treatment and its effects. These discoveries included the use of hypnosis to stir the emotions, thereby affecting the palpable symptom; a phenomenon known as abreaction; a better understanding of the effects of catharsis; the connection of sexuality and its repression to the appearance of symptoms; and the crucial effects of a distorted aspect of the relationship between doctor and patient, the transference. Thereafter, Freud's work with Liebeault and Bernheim impressed on him that psychological motivation in the unconscious could be causative in the development of symptoms. Freud's understanding of the unconscious and of repression was accentuated thereafter in his formulations. His increasing scientific interest in the patient's resistance to accepting unconscious material led him to relinquish hypnotic methods and to shift his technique toward the use of free associational processes.

Several key concepts contributed to the coherence of the psychoanalytic method: the reactivation of the patient's past in the transference relationship with the therapist; an understanding of the role of repressive forces; the continuing importance of forgotten events; and the use of dreams in understanding both the unconscious and the nature of psychological conflict. In fact, Freud's *The Interpretation of Dreams* (1900) was actually a synthesis of all of his major contributions to that point, and it represents his master work.

In his work with the dream, Freud uncovered many secrets of the personality and its dynamic operation. He was able to understand needs and wishes, to formulate the sense of manifest, conscious ideas and their corresponding latent sources, and to grasp the idea that symptoms generally can be psychopathological compromises between unconscious needs and the frustration and repression of these needs. Freud proposed that such compromise formations, in the form of psychopathological conflict, are the essential cause of emotional distress. In his study of patients, especially those with hysterical symptomatology, he noticed the importance of sexual feelings in neurotic phenomena. He noted that alien sexual material that was expelled from consciousness gained expression instead in dreams and symptoms.

FREUD'S COMPLEMENT OF THEORIES

Freud consolidated his observations in a series of theoretical perspectives that he systematically developed in connection with the different components of psychological and psychopathological functioning he studied. His theoretical evolution encompassed a broad range of phenomena, and therefore the scope of his interests and inquiry necessitated a number of theoretical areas that were amalgamated to comprise an overall account of functioning in both normal and abnormal spheres. Freud's original contributions include explications of childhood psychosexual development, the mental structure based on id, ego, and superego functions, identification of varying levels of consciousness, psychic energy that is based on instinctual drives or impulses, specification of a complete individual history that clarifies the psychologically relevant events, and the adaptational propensities that relate to ego strength. These component theories that in totality form the Freudian view of development, psychological functioning, and etiology of psychopathology are briefly presented in the following sections.

The Developmental Theory of Psychosexual Stages

Freud's work presents a developmental theory of personality based on shifting sites of sexual experience. Individuals pass from oral to anal to phallic stages, with the Oedipus complex developing before the latency period. At each stage, the child is faced with specific anxieties that need to be resolved. The resolution of the Oedipus complex introduces repression over these crucial childhood sexual developments to set the stage for normal latency development. The orderly sequence in which psychic energy is expressed in the developing individual comprises the psychosexual theory of personality development. This theory not only describes the progression of development in terms of oral, anal, phallic, and oedipal strivings, but also presents derivative characterology, which constitutes a form of typology. Typology is implicit in the theory of psychosexual development, because specific adult character traits are assumed to derive from activity in the infant's psychosexual development and from the influence of fixation and regression with regard to these stages. Freud's typological system based upon the theory of psychosexual stages is presented in chapter 14.

The Structural Theory

In addition to describing chronological development, Freud also outlined the structure of mental functioning. The structural agents of mental functioning that he proposed both generate aspects of development and result from resolutions of conflicts and developmental pressures. The repository of the original infantile needs and strivings, which Freud originally saw in terms of sexuality and to which he later added aggression, is the *id,* which imparts timeless wishes and erotic impulses to the developing person. These strivings are based on the pleasure principle, the primitive, primary process of mental functioning, without recognition of the properties inherent in reality. Consequently, the id dominates infant functions on the basis of the pleasure principle. But the need to recognize elements of reality soon becomes more pronounced, and to assist in the ability to adapt realistically to properties of its surroundings, the developing organism builds up the agency known as the *ego.* The very important group of ego functions enables delay, mastery, frustration tolerance, and perception of reality based on logic and recognition of the actualities of the world. The ego operates on the more logical, secondary process of mental functioning and orients the organism on the basis of the reality principle.

The principles involved in the social context in general and the family in particular, and the regulation these impose over the individual's psychological functioning, Freud grouped under the agency of the *superego.* Superego functioning provides a broader context for reality orientation than the ego because it takes into account the teachings of the previous generation, through incorporation of parental precepts and parental interpretations of social requirements. The superego's functioning is marked by sternness, rigidity, and even primitiveness; in this regard, the emotions of shame and guilt are associated with the superego and are generated to curb impulse activity. While aspects of the superego are identified with conscience, much of the superego is itself unconscious, so that there is a substantially irrational component to those functions governed by the superego. This outline of Freud's contributions with respect to the agencies of the psychological apparatus—ego, id, and superego—their interaction and differential involvement with reality, comprises the structural theory, or intrapsychic agency, that is one of the foundations of Freud's theory of psychopathology.

The Topological Theory

The perspective on psychological functioning that categorizes psychological material as conscious, preconscious, and unconscious represents Freud's topological theory. In his view, the bulk of psychological functioning is at the unconscious level, and man's major motivations and strivings derive from this locus. Unconscious functioning comprises the totality of the id, a major portion of the superego, and parts of the ego such as those having to do with instituting defense mechanisms. Preconscious material is that which has the potential to become accessible to consciousness, given the proper conditions of attention and concentration. While much narrower than the unconscious range of material, the preconscious zone is still broader than that of consciousness. Consciousness represents the material that the individual is currently focusing upon. The main consideration regarding consciousness, however, is the quantity of material potentially accessible to it.

The Economic Theory

The interplay between unconscious, preconscious, and conscious components of mental functioning can also be regarded from the point of view of Freud's economic theory. This theory considers the deployment of drive energy that is striving for expression and accessibility to consciousness. In relatively normal development, components of this energy become neutralized at each stage of development. As a result, this neutralized energy can be used for the autonomous function of the ego while the remaining quantity is expressed as id-dominated energy. Impediments to normal development produce an investment of drive energy into pathological processes and maladaptive behavior. Therefore, the quantity of drive energy invested in the various areas of psychological functioning represents the scope of the economic theory. This aspect of Freud's

thinking provides the quantitative basis for the organism's psychological functioning.

The Genetic Theory

The particular form that the conflict between impulse and defense
takes is determined by the biological quality of impulse and the
personal history of the individual. From this consideration Freud
developed his genetic theory. The genetic theory traces the individual's development and determines the influential historical events
and experiences that led to the nature of present psychological
functioning. An important element of psychoanalytic treatment is
the reconstruction of the individual's development and history to
determine the origin of current symptoms and pathology as well
as interests and inclinations. In the psychoanalytic survey of genetic development, the contributions of various instinctual activities and proclivities along with their vicissitudes are also assessed.

The Adaptive Theory

Freud's contributions in relation to psychopathology and diagnosis can be appreciated from two points of view. First, in common with other psychopathologists and neurologists in the late
nineteenth century, he recognized hysterical symptoms as a form
of neurosis. He was then able to discriminate neurosis from psychosis on the basis of the patient's capacity to form sustained and
meaningful object relations. The strength and flexibility of the patient's ego functioning was also a consideration in assessing the
presence of neurotic phenomena, and this relation of the ego to
the environment reflects Freud's adaptive theory, which includes
a focus on reality testing and secondary process thinking.

Secondary process thinking derives from the logical capabilities
of ego functioning in accordance with adaptational needs governed by the reality principle. It contrasts with primary process
thinking, which is influenced more directly by the wishes and instinctual strivings reflecting id functioning in accordance with the
pleasure principle. With Freud's demarcation of primary and secondary process thinking, he contrasts the irrationality of primary

process thinking with secondary process thinking that reflects adaptational ego strengths. Thus, this stage of differential diagnosis and clarification of psychopathology represents in Freud's work a relatively gross distinction between the major emotional disorders—neurosis and psychosis. Freud's recognition of these disorders as essentially psychological in their importance is his major contribution at this level.

THE CONCEPTS OF FIXATION
AND REGRESSION

The second contribution to psychopathology and differential diagnosis by Freud involves the different kinds of character traits associated with the various stages of psychosexual development, discussed in further detail in chapter 14. Implicit in Freud's theory of personality development is the idea that occurrences in early stages have determining ramifications for the type of personality and character structure that eventually crystallizes in the functioning of the adult.

Two psychological constructs in Freudian theory are relevant to the emergence of various types of adult functioning. First, Freud's concept of *fixation* relates to increased reliance on personality dispositions and character traits that emerge at a given psychosexual stage of development. Traumatic events or unresolved needs at that stage form a psychological point around which traits cluster into a type of personality functioning. The second Freudian construct central to the development of various types of adult functioning is *regression*. Regression involves the utilization of a previously surpassed cluster of behaviors that occurs when stress forces the individual to give up more recently developed behaviors. The mechanisms of fixation and regression work together to create four very general types of personality orientation. These orientations are outlined in part 5 of this volume, on typologies. Before presenting Freud's typologies, the next chapter outlines earlier typologies based on dichotomies and body types, revealing the limited personality spectrum covered before Freud introduced his character typology system.

SUMMARY OF DIAGNOSTIC FORMULATIONS

Although Freudian theory is grounded in a biological epigenetic framework, Freud's contributions nevertheless inexorably steered the study of psychopathology toward a psychological orientation and away from a narrow biological one. He unearthed a wealth of information and developed a plethora of possibilities for the understanding of psychological functioning. His display of an inner psychological existence profoundly energized investigation into verbal therapy. Treatment would not have to rely upon the magic of medication; it was now clear that it was within the power of the individual to literally help himself. Table 12.1 presents a distillation of Freud's conceptualization of psychopathology, diagnosis, and psychodynamics.

TABLE 12.1: Freud's Theories and Salient Features of His Discoveries

Theories

- Structural: Formulation of the intrapsychic agency of ego-id-superego.
- Topological: A system describing material as unconscious, preconscious, or conscious and indicating transformational possibilities between levels.
- Economic: Description of the interaction between drive energy striving for expression, and accessibility to consciousness with respect to behavior.
- Psychosexual: The relation of character formation to the progression of early stages of development—oral, anal, phallic, and oedipal.
- Genetic: A tracing of development and locating of historical events that affect current behavior.
- Adaptive: The relation of the ego to environmental conditions, focusing on reality testing and secondary process.

Some Key Concepts of Psychoanalysis

- Intrapsychic conflict
- Primary process and secondary process thinking
- Repression
- Infantile sexuality and libido
- Unconscious processes
- Oedipal theory

TABLE 12.1, *continued*

- Pleasure principle versus reality principle
- Fixation and regression

Treatment Concepts

- Psychoanalytic method involving transference concepts connecting past and present.
- Importance of resistance in achieving personality change and symptom relief.
- Verbal communication and free association as the royal road to unconscious conflict.
- Use of symbols and dreams.
- Working-through required for complete treatment.

PART V
Typologies and Followers of Freud

CHAPTER 13
Typologies

In an attempt to create a parsimonious view of personality, investigators as far back as the ancient Greeks have noted differences in temperaments and emotional dispositions of personality, and they have formed typological systems on the basis of those differences. Precursors to the elaborate typologies of the modern era may be found in the work of Empedocles and Hippocrates during the fifth century B.C.

As briefly described in chapter 1, the philosopher Empedocles proposed a doctrine of four basic elements that aimed to encompass all the complexities observed about the universe. These essential substances were fire, earth, water, and air. In the Hippocratic tradition, these fundamental elements were related to corresponding humors of the body—blood, phlegm, yellow bile, and black bile. Each of these humors corresponded with an organ of the body—heart, brain, liver, spleen—as well as with a characteristic temperament—sanguine, phlegmatic, choleric, melancholic. Consequently, personality disposition could be typed on the basis of a presumed constitutional factor. The relationships between the types of temperament and excesses of particular humors is shown in table 13.1. The table also shows the cosmic elements cited by Empedocles and their distinct properties as they were amalgamated with the typology of Hippocrates.

In Hippocrates' typological system, the constitutional humors were believed to be present in different proportions in the body. If the proportions were balanced, a person would be healthy, both physically and in terms of personality functioning. As the proportions of the humors became less than ideal, various pathological disturbances could appear, and corresponding temperamental types would become predominant. As mentioned earlier, modern colloquial usage labeling personality types as *melancholic, sanguine,*

TABLE 13.1: Typologies of the Classical Greeks

EMPEDOCLES		HIPPOCRATES			
Elements	Properties	Humors	Organ	Qualities	Temperament
Fire	warm and dry	Blood	heart	heat	sanguine
Earth	cold and dry	Phlegm	brain	dryness	phlegmatic
Water	cold and moist	Yellow bile	liver	moisture	choleric
Air	warm and moist	Black bile	spleen	cold	melancholic

or *phlegmatic* derives from these early typological efforts. The central, enduring components of personality that concerned these ancient investigators are encoded in contemporary language.

The influential Hippocratic typological theory is noteworthy in that no direct evidence of humors was available to the ancients. However, the presumption that something tangible and material predetermined both physical and psychological functioning was an essential construct, and such conceptualizing has relevance to many of the typologies subsequently devised to categorize personality functioning. Some later investigators, such as Kretchmer and Sheldon, relied particularly strongly on constitutional elements and have shown a predominantly tangible, material bias. Others, such as Freud, tried to incorporate both biological and psychological features into the underpinnings of their typologies. Still others, such as Horney and Fromm, have restricted the explanatory concepts related to their typologies to psychological and interpersonal factors.

Toward the end of the nineteenth century, when abundant descriptive data was carefully accumulated regarding types of personality and differential psychopathologies, concern about classification of mental disorders contributed to the development of systematic typologies. The first efforts at these classifications involved the formation of dichotomous typologies.

DICHOTOMOUS TYPOLOGIES (PSYCHOSIS)

Among modern investigators, the decisive steps in forming dichotomous typologies were taken by Kraepelin with respect to psychosis, and by Janet with respect to neurosis. Kraepelin formed a fundamental dichotomy among psychoses, joining mania and melancholia within an overall manic-depressive psychotic diagnosis. He conceived of this psychosis as based on a single pathological state, and contrasted it with the diagnosis of dementia praecox. The features associated with these dichotomous categories have been presented previously. Briefly, the distinguishing qualities of manic-depressive psychosis, as construed by Kraepelin, included the following: onset is in the patient's mature years; periods of remission occur between psychotic episodes; psychotic episodes frequently alternate between manic and depressive conditions; and last, the pathological condition tends to assume a relatively stable quality throughout the patient's life. In contrast with these features of manic-depressive psychosis, the characteristics that Kraepelin believed to define dementia praecox included the following: onset tends to be during adolescent years; psychotic episodes include delusions, hallucinations, and bizarre speech or activity; the condition involves a gradual, long-term deterioration in functioning; and the condition generally becomes chronic.

The concept of dementia praecox as one of the types in Kraepelin's diagnostic system was soon supplanted by the observations of numerous investigators that there were several subtypes of the psychosis that needed to be differentiated from one another. Kraepelin gradually refined his categorization of dementia praecox to include the various subtypes that other investigators defined. These subtypes were catatonic, presenting mute and excited behavior, hebephrenic, characterized by inappropriate reactions, and paranoid, emphasizing delusions of persecution.

Swiss psychiatrist Eugen Bleuler reorganized the classification of dementia praecox, which he renamed *schizophrenia,* a word of Greek derivation, meaning the splitting off of the mind—by implication, from the order of reality. Bleuler amalgamated and refined the overall notion of schizophrenia into various specific subtypes. Even Bleuler, however, sought to establish some unity within this disorder, by elaborating four central characteristics shared by every subform. These characteristics, now known as Bleuler's "four A's," can still be productively and incisively utilized in determining the presence of schizophrenia, particularly when such obvious pathogenic markers as delusions, hallucinations, and overtly bizarre behavior are absent.

The first of Bleuler's A's, *autism,* refers to the preoccupation with inner subjective determinants that limits involvement with and appreciation of external reality in appropriate or accurate terms. The second A, *affect,* refers to the disturbance in mood or emotion that appears in schizophrenia. This may take the form of inappropriate laughter, as in hebephrenia, the flat affect of the simple schizophrenic, the excitement in catatonia, or the depression that often accompanies various schizophrenic reactions.

As can be seen, during the early stages of the history of diagnosis, when typologies constituted the prevailing diagnostic form, investigators such as Bleuler were refining and broadening conceptual penetration into personality functioning, as reflected by diagnostic constructs. Bleuler's third A is for *ambivalence,* the subject's approach-avoidance conflict with respect to emotional reactions or attachments. Bleuler's last A is that of *association,* referring to failure to adhere to a logical relationship to reality, as signified by loose or tangential associations, circumstantiality, and other signs of disordered thought. Thus, Bleuler sought to classify psychological features that were observable and could be utilized conceptually to establish the essentials of a major pathological diagnosis regardless of which subclassification of the disorder was manifested.

In spite of these refinements aiming to establish various subtypes of dementia, the organizing idea of a fundamental distinction between the two most important psychoses—manic-depressive and schizophrenia—continues to have a strong influence in the psychiatric field even today. The emphasis on hereditary factors, presumed organic or metabolic agents, and drug treatments, with a deemphasis on motivational possibilities, reflects the biological tradition of Kraepelin. Thus, Kraepelin's dichotomous conceptualization has been extremely influential, despite its apparent oversimplifications regarding the complexity of schizophrenia, the factors that are critical in distinguishing the classes of psychosis he sought to differentiate, and the personality components of the individuals included in the various psychotic categories and subcategories.

DICHOTOMOUS TYPOLOGIES (NEUROSIS)

As Kraepelin dichotomized the psychoses, Pierre Janet differentiated neurotic psychopathology by separating hysteria from neurasthenia or psychasthenia. Consistent with attitudes of his era, Janet tended to associate these categories with sex differences. Neurasthenia was thought to occur predominantly among men, while hysteria was a phenomenon believed to be generally limited to women. In fact, the term *hysteria* derives from the Greek word for womb, and the original concept of hysteria was that a displacement of the womb was the physiological basis for its occurrence. Of course this tradition, encoded in language, itself reinforced the finding of hysteria almost exclusively among women. The combination of early biological thinking and later efforts to understand psychopathology on the basis of physiology, as demonstrated by this view of hysteria, has contributed to the strong tendency for typologies to rest on basic physiological underpinnings. These often subtle and at times arbitrary organic determinants are made more or less explicit depending on the theoretician in question.

In a sense, the study of psychopathology has been attempting to become increasingly free of the constraints dictated by the repeated reliance upon physiological influences to account for the differences between people and for the particular psychological disturbances that individuals develop. The importance of this struggle to separate psychopathology from physiology appears strongly in the consideration of treatment approaches. The physiological influence, which throughout the history of psychiatry kept appearing as a major thematic strand, again made a strong impact with the advent of typologies. That is, inherent in the conceptualization of personality in terms of typologies is the idea that instincts or organic proclivities are determined and relatively fixed. The fundamental proposition implied in such a position is that personality has a genetic bias. One question that emerges perhaps inevitably from this position is whether—or to what extent—psychopathology is also genetically determined.

A second question arises also, concerning a subtle and even insidious bias involved in the specification of the nosology itself, in which chemical advances tend to rule out continuing psychological considerations. This possible bias regarding fixed organic types may influence the devising and specification of the various nosological categories that make up the nomenclature. To present one example, a recent medical advance is the more effective regulation of manic-depressive psychosis through the application of chemotherapy, in the form of lithium carbonate. However, the dramatic nature of this advance has the effect of automatically diminishing consideration of the psychological point of view regarding the individual struggle of the person suffering with this condition. This sort of pharmacological advance may tend to reduce the person to a physiological entity who lives with the condition of depression or excitement, however these conditions are controlled. Even though this psychopharmacological approach can be especially helpful, it may nevertheless effectively deflect attention from any real psychological approach to the problem. Further, the pharmacological approach tends to reinforces the assumption that such distress is biologically and/or genetically determined, and that further explanations then become unnecessary at best, and irrelevant at worst.

Yet, the success of a chemical agent in ameliorating any psychological or mental distress is not proof positive that the distress in question is, in its complex totality in the context of a particular individual, genetically determined. The corollary to be considered is that the cause of the ailment notwithstanding, a person with a problem is experiencing a psychologically distressing phenomenon, and this consideration needs to be central in any diagnostic scheme, especially one with treatment implications. Extending this epistomological problem further, it is evident that there is a tendency in contemporary nosology to regard the psychotic disturbances as basically biological and genetic in causality, while the less severe neurotic and characterological disturbances are more easily viewed as deriving from environmental and adaptational conflicts of a more psychological kind. Yet, in the formulation of typologies, investigators and theorists tacitly imply, for the most part, that characterology emanates from biological roots exclusively. It is within this framework that the further presentation and discussion of typologies will be made here.

When Janet presented his dichotomy between neurasthenia and hysteria, the implication that genetically determined sex differences relate to specific psychological disturbance was an exemplification of the power of this biological bias. Such assumptions have obviously severely limited the progress of appreciating psychopathological phenomena in terms of the essence of psychological functioning.

Kraepelin's dichotomy and conception of psychopathology as well as Janet's division of psychopathology achieved enough acceptance in the field to initiate a search for personality characteristics and, especially, for somatic characteristics that could predispose an individual to develop one type or the other of psychosis or neurosis. As a result, investigations of dichotomous types of personality, physique, and traits arose. Some of these types were identified with manic-depressive psychosis or hysteria; others were believed to underlie schizophrenia or psychasthenia. Several typological systems reflected this belief in an underlying dichotomy of personality.

In the following section Jung's typology will be presented as another example of a dichotomous typology. Presentations of the typologies of Kretschmer and Sheldon, which reflect the assumption of strong physiological predispositions in personality, will then follow.

CARL JUNG

Outside of the work of Freud and his followers, several efforts were made to categorize important attributes of temperament and psychosis in order to pursue diagnostic refinements. Some of these theories, such as those of Kretschmer and Sheldon, involve complex anatomical speculations, while others, such as Carl Jung's, avoid physiological speculation, instead focusing on psychological explanatory dimensions.

In his division of personality types, Jung emphasized the partition between introversion and extraversion. Among Jung's many theoretical formulations regarding personality and treatment, the introversion-extraversion concept has had substantial influence on issues relating directly to diagnostic nosology. The defining essence of this typology for Jung was the conception of the *introvert* as focused and directed by internal signals, while the *extravert* looks to outside data as the essential guide. The introvert places great emphasis on subjective experience as fundamental for the interpretation of reality and for securing satisfactions, while the extravert forms an interpretation dependent on external experiences and qualities and seeks satisfactions from outside contacts and social arrangements.

In the early part of the twentieth century, Jung developed the formulation of introversion as the basis for personality functioning in schizophrenia. The tendency in both schizophrenia and in introversion was for the person to be drawn inward, to make reference to internal thoughts and feelings. Such internal reference served in introverted individuals as the basis for organizing the understanding of reality and for introverted behavior tendencies; it also minimized interpersonal bonds. Jung related the neurosis of neurasthenia or psychasthenia to schizophrenia, and so construed neurasthenia as the neurosis associated with introversion.

The disorder Jung related to extraversion was the neurosis of hysteria. In the behavior of the hysteric, the dramatic, outgoing, externalizing tendencies could readily be identified with the qualities of the extravert. For example, the tendency of the hysteric patient to focus on external stimulation and involvements and to try to use these to resolve any personal dilemma exemplifies the external focus that Jung attributed to the extravert. For the hysteric in particular, the tendency to focus on symptoms of a bodily and physical nature and to symbolize internal conflicts and efforts to resolve them through bodily experiences also exemplifies the avoidance of introspection that Jung attributed to the extravert. Further, for the hysteric the pressure of affect is associated generally with external events, which in a sense can include bodily phenomena and symptoms as a focus outside one's reflective side or personality. At the same time, the actual affect experienced internally remains quite shallow. This also fits well with Jung's extravert concept.

Along with Jung's introduction of the introversion-extraversion diagnostic dichotomy, Hermann Rorschach, in his investigation of psychodiagnostics through the ink blot projection technique he devised, also distinguished between two types of personalities, which he called *introversive* and *extratensive*. These types reflect strong parallels to the typology of Jung. Rorschach's introversive type represents those who respond primarily to stimulation from within and utilize internal fantasy and other internal resources in attempting to manage distress, bind anxiety, and seek solutions to challenges. Rorschach's extratensive type responds primarily to external stimulation and therefore relies on overt activity in seeking to manage stress, limit anxiety, and solve problems. Rorschach's conceptualization is further allied with Jung's in the sense that Rorschach's extratensive type is responsive to color stimuli in the ink blots. This sort of responsiveness means that the person is attuned to the external environment, is therefore enlivened by external cues, and is driven by the pressure of feeling toward action rather than contemplation. In contrast, the intratensive type is more responsive to kinesthetic and fantasy cues, and therefore corresponds to Jung's more inner-directed type, who is compelled by inner subjective experience including fantasy and reflection.

It is interesting to note the historical fact that Rorschach and Jung formulated these similar typologies independently. This coincidence reflects the current existing at the time that led investigators to seek dichotomies and to polarize people along obvious dimensions. Of course, the problem with all such dichotomies is that people are rarely distributed bimodally with respect to any one trait. Rather, the tendency is for any trait to be distributed across the range of possibilities. This would apply in areas such as intelligence, as well as in a personality trait such as how outgoing a person is. Another example would be the traits of passivity and aggression. Most individuals are neither wholly passive nor wholly aggressive, but are rather a mixture, showing both traits in varying degrees. Jung made an effort to address this general way in which traits are distributed by theorizing unconscious extraversion in a person who appears introverted. What this shows is that the complexity of psychological functioning does not always lend itself to the simple categories that have been historically developed. Therefore, new constructs and more elaborate themes are added to dichotomizations, to enable them to account for more of the findings derived from the study of large numbers of people.

Another derivative of the fact that psychological complexity works against simple dichotomies is the effort by many succeeding typologists to categorize individuals in terms of a system oof three or more parts. Ernest Kretschmer developed a typological system that may be considered dichotomous, since it was originally based on two major body types. When he introduced a third body type, however, his system became a precursor to the typology of Sheldon.

ERNEST KRETSCHMER

In Kretschmer's system, efforts to develop meaningful diagnostic classifications were rooted in body types. Nevertheless, Kretschmer started his division on the basis of the two fundamental disorders: schizophrenia and manic-depressive psychosis. The concept of two types of temperaments—one *schizoid* and the other *cycloid*—was related to the division between psychoses. The schizoid temperament Kretschmer characterized as unsociable, reserved, and serious. Deterioration of this schizoid state could lead to disassociation, eccentricity, and even schizophrenia. This aspect of Kretschmer's thinking is strongly related to Jung's formulations about introversion.

The other temperamental type that Kretschmer conceived, the cycloid, was characterized as sociable, cheerful, interpersonally involved, and rather impulsive. The area of disturbance with this temperament was the tendency toward great variability in mood. This cycloid disposition corresponds to Jung's formulation of extraversion. Kretschmer's formulation postulates that under extreme distress the cycloid personality would develop manic-depressive psychosis.

The original step which distinguishes Kretschmer's dichotomous system from earlier ones is the relationship he drew between his two temperamental types and physique. He believed that heavier, broader, and shorter body builds—which he called *pyknic*—correlated with personalities in the cycloid and manic-depressive sector of his dichotomy. In the schizoid sector, on the other hand, body builds tended to be elongated, in what he termed the *asthenic* or *leptosome* type. An athletic body type was correlated in Kretschmer's research with individuals less likely to display psychopathology.

Kretschmer found that the cyclothymic personality associated with the pyknic body build could be subdivided into three temperaments. The *hypomanic* was lively and effervescent, the *syntonic* was practical, and the *melancholic* discouraged but calm.

The schizothymic temperaments varied along a continuum; at one end was the hypersensitive state, and at the other end, the phlegmatic state. Along this continuum three types emerge. The *hyperesthetic* type is tense with inner sensitivity, the *anesthetic* type is eccentric and apathetic, while in between is a middle type, decisive and logical.

As this outline of aspects of Kretschmer's formulation reveals, there appears always a need to subdivide the distinctions that form the basic dichotomy. This indicates that the actual nature of people, in either their normal or diseased state, never really falls into a neat dichotomous package. In effect, Kretschmer accumulates a large number of traits that can be clustered to compose a working nosology. His effort to correlate these clusters of traits with body build reflects the striving of so many investigators to find a way to reduce personality and psychological functioning to some physiological hypothesis. Thus, what emerges in Kretschmer's theory is a fundamental support of the biological tradition, in which inexorable personality imperatives are suggested by body build. Although the typologies of Jung and Janet also distinguished or dichotomized types, it was with Kretschmer that manifest physical qualities were considered basic to diagnostic indications of personality. On the psychological level, Kretschmer contributed to organizing psychopathology into diagnostic parsimony through his use of a dichotomous system further subdivided to consider variations in normal, prepsychotic, and psychotic states.

W. H. SHELDON

Sheldon became a student of Kretschmer's theories and developed his own formulation. Sheldon's scheme reflected Kretschmer's influence regarding the importance of physical components, but it introduced different views of personality. With respect to physical types, Sheldon distinguished three separate structures. The first is the *endomorph,* in which somatic structures are relatively weak and underdeveloped, with a round and plump body build. The second is the *mesomorph,* in which the structure is firm and strong, in an athletic body build. Finally, the *ectomorph* is long and slender, with poor muscle development. Corresponding with each of these body types are three temperamental dispositions. Associated with the endomorph is *viscerotonia,* emphasizing needs for comfort, affection, and gregariousness. Associated with the mesomorph is *somatotonia,* a need for muscular work and assertiveness. Psychologically, interest in power also corresponds with the mesomorphic type. The ectomorph is associated with *cerebrotonia,* a disposition involving inhibition and withdrawal.

Different disorders presumably corresponded to the body types that Sheldon proposed, much as to Kretschmer's types. The thin persons were considered prone to schizophrenia, the rotund types were considered predisposed to manic-depressive distress, while the athletic types were considered less disposed to mental illness.

The major problem with Sheldon's linkage between temperament and body type is the same difficulty that generally relates to efforts to associate psychological functioning with physiological processes or anatomical structure. Placing the roots for various psychological differences or disturbances in anatomy implies that temperaments are predetermined and fixed. Therefore, the influence of salient family patterns and other sources of social training is seen as having no fundamental effect on personality functioning and the character structure that develops. This kind of limitation is also inherent in any diagnostic system that seeks to divide disturbances into only two or three components and then investigates correlations with bodily phenomena.

The essential deficiency of this approach was acknowledged by Sheldon, and he therefore sought a means to rank the relative importance of his three dispositions as well as his three body types as they are manifested in any given individual. This ranking introduced a means of reflecting the complicated variability of human makeup. However, its explanatory power remained relatively inadequate, since the theory leads to an after-the-fact assessment of the findings about individuals. Further, the mixture of components, even when their relative strengths and weaknesses in the individual are weighed, has to remain fixed and permanent in Sheldon's scheme. This permanance implies a total determinism in human nature and a rigidity with regard to any means of change that does not involve the individual's physical makeup. In the absence of any arena for analysis of the influences of personal development and adaptation, such theories thus support genetic determinism. Further, contemporary experimental and clinical data do not verify the body type theory.

SUMMARY

The approaches of Kraepelin, Janet, Jung, Kretschmer, and Sheldon crystallized in the study of psychopathology the notion that it was meaningful and useful to categorize types, that doing so would help to organize the varieties of psychopathology around a more conceptually manageable array of components. The focus on physical elements as indicators of personality ignored the important influence of experience and adaptational factors in the development of personality. It was Sigmund Freud who introduced and strongly shifted the focus onto experiential factors, even though he retained a biological foundation in his theory. In the following chapter the influence of Sigmund Freud on typologies will be presented.

SUMMARY OF DIAGNOSTIC FORMULATIONS

The systematization of typologies has its origin with the Greeks. The overall, underlying debate inherent in the history of typologies concerns the ever-present theme of whether personality develops on the basis of biological or psychological factors. What this debate means, in terms of the practical aspect of the access of personality disturbance and emotional distress to treatment, is also the underlying issue when considering typologies.

Taken together, the work of Jung, Rorschach, Kretschmer, and Sheldon, along with previous diagnostic differentiations and relationships established by Kraepelin, Janet, Bleuler, and even the ancient Greeks, formed a network of relationships with respect to concepts of psychopathology and diagnosis.

Tables 13.2 and 13.3 present some of these relationships. Table 13.2 indicates relationships involving ancient and modern typological and diagnostic efforts; table 13.3 presents a matrix of other typological systems. It should be noted that with the exception of Jung's, these typologies rest on a foundation of tacit biological substructures.

TABLE 13.2: Ancient and Modern Typological and Diagnostic Systems

Ancient Greeks

- Humors related to temperament, with such derivative terms as *phleg-matic* and *melancholic* applied into the twentieth century.

Dichotomous Typologies

Kraepelin
- Manic-depressive versus dementia praecox (psychosis): criteria for differential diagnosis emphasize onset components and course of disorder.

Janet
- Hysteria versus psychasthenia (neurosis): criteria for differentiation based on physiological weakness of the nervous system, in turn related to sexual differences.

Further Diagnostic Criteria

- The inclusion of numerous subtypes within dementia praecox.
- Bleuler's description of disturbances of autism, affect, ambivalence, and association, seen as essential components of all subtypes of schizophrenia.

TABLE 13.3: The Typological Systems of Jung, Kretschmer, and Sheldon

JUNG'S DICHOTOMOUS TYPOLOGY		
	Introvert	*Extravert*
Governing stimuli	Internal	External
Pathological inclination	Schizophrenia	Hysteria
Rorschach correspondence	Introversive	Extratensive
KRETSCHMER'S TYPES		
	Schizoid	*Cycloid*
Interpersonal disposition	Unsociable	Sociable

TABLE 13.3, *continued*

KRETSCHMER'S TYPES

	Schizoid		*Cycloid*
Motivational direction	Introversion		Extraversion
Related psychosis	Schizophrenia		Manic-depressive
Body type	Leptosome/ Asthenic (thin)	Athletic (intermediate and less prone to pathology)	Pyknic (rotund)
Temperament	Schizothymic Hyperesthetic (tense, sensitive)		Cyclothymic Hypomanic (cheerful, lively)
	Anesthetic (eccentric, indolent)		Syntonic (realistic, practical)
	Logical (active, decisive)		Melancholic (discouraged, calm)

SHELDON'S TYPES

	Ectomorph (thin)	*Mesomorph (athletic)*	*Endomorph (rotund)*
Temperament	Cerebrotonia (restraint: tendency toward inhibition, withdrawal)	Somatotonia (self-assertion: interest in muscular activity, power, risk taking)	Viscerotonia (sociability: enjoyment of affection, comfort)
Related mental illness	Schizophrenia	Not prone	Manic-depressive

CHAPTER 14

Freud's Personality Types

Even though Sigmund Freud's theory of psychosexual development and the various character types that derive from each stage have biological underpinnings, environmental factors related to the gratification and frustration of the individual's needs play an exceedingly important role in the development of character, in his view. The following review of psychosexual stages as they relate to character development essentially represents Freud's theory of typology.

The Oral Types

The oral types of characterology develop from fixations associated with the first stage of development, during which oral processes and satisfaction play an overwhelmingly important part in the infant's existence. Unusual gratification during this phase, either because of the pressure of the individual's predetermined biological proclivities or because of environmental influences in childrearing, presumably can lead to fixation of one of two oral types. One is the *oral passive* or *oral incorporative* type, from which a dependent, optimistic, but immature disposition develops. Individuals in which this type of character structure predominates utilize passivity as a means to incorporate care extended by others and are limited in their ability to assert the effort or tolerate the frustration required for achieving direct satisfaction of their own needs. This type of character structure presumably derives from fixations involving nursing and sucking and an overemphasis on the attitude of being fed, which are the infantile bases for the lines of development of this particular character structure. The overimportance of this oral phase fixates the passive-dependent character style as a lifelong attribute of central significance.

A second type of oral fixation occurs because of excessive gratification or frustration during the later part of the oral phase associated with biting and assertive activity. Under such circumstances an *oral aggressive* type develops. Similar to the oral passive type, the oral aggressive or sadistic type yearns for nurturance, and yet anticipates disappointment. This expectancy of malevolence may be expressed characterologically through cruelty or hostility, either in terms of overt behavior, or verbally, in the form of sarcasm in the context of interpersonal functioning.

The Anal Types

Personality types based on anal experiences correspond with the central activities and location of importance in the infant's next phase of development. The characteristics that Freud noted here make up the obsessional character; they consist of a cluster of traits including the triad of orderliness, obstinancy, and parsimony. This characterology, which also involves interpersonal stubbornness, was related by Freud to strict toilet training experiences. The experience of toilet training represents an actual interference with what Freud considered an instinctual impulse, now in the process of being controlled and regulated. If special attention and praise is received from the parent in connection with gentle toilet training, then pleasure becomes associated with characterological control mechanisms that derive from mastery of sphinctor control. On the other hand, if forceful parental regulation evokes hostility and resentment, then stinginess and overcontrol or messiness and disorder can become characterological expressions of aggression throughout life.

In the character types that correspond with the emotional reactions to toilet training gratifications or frustrations, both constitutional and experiential factors play important roles. The infant's biological striving for personal mastery and self-regulation may put it in conflict with even modest parental training techniques, and the child with limited biological proclivities for self-regulation may react intensely to rigid parental control techniques. Thus, the subtle interplay of temperamental predispositions and interpersonal influences can lead to the predominance of anal personality types. One of these is the *anal expulsive* type, while the other is the *anal retentive* type.

The anal expulsive type utilizes disorder as an expression of aggression and is therefore also called the *anal aggressive* type. This aggressiveness, although controlled and disguised, is central in such an individual's personality functioning and therefore defines the personality type. The anal retentive type involves the triad of characteristics that are opposite to those of the disorderly or anal aggressive type. The central characterology of the anal retentive type is an excessive degree of orderliness and stinginess, including the stubborn withholding of emotional warmth and interpersonal closeness and an obstinate, unyielding rigidity. Such characteristics presumably reflect the infant's original response to the particular parental method and attitude during the period of toilet training. This creates personality imperatives that revolve around the concepts of delay of gratification, withholding of the offering of pleasure to others, and issues of control.

The Phallic Type

The next phase of development following the anal stage involves a focus of attention on the genitals. The personality type that derives from a fixation at this stage was called by Freud the *phallic* type. The phallic type centers on ambitiousness and exhibitionism and generally reveals characteristics of narcissism and self-aggrandizing pride. Such a person seeks to be the center of attention and frequently senses too readily or even exaggerates deflation, thwarting, and lack of appreciation from others. In the phallic stage of development, which is the source of the personality traits that define this type, concern and attention to the genital organs are central. The quality of the genital organs and the certainty of this quality are major preoccupations; there is often a fear that the genitals are not adequate, that they may have been damaged, or that they may become damaged. This concern about damage to the genitals is known as *castration anxiety,* and efforts to manage this anxiety generate the personality traits that center on the individual's sense of adequacy as well as traits that comprise the *phallic exhibitionistic* personality type.

Important dimensions of castration anxiety and its derivative, the phallic exhibitionistic type, are an essential concern about self-esteem and difficulty regulating self-esteem in a steady and sustained manner. For example, threats from authority figures or questions raised by authority structures will trigger intense anxiety regarding self-worth in the phallic personality type. At times, this anxiety may be masked by feelings of depression, which are associated with the felt loss of authority support, and which can then generate regression to earlier levels of functioning, such as needs for oral gratification.

Another manner in which castration anxiety may be expressed is the formation of narcissistic exhibitionistic strivings designed to assure phallic exhibitionists of their specialness. In this pattern, when the accolades this type of person depends upon do not materialize to full strength or are not perfectly consistent, a major sense of deflation is experienced. This sense of deflation and devaluation often triggers rage or depression, which stem from the feelings of being wounded. While the wound is readily ascribed to lack of external interpersonal support, the underlying cause is the castration anxiety that actually stems from the issue of whether the genitals are sensed as wounded or intact, inadequate or adequate.

One other less dramatic form in which castration anxiety may be experienced is the more or less chronic sense of self-devaluation felt by those concerned with their inadequacy. Again, while the sense of inadequacy may be directed in this character formation to failures of achievement in work or in interpersonal relationships, the underlying source is anxiety about genital adequacy. Among the common ways of coping with the castration anxiety that is manifested by the sense of self-devaluation and inadequacy is restriction of what is attempted, from which then naturally follows limitation of success, which in turn supports the sense of inadequacy. Such persons may develop passive or inertial responses to demands, which may protect them against threat, yet also generate increased hostility from others. Thus, the passive-aggressive feature within the phallic stage reflects the entire conflict: namely, to protect oneself, and to retain power. Unfortunately, such behavior also calls forth increased threat of punishment from external sources. While the basis for the phallic exhibitionistic personality type—including the form in which self-devaluation and inadequacy are central—is early concern about the intactness or inadequacy of the genital organs, this concern about adequacy may also extend to encompass the child's entire emerging sense of adequacy as a boy or girl. In this sense, the issue of assertiveness can become a derivative problem.

The Oedipal Stage

In early psychoanalytic writings, the phallic and oedipal stage of development were considered together, but they were later separated, since they reflect different emphases and derivative character traits. In the oedipal phase of development, the major focus is the triangular relationship that develops between the child and its two parents. In this fateful constellation, the child seeks closeness, affection, and sensual fulfillment with the parent of the opposite sex while simultaneously seeking to eliminate the rival for this position, the parent of the same sex. The intense feelings of yearning for the opposite sex parent and hostility for the same sex parent give this phase of development its distinctive emotional and interpersonal quality. When these complex sets of feelings are not sufficiently overcome, distinctive clusters of personality traits become part of the adult character structure. An intensely competitive individual who has difficulty befriending people of the same sex is one such type. Another is the person who is unable to establish loyalties governing new, mature relationships, who instead must remain exclusively attached to the oedipal object.

Traits deriving from unresolved elements of the Oedipus complex include urges toward conquest in interpersonal relationships, inappropriately competitive strivings to win, and preoccupations with achieving at any expense. In Freud's conception of neurotic conflict in adults, the majority of neurotic patterns and complaints and associated anxiety derive from the Oedipus complex that forms this phase of development and from which issue so many derivatives in the character structure.

FREUD'S TYPOLOGY CONSIDERED

The difficulty with the typology that derives from Freud's theory of psychosexual development is its complexity, since important consequences are based on early experiences in life that have unconscious implications. Because of the unconscious elements that give weight to the formation of enduring character traits, the precise development of the personality cannot always be specified or observed directly. This complexity is also extremely valuable, however, because it provides a typology and a chain of events congruent with the richness and diversity of human psychological functioning. Many aspects of human functioning that are major concerns for individuals but are difficult for scientists to investigate are given full value in this theory. These aspects include the development of sexuality, toilet training experience, and competitiveness, as well as the intense anxiety and threat that are associated with these concerns. Freud's premise was that the long-range nature of all these preoccupations and inner fears realistically matches what people are quietly and privately concerned about in their daily living.

Although instinctual components were considered important by Freud in forming the fixations at each stage of development and the accompanying derivatives that form the personality types, he also takes a vigorous adaptational stance, in which environmental responses and pressures play a significant part in determining character formation. In fact, the complexity of Freud's psychosexual stages of development and their derivative typologies provides an additional positive in this theory. This positive is the fact that derivatives from various stages of development can play a role in the finished character structure, so that the wide and complex variability between people can be theoretically accounted for. This relationship between Freudian theory and the complexity of human functioning and personality structure makes this approach a particularly compelling, fertile theory for investigating the genesis of psychopathology and its differential diagnosis. It should also be noted that this theory of psychosexual development and its derivative influence on character reflects only one aspect of Freud's total theory.

A HISTORICAL BENCHMARK IN THE FIELD OF PSYCHOPATHOLOGY

At this point in the history of psychopathology, a major benchmark regarding the institutionalization of personality codification was established. Clearly, the development of typological systems during this period, including the work of Kraepelin, Janet, Jung, Kretschmer, and Sheldon, departed from the hit-or-miss formulations of earlier studies of psychopathology, especially with regard to diagnostic references. No longer was the particular investigator of psychopathology relying on hypotheses regarding depression or an aspect of depression, mania or an aspect of mania, or some isolated mental phenomenon such as hallucinations. With the onset of modern thinking regarding typologies, investigators turned their attention to entire systems that included a host of diagnoses and their constituent personality properties. Despite the biological implications of typological theories, these systems strove to develop larger conceptions of psychopathology and diagnosis that were based upon implicit notions of the coherence of personality. This newly accepted point of view and the quantum leap in the crystallization of the understanding of psychopathology finally created a new discipline, which may be roughly characterized as embracing the broad context of personality, the vicissitudes of disturbance of this personality called psychopathology, and the codification of this psychopathology into differentially based diagnostic nosologies.

With the appearance of Sigmund Freud, a massive infusion of dynamic theory vitalized the entire descriptive nosological approach, consolidating into its contemporary forms this new field of personality, psychopathology, and differential diagnosis. The work of the neo- and post-Freudians can be considered a fortification of this vitalization, ultimately leading to ever-newer and different dynamic psychologies, including, for example, ego psychology, object relations theory, and self psychology.

In the following chapters, the typologies developed by other psychologists and psychoanalysts reflecting post-Freudian contemporary theory will be presented.

SUMMARY OF DIAGNOSTIC FORMULATIONS

The Freudian typology based upon psychosexual development created a new approach to the understanding of psychopathology and practically generated its own diagnostic nosology. In this typology, concern is focused on specific conflict related to development, and each conflict generates specific anxieties. Thus, Freudian character typology implicitly relates psychopathology and its diagnostic differentials with the important personality barometer of anxiety. In table 14.1, this Freudian character typology is presented along with the derivative character patterns.

TABLE 14.1: The Freudian Character Typology

PSYCHOSEXUAL STAGE FIXATION	CHARACTER TYPES	
Oral	Oral Passive	Oral Aggressive
	A passive-dependent character style containing traits such as dependency, optimism, and sense of inadequacy. Also known as oral incorporative type.	Pessimistic, expecting disappointment; character traits include cruelty, hostility, sarcasm, and bitterness. Also known as oral sadistic type.
Anal	Anal Expulsive	Anal Retentive
	Character traits are messiness and disorderliness, which become symbols for aggression and resistance to control throughout life. Also referred to as anal aggressive type.	Involves triad of characteristics: orderliness, stinginess, including withholding of emotional warmth, and stubborness, all reflecting control preoccupation.
Phallic	Phallic Exhibitionistic	
	Traits include ambitiousness, exhibitionism, narcississm, and pride, with sensitivity to deflation, thwarting, and lack of appreciation from others. Castration anxiety, on which character trait development hinges, is the central concern; regulation of self-esteem is a derivative concern. Passive-aggressive patterns obtain.	

TABLE 14.1, *continued*

PSYCHOSEXUAL STAGE FIXATION	CHARACTER TYPES
Oedipal	*Oedipus Complex*
	The family triangle is the central issue, with closeness to opposite sex parent and hostility to same sex parent. Traits and patterns include loyalty to oedipal object, which closes off opportunities for mature relationships, extreme competitiveness, and need for conquest.

CHAPTER 15

Followers of Freud:
Horney, Fromm, and Erikson

Freud's typological system influenced investigators generally, and Freudian adherents specifically, to create other systems of types. This ferment and growing typological orientation further contributed to the momentum toward categorizing pathology through the development of allegedly universal diagnostic systems. Consistent with this historical development was the work of several investigators who attempted to refine Freud's principles to depict social factors as being more influential than did Freud's system, with its roots in biological phenomena. These culturally oriented psychoanalytic typologists did not rely on the typical Freudian stages of development for their conceptualization of personality types. Instead, they proposed a range of types presumed to encompass the universe of neurotic pathology that earlier psychoanalysts focused on, but which in their systems derived exclusively from the social interactions occurring during the individual's development. Thus, these post-Freudian psychoanalytic investigators essentially presented social and interpersonal systems of typology. The most extensive contributions within this social tradition were those of Karen Horney, Erich Fromm, and Erik Erikson; of the three, Erikson retains the closest connection with Freud's original developmental theory and its biological underpinnings.

KAREN HORNEY

In the psychoanalytic theory of Karen Horney, the concept of basic anxiety and the person's need to secure a sense of safety are the crucial constructs. If the child's need for security is not met by its parents, feelings of helplessness, fear, and hostility are generated. When the child seeks to mask such feelings, and especially to repress the hostility in order to maintain whatever parental ties are available, basic anxiety is experienced. Basic anxiety is the persistent feeling of being alone and helpless in a dangerous, hostile world. Specific personality characteristics are then developed to manage this basic anxiety.

Both the anxiety and the characteristics developed to seek security emanate from the interpersonal relationships and conflicts between the developing child and its family. A series of protective mechanisms can become permanent parts of the personality, forming a character structure as a result of repeated, consistent conflicts during development. These protective mechanisms evolve into three types of neurotic personality.

The Self-Effacing Type: Movement Toward People

The first of the characteristic protective mechanisms described by Horney is known as *movement toward people,* and it results in the *self-effacing* type, the individual who in order to feel secure and protected strives to sustain affection and approval from another person. In this neurotic character type, the drive toward securing safety through compliance is compulsive and occupies the foreground of personality functioning, eclipsing all other personality tendencies. Consistent with the basic social and interpersonal orientation of Horney's theory, this type of person is therefore described as moving toward people in a manipulative manner in order to exchange compliance for protection. This compulsively driven central exchange or social interaction betrays the infantile developmental roots of this character type. Such personality types were called self-effacing by Horney, to reflect their apparent efforts to minimize themselves in order to gain acceptance, protection, and security.

In Horney's theory, a range of neurotic needs drives the individual's behavior. The particular needs from which moving toward people evolves include needs for affection and approval, for a dominant partner in life to serve a protective safety purpose, and for narrow and restricted limits in living and self-expression. This cluster of needs helps the person guard against the appearance of hostility, which would interfere with the compulsive movement toward gaining security through people. The basic driving force, however, is an underlying hostility, which is defended against by the compliant character structure that evolves. From this hostility springs a hidden but central need to control and manipulate.

The Expansive Type: Movement Against People

The *expansive* type is characterized by an aggressive personality compulsively involved in *movement against people*. Interpersonal relationships are viewed as a constant hostile struggle in which only the strongest can survive. In order to alleviate basic anxiety and the underlying feelings of helplessness and insignificance contributing to it, such a personality type uses behavior that is domineering and controlling in an uncompromising effort to achieve superiority. Therefore, all relationships for this expansive type are based on interpersonal manipulations to gain power and admiration, without ever expressing feelings of weakness or fears of rejection. The neurotic needs that cluster to form this personality type include needs to exploit other people, to gain power over others, to strive singlemindedly for achievement and fulfillment of ambition, and to gain admiration, which serves a need for continuous prestige. This expansive type, motivated by an underlying anxiety about personal insignificance, reflects a compulsion for mastery that enables the individual to gain a sense of security at the expense of interpersonal equality, warmth, and closeness.

The Resigned Type: Movement Away from People

When neither of the previous two personality motives has proven workable in containing basic anxiety, a third type develops, characterized by detachment from people. The central effort of this *resigned* type is to gain a sense of safety by securing emotional distance from people. The characteristic stance therefore involves *movement away from people*. A compulsive development of self-sufficiency and independence from others is generated, so that the individual can eschew interpersonal participation on the level of emotional involvement or cooperation. This type of person lives a withdrawn, private, isolated life. Intense sensitivity to any interpersonal influence or obligation to people requires avoidance of any closeness. Detachment from feelings establishes a reliance on a cognitive orientation, with an emphasis on an orderly sequence of thought. In contrast to the other types, who compulsively use yielding or domination as ways to avoid interpersonal conflict, this type of person avoids interpersonal conflict through detachment from people and the cultivation of privacy.

The basic neurotic needs that cluster within this type include the needs for self-sufficiency, independence, perfection, and a position that cannot be criticized. This type is known as resigned because of its abandonment of efforts at interpersonal engagement through dependency or hostility, in favor of a detached status.

In conceptualizing these three major personality types, Horney's view was that in an individual, one type predominated, while the other two could play secondary and essentially unconscious roles. This conceptualization was limited to an analysis of the neurotic range of psychopathology, which was the domain Horney investigated. In her view, the neurotic individual strives to attain an idealized persona or self-image based on one of the three neurotic types, in an effort to cope with the anxiety aroused by facing a hostile, unaccepting world. This distorted idealization of the self generates a pathological pride system, in which neurotic claims and entitlements towards others are systematically employed to limit anxiety and interpersonal closeness. Pursuit of this elaborate pride system, based on ideal rather than real conceptions of self, demands intensely driven and compulsive strivings in one of the personality directions described in Horney's typology. This aspiration toward the ideal acts as a tyrannical force, pressuring the individual toward perfection within the central character structure, and resulting in a constant experience of self-dissatisfaction.

Horney's emphasis on three character types derived from striving for an unreachable idealization is based on her important recognition of the infant's need to hide its true reactions from caretakers who are unaccepting or rejecting of the child's responses. The resulting alienation creates the need to seek security by compulsively attempting to build an essentially unworkable character, which contributes to neurotic suffering.

ERICH FROMM

Erich Fromm was another theorist who appreciated the experience of personal and social alienation, and he also developed a typology of the neurotic styles that individuals utilize to manage this alienation. In the mid-twentieth century, he developed his own interpersonal typological system, which influenced the field of psychopathology and diagnosis in advancing the importance of cultural variables on the development of personality and conflict. Central for Fromm were individuals' strivings to find security and connections with people in life. Fromm held that by becoming united with other people, one could achieve a sense of independence—if one's personal integrity were not sacrificed. This altruistic approach develops through interpersonal involvements in work and love. The context for this personality texture is a harmonious community based on interpersonal support. Fromm translated his social orientation to individual functioning by developing a system of character traits. Each of these traits signifies a typology, because one of these traits usually plays a central, defining role, although others may also be manifested. Within this typology are one major productive orientation and several nonproductive orientations. The four nonproductive orientations are the *receptive orientation,* the *exploitative orientation,* the *hoarding orientation,* and the *marketing orientation.* The one positive orientation is entitled the *productive orientation.*

The Receptive Orientation

In the receptive orientation the basic posture is to dependently seek to fulfill needs and wants from sources external to the self. Other people and power sources are looked to for security and well-being. Individuals with receptive orientations have the wish for things and affection to be given to them, rather than risking an active effort in response to their needs. Such people are ineffectual without assistance from others. This receptive orientation corresponds with Freud's oral passive type, but Fromm goes further in suggesting that societies in which this type is encouraged are those with rigid power structures, where the mainstream group needs to use others.

The Exploitative Orientation

In the exploitative orientation also, other people are relied on to gratify the individual's needs. The major difference between this orientation and the receptive orientation is that active coercion or manipulation takes the place of a passive-receptive stance. In this type, security is satisfied on the emotional level by a kind of greed based on conquest, usurpation, and outright covetousness. Hostile possessiveness is a major characteristic of this type, in the sense that the prize sought after becomes valued by virtue of its possession by another. When this trait of covetousness exists in an intense form, the individual is attracted to conquest through force. Thus, this type is a domineering individual, bearing some similarity to Freud's oral aggressive type.

The Hoarding Orientation

In the hoarding orientation, whatever can be attained and hoarded is used to assure the absence of anxiety or its continual reduction. The things hoarded include the tangibles of practical life, as well as the components of the inner life. Individuals with this orientation withdraw from people and are detached, isolated, and miserly. They guard their possessions from external involvement. In conceptualizing the hoarding orientation, Fromm was apparently influenced by Freud's formulation of the anal retentive type. During advanced years, such persons can become extremely rigid and stubborn and can also become somewhat isolative and suspicious, thinking that people may want things of them.

The Marketing Orientation

In the marketing orientation, the success with which an individual is able to aggrandize and sell himself is taken as the indicator of the person's stature. Thus, the merit of the individual is regarded in extremely materialistic terms. A person's external facade assumes more importance than his or her integrity, wisdom, and skillful, solid achievement. In this type, relating to others is always superficial, because the focus on externals reduces consideration of personal awareness and emotional interactions. A sense of alienation, without deep relationships and with limited self-knowledge, further defines this type.

The Productive Orientation

The productive orientation represents the only positive one, what Fromm regarded as the essential aim for human beings. Since in this type an ideal is presented, Fromm conceptualized it more extensively, in terms of what a person might strive for. The goal is for the individual to develop and actualize his talents and abilities. Fully creative aims are engaged by this type. As an ideal, this type is not frequently seen, but is regarded more as a goal to encourage personal transformation and social change.

Fromm's Later Types: The Necrophilious and Biophilious

Two final orientations were later appended by Fromm to complete his typological categorization of people with respect to character formation. The *necrophilious* type is preoccupied with features of death, decay, and sickness, and people of this type are substantially focused on historical family events characterized by morbid feelings. In addition, such people are interested in noctural experiences, especially phenomena of death, its vicissitudes and rituals. The *biophilious* type is the opposite of the necrophilious. The biophilious person is optimistic and focuses on the vitality of life.

Social Determinants in Fromm's Theory

Fromm's typological discriminations were strongly related to his ideas about people's strivings and the social systems that contain them and so strongly influence them. His concern that people strive to be self-actualized and positively related and that they find ways to benefit from freedom formed the essential template that generated the productive characterologies he delineated. His approach to typology also forcefully reflected his efforts to understand the variety of social systems that exist. Each of these social systems in his view tends to promote a particular kind of character structure, one often antithetical to the adequate satisfaction of human needs, as in the nonproductive types. The emphasis Fromm placed on cultural and societal values in the development of personality and psychopathology is revealed in the hierarchy of characterologies implied by his typology. His personal interest in the direction mankind needs to follow both in social functioning and personality ideal is also strongly implicit in his typological system.

In focusing on external pressures in particular societies, Fromm incorporated cultural factors as a basic determinant of the individual's developing personality trends. In his view, for example, a social structure based on a feudal or slave system fosters the receptive orientation, while societies emphasizing conservative religious and business practices may promote the hoarding orientation. Facism is cited as promoting the exploitative orientation, while Fromm proposes that capitalism promotes the marketing orientation.

Thus, an important contribution that derives from Fromm's broad appreciation of cultural and individual interplay is his placement in the foreground of the profound effects that the wider culture may have on individual character formation. In contrast to Fromm's broad perspective and demarcation of types of individuals with relatively limited reference to stages of personal development, Erik Erikson has built upon Freud's psychosexual stages of development to form an elaborate theory of the various phases of individual development.

In the next section, the eight stages of man delineated by Erikson will be described, and the type of conflict associated with each stage will be related to character formation.

ERIK ERIKSON

The theoretical positions elaborated by the followers of Freud who have been considered thus far remain within the psychoanalytical tradition, but reflect an increasing social emphasis. The main contribution of these various typologies was to bring focus to the social and interpersonal approaches to personality development. Accordingly, the demarcated stages of personality development and evolution presumably deriving largely from biological influences were minimized, since these psychoanalytic theorists emphasized a greater social focus. But in Erik Erikson, a major influence on psychoanalytic theory emerges who has embraced the importance of predetermined stages of personality development and their biological implications, while also retaining an intense emphasis on the social influences affecting personality formation.

In the theory of personality development presented by Erikson, the evolving individual passes through a series of stages, covering the entire life span. Consequently, an array of typologies is absent from Erikson's conceptual approach; his emphasis is on the complexities—biological and social—affecting each stage and accruing from infancy to old age. During each stage a characteristic conflict and crisis must be dealt with, and the resolution of the crisis of each period bears implications for the management of the next stage.

Erikson's theory also emphasizes personal identity and aspects of functioning associated with ego development. This ego psychology component of his theory reflects the importance of cultural and interpersonal pressures, while his developmental theory of personality builds upon the importance that Freud attributed to the biological foundation of personality.

Through the following descriptions of Erikson's stages, it will become apparent that this sequence amounts to an encapsulation of the stages of man.

The Oral-Sensory Stage

In the first stage of life, the *oral-sensory,* the infant relates entirely to a nurturing figure for security. Thus, dependency characterizes the infant's psychological position. The biological aspect of this stage involves the importance of the oral process, reflecting a parallel between Erikson and Freud and establishing the correspondence between this stage of Erikson's developmental theory and the oral stage of development proposed by Freud. However, Erikson adds an additional emphasis on the interpersonal relationship at this stage, whereby the child's adaptation to the world can take on a cast characterized by trust and collateral traits, so that anxiety is controlled. When the development of trust in people fails, security is threatened. Thus, the central issue of this stage concerns *trust versus mistrust,* and the derivative influences of these traits on the child's personality. For example, the extent to which the mother responds to the infant's needs with warmth and reliability determines the infant's overall sense of security in the world. This sense of security, or trust, becomes so important that it influences the foundation of the personality in terms of whether the emerging individual can experience greater freedom in the world, especially in terms of accomplishing the series of important developmental tasks that must be faced. The beginning of a sure sense of identity is also determined by this foundation of basic trust. When basic trust is not established because of parental inattention or unpredictability, the personality traits of suspicion and fear are generated. It is apparent, especially in connection with distrust, that there are implications for a paranoid personality disposition as a pathological derivative from this stage.

The Muscular-Anal Stage

Erikson's second stage of development, the *muscular-anal,* corresponds to Freud's anal stage. However, Erikson emphasizes during this period not only sphinctor control in the context of the toilet training, but the child's general interest in developing skills and its pride in doing new things, experiences that are essentially based on the child's muscular advancement. The psychological dimension of retaining and controlling versus yielding is seen by Erikson as the basic contrast during this period. The developmental task here can be accomplished in ways that are either loving or hostile. A central experience that relates to parental reactions to the child's emerging autonomy involves whether the child is enabled to promote its personal wishes autonomously or is made instead to feel shame and doubt about these strivings. To the extent that autonomous functioning is interfered with, pervasive qualities of self-doubt and of shame in relation to other people become solidified. The conflicts related to toilet training can be extended to other areas of functioning, and the relationship between child and parent during such training generates enduring traits. Implications for independent functioning as opposed to psychopathology involving dependency can be seen as deriving from this stage, while the conflict in this period revolves around the theme of *autonomy versus guilt*.

The Locomotor-Genital Stage

Similar to Freud's stages of phallic and oedipal development in time span, the *locomotor-genital* stage in Erikson's theory is based on the assertiveness that the child develops to fulfill his ambitions. This desire to fulfill ambition is defined as the child's initiative. The main ambition is the child's striving for recognition and closeness with the parent of the opposite sex, within the context of an overall oedipal pattern. As the child develops activities and fantasies surrounding oedipal issues, parental responses can encode an appreciation of assertion or initiative or a persistent sense of wrongdoing that will bear upon the comfort that the individual will have throughout life; that is, the child whose parents foster a sense of wrongdoing will develop persisting traits with strong guilt components. A disposition enabling assertion, as opposed to psychopathology involving inhibition of this assertiveness or initiative, can be related to derivatives of this stage. The derivative conflict theme characterizing this period therefore revolves around *initiative versus guilt*.

Latency

Erikson's *latency* stage corresponds to the latency stage described by Freud as relatively calm in impulse terms. Erikson adds a great deal of emphasis on the child's achievement in the spheres of cognition, deliberation, and the development of orderly thought patterns. Consequently, the essential conflict of this stage involves *industry versus inferiority*. The characteristics that are added to the child's ego identity depend upon parental reactions to the skills and new efforts that the child concentrates on exploring. A sense of competence emerges when adequate support for new efforts is received, while limited positive attention leads to the solidification of traits of inferiority. Erikson's association of feelings of inadequacy with conflicts during latency contrasts with Freud's derivation of inferiority from the phallic period.

Adolescence

During the stage of *adolescense,* identity concerns become central. The task for the adolescent is to construct an integration of self-knowledge, as well as to absorb feedback from others. In addition, the blending of family and personal history with this integration of self-awareness also becomes a vital task. The fusion of these aspects begins to comprise the person's profile of the self. In ego terms, this kind of self-awareness reflects the development of an observing ego, which reduces the anxiety involved in self-doubt and the probability of identity crises occurring. Without success in this task, it is impossible to move into adulhood with clarity and sureness about oneself. If an identity crisis develops, the adolescent experiences great difficulty in clarifying who he is and what he wants, both in the present and in the future. In fact, under the pressure of a prolonged or unresolvable identity crisis, roles that are counter to the norm are sought, and the adolescent becomes anchored in maladjustments. Clearly, when there is a failure of crisis resolution during the adolescent phase and successful formation of a positive identity does not take place, the individual is not prepared to master the succeeding stages associated with mature functioning. The main theme of this period, therefore, revolves around *identity versus role confusion.*

Young Adulthood

Young adulthood involves the establishment of independence and the consistent appearance of adult and mature behavior. During this stage, which usually lasts until middle age, the emphasis is on the formation of close and intimate relationships. Both friendship and sexual intimacy serve as means for cementing the tasks of this stage, since success at forming intimate bonds is based on a secure sense of self-identity. For the individual who successfully resolves the challenges of this stage, historical loyalties, as to parental figures, evolve to include new loyalties without a sense of disloyalty to past figures arising. If the person cannot form intimate involvements, a life of relative social isolation is embraced in which a rejecting or aggressive attitude may be maintained against others, based on the inability to achieve intimacy. Thus, closeness becomes associated with anxiety. Therefore, the main concern of this period relates to *intimacy versus isolation.*

Adulthood

Extending throughout midlife, the stage of *adulthood* represents the person with potential to reach beyond the immediacy of his family circle. Adulthood necessarily means expressing in action that which has been incorporated and incubated throughout life, so that others can have the benefit of such a synthesis. Thus, the central issue of this stage goes beyond family; it extends into the future, and therefore contains generational implications. Knowledge and techniques are generated and shared so as to benefit a new group of people, giving additional meaning to the central issue of this stage, that of generativity. Without such generativity, a crisis of stagnation occurs, creating feelings of personal emptiness. If this happens, the individual may become self-centered. The major theme of this stage is thus *generativity versus stagnation.*

Maturity

In the last stage of life, *maturity,* a person is in a position to gain an overall perspective on his life and can therefore obtain a more profound sense of it and understand its substance. If the person can come to terms with the broad sweep of his development, then he can experience the final challenge—that of cohering and sensing ego-integrity. If this personal assessment evokes disappointment, then a sense of despair ensues, characterized by disgust, by fear of death, and even by contempt for people. Thus, the major theme of this stage can be called *ego-integrity versus despair.*

Characteristic Strengths of Each Stage

Erikson's stages of development comprise a system that differs from that of typologies. In Erikson's sequence of characteristic conflicts and qualities for each stage, social variables are fundamental but are rooted in a necessary biological and transcultural sequence of development, meant to obtain for all people. Associated with each of the eight stages is an opportunity for a characteristic strength to evolve; Erikson conceives of these strengths as basic virtues. These qualities are essentially the resiliency that results from a successful traversing of developmental tasks, and they reflect healthy adaptations. According to Erikson, when the particular stage of development is mastered in an adaptive manner, a characteristic human strength develops and can then be reinforced during the entire course of life.

In the first stage of life, when basic trust is established through the appreciation that needs can be met, the characteristic of *hope* evolves. Hope is a confidence that persists in spite of the absence of immediate gratification or in the face of rejection. Next, the characteristic of *will* is developed from the mastery of autonomy. Will provides the individual with a disposition to utilize freedom and spontaneity as well as civilized self-control in life. In the next stage, with successful exercise of initiative and assertiveness, the ability to develop goals and persist in achieving them evolves as the virtue of *purpose*. Mastery of assiduousness, along with the necessary skills to carry through important assignments from beginning to end, then contributes to the development of the characteristic of *competence*. Authentic and loyal relationships with others based on clear identity issues and a resilient ego give rise to *fidelity* as a major characteristic. Successful participation in intimacy leads to the virtue of *love*. From generativity, which more or less involves altruistic behavior and the capacity to show concern, arises the disposition of *care*. Finally, concern for life's experiences within the generational perspective leads to a sense of ego-integrity and gives rise to *wisdom* as a final characteristic.

The characteristics associated with the successful resolution of the crisis corresponding with each stage are identified not only with the development of individuals, but with the evolution of mankind. From this position it can be seen that the biological orientation implied by stages of development is accompanied by extensive social and cultural concerns. The essence of each stage in the developmental sequence is a crisis to be resolved, and intense anxiety accompanies the crises that are faced in succession throughout life. Thus, the individual is involved in mastering particular anxieties throughout the span of life.

The issue of anxiety as an essential phenomenon in the understanding of personality and psychopathology was certainly cemented during the twentieth century largely through the impetus of the work of Freud, and it has continued to be a strong underlying component in the work of his followers. As will be seen later, the central concept of anxiety also constitutes an important hinge on which current nosological systems were based. In addition, the development of object relations theory also places anxiety in a central position as a major phenomenon of personality functioning.

Anxiety and its management was also given a crucial role by both Alfred Adler and Harry Stack Sullivan, in their emphasis on the social and the interpersonal that separated them from Freudian theory. In the following chapter, the treatment of anxiety and its importance in personality and psychopathology will be addressed as it relates to the work of Adler and Sullivan.

SUMMARY OF DIAGNOSTIC FORMULATIONS

The post-Freudian typologies continue to emphasize the important role of anxiety as a psychological construct and as a universal experience which emerges as the fulcrum of adaptation. In the theories of Horney and Fromm, typologies or character dispositional types—that is, defined patterns of personality functioning—are construed as responses to the issue of personality development interactions with respect to the management of anxiety.

Erikson emphasized the importance of social and cultural influences on personality while retaining the view that biological factors have substantial influence in personality development. He delineated a sequence of stages comprising the life span. Each phase contains a specific conflict or crisis requiring resolution; the result is adaptive or pathological, and a particular strength that can persist through life derives from success at each stage.

Table 15.1 presents the systems of Horney and Fromm, while table 15.2 presents the stages of Erikson.

TABLE 15.1: The Systems of Horney and Fromm

Social and Interpersonal Typologies Based on Management of Anxiety

HORNEY

Horney focused on basic anxiety that accrues from rejection and hostility in a maladaptive family situation. Attempts to manage this anxiety by the development of a pride system center on an ideal associated with three main strivings:

Self-effacing: Movement Toward People—Safety and security through compliance and dependency.

Expansive: Movement Against People—Safety and security through domination and aggressivity.

Resignation: Movement Away from People—Safety and security through detachment, isolation, and noninvolvement.

FROMM

Fromm focused on strivings to attain security in a social system and by implication thereby to manage anxiety. His main types are:

Receptive Orientation—Security is sought passively from others.

Exploitative Orientation—Security is sought forcefully from others.

Hoarding Orientation—Security is sought by saving whatever one possesses.

Marketing Orientation—Security is sought through salesmanship.

Productive Orientation—Security is gained through effort and self-actualization.

TABLE 15.2: Erikson's Eight Stages of Man

Stage	Characteristic Conflict	Adaptive Result	Pathological Disposition	Sustained Strength
Oral-Sensory	trust/mistrust	basic trust	paranoid	hope
Muscular-Anal	pride/shame, doubt	autonomy	dependency	will

TABLE 15.2, *continued*

Stage	Characteristic Conflict	Adaptive Result	Pathological Disposition	Sustained Strength
Locomotor-Genital	initiative/ guilt	ambition	inhibition	purpose
Latency	industry/ inferiority	competence	inadequacy	competence
Adolescence	identity/ isolation	identity	immaturity	fidelity
Young Adulthood	intimacy/ isolation	intimacy	rejecting/ aggressive	love
Adulthood	generativity/ stagnation	generativity	self-absorbtion	care
Maturity	integrity/ despair	integrity	despair	wisdom

CHAPTER 16
Adler and Sullivan

In Freud's pioneering work on psychopathology, he was among the first to elaborate the importance of anxiety in personality functioning. The term *anxiety* derives from the Greek word *agon*, the struggle or contest between opposing forces; Freud regarded anxiety as generated from the individual's difficulty in mastering instinctual drives. This conception of anxiety is an example of the emphasis that Freud placed on the biological perspective, even as he developed a complex network of psychological theories. Among the theorists strongly influenced by Freud's emphasis on early childhood experiences and the role of anxiety in determining personality patterns and psychopathological functioning were Alfred Adler and Harry Stack Sullivan. Both of these investigators emphasized social and interpersonal phenomena as sources of anxiety. They also stressed social and interpersonal phenomena as bearing the pathological effects of disturbed patterns developed in coping with anxiety.

ALFRED ADLER

Alfred Adler, one of Freud's early colleagues, was the first to depart from the biological aspects of Freud's views, especially with regard to his references to instincts. Adler developed an approach based on the primary impact of social forces, on viewing them as central in human development. In contrast to Freud, Adler deemphasized the roles of both sexuality and unconscious functioning as motivational forces; this led to a theoretical perspective in which personal development is under significant individual and personally creative influence. This social-personal view relates Adler to the later advent of the human potential movement. The personality theory that Adler formulated is known as *individual psychology* because of its emphasis on the individual's role in forming his own destiny.

The Role of Anxiety

In Adler's perspective, the sense of inferiority and the anxiety attendant on this feeling are the central emotional factors in people's existence. This theoretical formulation, regarding such inferiority feelings as the ordinary condition that people experience, removed the sense of inferiority from the sphere of pathology. In Adler's view, inferiority feelings serve instead to motivate each individual to attempt to advance, to try to rise above a basic sense of inferiority.

Early in life the child's sense of inferiority relates to its anxiety in the face of the obviously superior position of its parents. This observation of Adler's demonstrates his view that the experience of anxiety begins as a social and interpersonally determined phenomenon; Adler's theory presents the central experience of anxiety in nonbiological terms. For the infant, it is the social sphere that provides the context in which dependency feelings develop. The simple contrast between the mastery and power of the parent and the smallness and vulnerability of the child creates an anxiety matrix with consequences for the child's feelings of security or relative helplessness. Thus emerged Adler's formulation of inferiority.

Under the best circumstances, these initial feelings of inferiority motivate the person's efforts to compensate, which means seeking opportunities for growth, finding solutions to challenges and, ultimately, making a positive psychological adaptation. When adaptive patterns are not established, the normal feelings of inferiority become increasingly amplified, resulting in the formation of the well-known *inferiority complex*. In the psychopathology of the inferiority complex, the inability to resolve the developmental problems of living constitutes the major dynamic.

Origins of the Inferiority Complex

Psychopathology derived from the formation of the amplified inferiority complex originates through three possible means: a physiological weakness; parental spoiling; or parental neglect of the child.

ORGANIC INFERIORITY

Adler's earliest conception of psychopathology connected the development of pathological or intensified feelings of inferiority to an actual deformity or inferiority in a part of the body, or to an organ deficiency. The abnormal physiology, he conjectured, stimulated compensatory functioning. If this compensation was unsuccessful, a pathological inferiority complex was formed.

The conception of inferiority developed by Adler and its intrinsic relation to the compensatory mechanism has led to the insight among clinicians that depression and other allied states are frequently diagnostic syndromes in which the defense of compensation is utilized to reduce the discomfort of inferiority feelings and other negative emotions. Therefore, it can be noted that the surfacing of the more intense dysphoric experience of depression and deflation of the sense of self-worth implies a failure of mobilization of an effective compensatory defense. Similarly, the lifting of depression frequently indicates the effective reinstitution of this compensatory defense. Clearly, such an understanding of the mechanism of compensation in relation to diagnostic syndromes has its roots in the work of Adler and his understanding of the construct of inferiority.

PARENTAL SPOILING OF THE CHILD

Spoiling involves the family's overfocusing on the child, so that the child becomes the major and consistent center of attention. The child in this social environment receives enormous gratification and endures minimal frustration. Such treatment contributes to the development of its inflated self-concept. As development proceeds and the child experiences the social world outside its immediate family, anxiety is mobilized when its position as a constant object of attention is contradicted. The psychopathology that develops in such situations is characterized by minimal concern and care for other people, as well as by only limited tolerance for the needs of others. Such unsocial attitudes evolve because of the lack of emphasis in the child's formative years on delays in gratification or appropriate attention to other people's interests. In turn, an inferiority complex emerges from the child's ultimate conclusion that its problems in securing continuous attention and high regard from others is due to a deficiency in its own makeup and capacities.

NEGLECT OF THE CHILD

The child who is raised by unconcerned parents rapidly experiences a sense of worthlessness regarding itself. Feelings of esteem and emotional comfort are absent. Instead, hostility and mistrust are generated, and become the emotions that accompany this form of the inferiority complex.

The Superiority Syndrome

With respect to the intensified inferiority feelings that underlie Adler's conception of psychopathology, the compensatory mechanism relied upon is an elaborate effort to achieve a sense of superiority. This striving involves hypercompensation or overcompensation to limit anxiety and ensure the absence of any palpable depression. A solid defensive core is established that enables the person to avoid internal despair. One example of such superiority strivings appears in individuals who pathologically manage inferiority feelings by maintaining an inflated view of their talents and achievements. The development of a facade of superiority serves to mask even from themselves their deep and painful sense of inferiority. In such cases these feelings of great superiority over others are not supported by actual achievements. Even when accomplishments are evidenced, a driven motivation to become extremely successful reveals a superiority complex when boasting and self-aggrandizement are joined with egocentricity and frequent criticisms of others. In such people, inferiority feelings drive maladaptive character development.

In the formation of psychopathology that Adler related to overcompensation, the individual's goal was to ameliorate inferiority feelings. Adler's concept of adaptive striving was ultimately encompassed by efforts to achieve superiority on the basis of healthy compensation. Adler considered this *striving for superiority* a motivation to improve and, indeed, to move toward perfection. For Adler, this positive, forward movement was identified with mastery of the environment as a form of superior adaptation. The goal of superiority—which amounts to a biological given—is directed teleologically, however, toward the future, and relates to Adler's concept of finalism.

Adler's Life Styles

Each person strives for an abstract, idealized potential through the development of a highly personal network of a distinct characterology which Adler called *life style*. For every individual, disruptive and paralyzing anxiety is minimized and psychopathology limited when a wholesome life style dictates overall functioning. This life style is essentially the individual's character, which develops from formative relationship patterns in the child's rearing. This characteristic life style is later, in a healthy individual, joined to the ideals of perfection or progressive purpose that are established as goals. Thus, the absence of psychopathology involves more than parental training of the developing child, since the individual strives for goals that are consistent with the development of improvements in the social structure.

It is from the child's training, however, that an individual life style emerges that thoroughly characterizes that person's specific functioning. So consistent is the individual's functioning that its essential nature can be detected at extremely early stages of life. One of Adler's lasting contributions to the understanding of personality dispositions and the diagnosis of psychopathology is the concept that the individual's earliest memory encapsulates significant features of his individual life style. Thus, Adler utilized consideration of the earliest memory as a means of diagnosing the individual's unique life style and particular psychopathology, and this utilization of memory as a diagnostic tool has become a general contribution toward the assessment of psychopathology.

Adler developed descriptions of four basic attitudes that roughly speaking define fundamental approaches to life.

THE DOMINANT ATTITUDE

The individual with the *dominant* desires to oversee or rule the environment. This need for dominance creates a collision course for the individual against other people and social norms, because the attitude of dominance receives its fuel and vitality more or less from inner experience and internal signals. From the point of view of the social context, there are few indications of the appropriateness of the dominating qualities that the individual imposes. Consequently, a self-centered style is promoted, with an absence of social feeling. Diagnostically, psychopathic behavior could be an example of the consequences of such development.

THE GETTING ATTITUDE

What Adler called the *getting* attitude generates characterological imperatives revolving around the trait of dependency, and consequently it creates diagnostic probabilities concerning depression. It is an unrealistic attitude in which a person develops a gradient of expectation involving obtaining nourishment from the world, and is bereft of any experience in the giving of nourishment.

THE AVOIDING ATTITUDE

Simply formulated, the *avoiding* attitude keeps the person detached and in hiding, so to speak, so that normal experiences with the world during formative years are significantly restricted. In this way the person avoids tension and anxiety and protects any inferiority position, but interpersonal relationships of course become effectively impoverished.

THE SOCIALLY USEFUL ATTITUDE

In the *socially useful* attitude, the only possible avenue to a healthy interaction with the world, the person is able to become giving and even altruistic, can engage in sharing experiences and in the overall give and take of experience.

As can be seen, Adler's conception of basic life attitudes contains implicit typological referents; therefore, within their social context, these attitudes can correspond to the typological systems of Horney and Fromm. Interestingly, Adler's types were originally reinterpretations of Hippocrates' four temperaments, with the choleric of Hippocrates corresponding to Adler's dominant type, the phlegmatic to the getting attitude, the melancholic relating to

172 TYPOLOGIES AND FOLLOWERS OF FREUD

the avoiding attitude, and the sanguine to the socially useful type. Not only are Hippocrates' types encoded in language, but his typological framework reappears through various periods in reinventions that suit the theoretical purposes of the psychopathologist.

In Adler's case, his concepts of abnormality stem largely from his special interest in social perspectives in human development. While for Adler anxiety and psychopathology result from antisocial parental influences, socially positive development depends upon the caretaker's teaching of social values that promote the security and self-esteem the child needs to grow as an individual and to overcome challenges constructively.

In addition to Adler's emphasis on the importance of the social context in compromises contributing to the individual's characterology, another major contribution was his incorporation of a future orientation within a primary theoretical position. The role of goals that an individual incorporated into purposes and strivings throughout life was emphasized by Adler as a major component in the forward outlook that contributed to the development of character styles. A creative energy—which amounted to a synonym for life force—was identified by Adler with the ego itself after the person's first few years of life. This creative energy embodied by ego functioning unified the personality, embraced future goals, and allowed individuals to move forward energetically and contribute to shaping their own development and culture.

At this point in the history of psychopathology, one can see that the proliferation of typologies and typologylike systems transformed the understanding of psychopathology and of its relationship to personality and diagnosis. In the construction of personality theory and in the deepest plumbing of character—in some important ways based upon the opening that Freud had made—the greatest leap was taken since the time of the ancient Greeks.

The central role of anxiety and the particular pathological characteristics that are developed to reduce and control this anxiety were also emphasized by Harry Stack Sullivan, who kept an unvarying focus on the interpersonal sphere from which anxiety, personality patterns, and psychopathology emerge. Sullivan's consideration of interpersonal relations in connection with anxiety and psychopathology will be presented in the next section.

HARRY STACK SULLIVAN

An important theorist whose main emphasis was the interpersonal influences on the structure of personality and psychopathology was Harry Stack Sullivan. In his view, both the existence of personality and its analysis could be established only through study of the nature of interpersonal relationships. A central construct for Sullivan is anxiety, and individual characteristics are developed on the basis of the constant need to reduce, overcome, and avoid tension. Personality attributes develop in relation to this management of anxiety so as to establish a firm and basic sense of security.

In Sullivan's approach, the most important source of tension is social insecurity; the basis for this social insecurity is interpersonal events, starting with the care the infant receives from its mother as she addresses both the physiological and social needs of the child. Whether the child develops feelings of security or insecurity is determined by the ways in which the mother relates to the child. Sullivan strongly emphasized the infant's capacity to be decisively affected by the emotions and behaviors of its caretakers. He maintained that the child can meaningfully appreciate the feelings of its caretakers, however subtly expressed, so that a mother who is not attuned to the child or to the need she is attempting to satisfy is readily sensed as a threat to the child's security. Moreover, even mild anxiety and rejection by the mother are quickly transmitted to the child in a crucial interpersonal transaction. This anxiety becomes associated through a process of diffusion with the reality beyond the mothering situation, and it sets the stage for the emergence of psychopathology.

In addition to his emphasis on the important psychological need for security, Sullivan also considered the infant's early discovery of its lack of power a contributor to the formation of personality and psychopathological patterns. The infant's sense of its helplessness determines the formation of qualities that are developed to gain power. Frustration in the achievement of abilities that assure power contributes to insecurity, as does frustration of another basic need, the need for physical closeness.

Sullivan's Personality Manifestations

Sullivan focused on three manifestations of personality that had particular long-term importance: *dynamisms, personifications,* and *modes of experience.*

DYNAMISMS

Dynamisms are continuing types of thought or behavior that characterize the individual. Since they emerge from interpersonal interactions, they ultimately characterize the individual's interactional style. The range of dynamisms that may appear coincides with the variety of traits that can characterize an individual, such as friendliness or aggressiveness. The self dynamism or self system is the individual's central trait; it is the self image that derives from the variety of interpersonal relationships that are experienced. Anxiety and threats to security contribute to the self system, along with characteristics devised to protect against threat and to please those whose attention is vital. Thus, anxiety and the defensive characteristics utilized to manage and reduce anxiety play a key role in the emergence of psychopathology. Further, special strategies are devised to conform to expectations and are used in place of spontaneous behavior.

PERSONIFICATIONS

During the development of the infant, various images of the self as well as of other people are established. The attributes that characterize such personifications can from then on be generalized as needed—the differentiations eliminated—to reduce anxiety, much as the use of compartmentalization can reduce anxiety. Some of these personifications are stereotypes; like other consistent perceptions, they allow for more automatic behavior. The personifications involving the self include the *good-me,* based on praised and accepted behavior, the *bad-me,* based on behavior associated with moderate anxiety, and the *not-me,* an unconscious personification developed through strongly negative consequences. Personifications of other people include the *good mother* and the *bad mother,* depending on associations with satisfaction or anxiety, respectively.

MODES OF EXPERIENCE

For Sullivan there were three different levels of experience underlying the ways in which the individual relates to others. The *pro-tataxic* mode is the earliest and occurs during infancy. In the protataxic mode of experience, random sensations and inner experiences that occur quite independently are not connected by the infant because of the undifferentiated nature of its experience and its limited awareness. In the second mode of experience, known as the *parataxic* mode, connections are drawn between some of the independent experiences that occur together, leading to the belief that things that take place together have an inherent connection. Since these connections are not logical, parataxic experiences have personal meaning. Such subjective investments lead to parataxic distortions when connections illogically formed are relied upon instead of objective connections. In psychopathology, such parataxic distortion is comparable to Freud's use of transference distortion. The *syntaxic* mode is the third mode of experience, in which the child comes to share the meanings held by all people in his culture through words. The syntaxic mode enables the child to think logically, to check conclusions, and to participate in consensual validation.

Further Conceptualizations

In addition to Sullivan's modes of experience, he also formulated six stages of development from infancy through late adolescence: infancy, childhood, the juvenile era, preadolescence, midadolescence, and late adolescence. During these stages, the self dynamism becomes more firmly formed and social interactions undergo increasingly complex vicissitudes.

The personality that emerges reflects three means of defense against anxiety, which become the basis for achieving feelings of security: dissociation, parataxic distortion, and sublimation. They form a cluster of mechanisms that protect the individual from anxiety. Anxiety is limited by retaining the parataxic distortion of reality.

In the use of dissociation, a recognition of anything that could threaten the self-system is avoided. Sullivan's use of dissociation is clearly similar to the Freudian term *repression,* in which material is expelled into the unconscious. Sullivan also utilizes the concept of selective inattention, which allows material to be avoided in a manner comparable to that of the Freudian preconcious. By employing sublimation, potential attacks on the self-system are transformed into favorable impressions. In this way, anxiety is avoided and part of the motivation that is seeking expression can be satisfied without threat to the self-system.

Sullivan also classified interpersonal relations into a personality-psychopathological nosology. The categories of personality that he named are: self-absorbed, incorrigible, negativistic, ambitious, asocial, inadequate, homosexual, persistently adolescent, and stammering. As their self-explanatory names suggest, these categories represent a wide array of personality dispositions.

Essentially, Sullivan's impact on the study of personality and psychopathology relates to his thorough emphasis on the importance of interpersonal interactions in the developing individual's efforts to manage anxiety and to maintain a sense of security and power with his or her culture. Although biological needs are considered, the overwhelmingly important determinants of personality, psychopathology, and styles of relating derive from attempts to maintain a secure sense of self by sacrificing the inclinations of the developing individual that are perceived to evoke anxiety in caretakers. To reduce this anxiety, important aspects of the self must be denied, disowned, and avoided, leading to consistent distortions of the self that are associated with psychopathology.

Sullivan, Adler, and Erikson form a group that in the first fifty years of the twentieth century contributed strongly to the development of a psychogenic stance in the understanding of the etiology of psychopathology. In recent years this stance has been extended to ego psychology and object relations theory. These newer dynamic conceptions, which will be explored in the following chapters, fall into two major points of view. On the one hand, directly building on Freudian biological instinct principles, there is the theoretical school known as ego psychology. On the other, there is the theory of psychopathology that largely departs from Freud's biological principles in favor of an emphasis on early bonds between mother and child; this is known as the object relations school.

In the following chapters, outlines of the contributions of the ego psychologists are presented, followed by a chapter on object relations from the British school.

SUMMARY OF DIAGNOSTIC FORMULATIONS

Alfred Adler emphasized the impact of social forces on psychopathology and developed the school of individual psychology. In this theory, the construct of inferiority identified a universal tension that the individual needed to manage in order to sustain healthy growth. The inferiority complex is derived from three means— organic inferiority, parental spoiling, and neglect—all of which concern issues of the child's self-image.

Adler posited that to manage the anxiety generated by inferiority feelings, compensatory behavior is developed that involves strivings and achievement drives to neutralize inferiority feelings. He called this a striving for superiority. He also derived four basic life styles, approaches to life in the service of managing the tension associated with inferiority.

Harry Stack Sullivan emphasized the importance of interpersonal relationships; he maintained that within this context, both biological needs and social insecurity are the sources of tension. The individual's goal is to relieve this tension or anxiety, and characteristic personality traits are developed to achieve this goal. In addition to security needs, Sullivan posited power needs and closeness needs. According to Sullivan, personality manifests itself with respect to the person's typical behavior, generalized sense of self in the world, and levels of thinking. Sullivan proposed six stages of development, from infancy to late adolescence, during which socialization develops its complexity. He also proposed typical defenses against anxiety which assure a state of security.

Table 16.1 presents various formulations of both Adler and Sullivan.

TABLE 16.1: Diagnostic and Dynamic Formulations of Adler
and Sullivan

ADLER

Origins of the Inferiority Complex

- Organic inferiority: A defect or weakness in a part of the body.
- Parental spoiling of the child: Spoiling results in the experience of anxiety when the child discovers that in the world at large it is not central at all times. Impatience results from this pattern.
- Neglect of the child: Neglect leads to feelings of worthlessness. Hostility and mistrust result from this pattern.

The Four Basic Life Styles

- The dominant attitude: The individual has a sense of ruling the environment.
- The getting attitude: The individual expects only to get things from the world.
- The avoiding attitude: The individual avoids tension and anxiety by being detached and by hiding.
- The socially useful attitude: The individual can give and share.

SULLIVAN

The Basic Features of Personality

- Dynamisms: Enduring behaviors and thoughts that characterize the individual.
- Personifications: Images of oneself and others that become generalized.
- Modes of experience/levels of thinking: Types of relationships drawn between events.
    Prototaxic mode: Random feelings and thoughts occurring in infancy without connection.
    Parataxic mode: Feelings and experiences are connected correlationally.
    Syntaxic mode: Universal understanding of meaning through words.

Stages of Development

- Infancy: From birth through speech acquisition.
- Childhood: From development of language to age 5 or 6.
- Juvenile era: Lasting five years, after beginning of school.
- Preadolescence: Ages 10–13.
- Midadolescence: Ages 13–17.
- Late adolescence: Ages 17 to early 20s.

TABLE 16.1, *continued*

Defense System Against Anxiety

- Dissociation: Equivalent to repression.
- Parataxic distortion: The repetition of childhood patterns.
- Sublimation: Socially undesirable behaviors are transformed into those that are socially acceptable.

Interpersonal Nosology (Styles of Behavior)

- Self-absorbed
- Incorrigible
- Negativistic
- Ambitious
- Asocial
- Inadequate
- Homosexual
- Persistently adolescent
- Stammering

PART VI
Contemporary Views: Ego Psychology and Object Relations

CHAPTER 17

Ego Psychology

THE FREUDIAN BACKGROUND

In the construction of his theoretical conceptualizations, Freud's clinical observation constantly stimulated alterations of theory. Some of the major aspects of the evolution of Freud's views will be briefly reviewed to provide a context for the emergence of ego psychology theories. While many accept Freud's theoretical network as the most powerful for analyzing and accounting for psychopathology, development, and the diagnosis of impaired functioning, the contributions of the ego psychologists were largely designed by them to continue to expand and broaden the application of the Freudian approach. Their revision and augmentation was accomplished by retaining a biological underpinning, utilizing adaptation as a principle for ego development, and investigating earlier aspects of parent-child interactions and their influence on ego functioning, mobilization of anxiety, object relations, and psychopathology engendered by ego deficiencies.

Psychoanalysis

It was Freud's theory of the inner life of the person that generated the revolution of psychoanalysis. The psychoanalytic conceptualization fused theory with technique. This technique resulted in a therapeutic process that would utilize a Socratic-like methodology cast in an associational framework that was essentially determined and guided by specific theoretical underpinnings. These psychoanalytic conceptions included the central precept of working-through, which placed historical adaptational considerations in a position of primary importance. The working-through process, in turn, required the therapist to understand repetitive patterns of behavior, as in the repetition compulsion, and to understand the defensive force of repression and the derivative unconscious behavior of acting-out. The therapist-patient relationship surfaced as the most salient therapeutic variable, and concepts derived from the therapist-patient relationship included transference and its vicissitudes—countertransference and resistance.

The essence of this therapist-patient matrix in the psychoanalytic setting, with its multiple axes of transference, resistance, repression, and so forth, set the stage in psychoanalytic thinking for the appearance of object relations theory and ego psychology. The psychoanalytic bridge to this newest thinking was constructed with elements that included concerns for historical analysis of the person, caretaker-child interaction, the management of anxiety in the formation of character structure, and the sense that diagnostic considerations of psychopathology refer to broad personality dispositions. This historical context locates psychoanalysis as the core scientific and clinical source for the appearance of ego psychology and object relations theory, which represent the most contemporary thinking in the conceptual development of psychopathology.

Freud's Theory of Drives

In his early work, Sigmund Freud focused largely upon the nature of drives and their vicissitudes for the diagnosis of psychopathology and for understanding its etiology. The agency governing these drives that essentially dictated psychological functioning was the id. Therefore, analysis of id functioning and its derivatives was central in early psychoanalytic conceptions of psychopathology.

The process of tension reduction, a major aspect of Freud's theory, corresponded with the operation of the pleasure principle, and it was based on the biological phenomenon of homeostasis. Analysis of psychological functioning in terms of what was unconscious, preconscious, or conscious was of critical importance in Freud's early theorizing.

In addition, Freud focused on what he considered to be basic drives. These were first seen as the sexual or libidinal drives and the self-preservative or ego drives. Freud later transformed this conception, describing life or libidinal drives in contrast to aggressive drives, or what he called the death instinct.

Emphasis on the Ego

In his new theory of drives, Freud placed greater importance on the ego. While in his early theory the ego was viewed as secondary to the id, later the ego emerged as an important theoretical construct that included in its domain the operation of defense mechanisms. For example, repression, the major defense against impulse, could now be understood within the province of ego functions. Thus, important aspects of the reality principle and elements of regulation and adaptation became prominantly associated with Freud's developing theories about ego functioning.

The Adaptive Role of the Ego

Anna Freud, Sigmund Freud's daughter, considered the ego to play an adaptive role and thus enlarged the ego's contribution to anxiety regulation and the development of pathology. Her work in analyzing and systematically categorizing the ego defenses was a foundation for the emerging area of investigation eventually known as ego psychology. Following her underscoring of Sigmund Freud's refocusing of the importance of the ego, Erik Erikson's consideration of social and cultural factors in the development of both normal and psychopathological phenomena added further emphasis on ego functioning.

At this point in the history of psychopathology and in the understanding of its vicissitudes, the post-Freudian ego psychologists and object relations theorists begin a systematic, in-depth analysis of early development. For the ego psychologists, this focus on early development was reflected in details of ego functioning. Now that psychopathology and its diagnostic superstructure was considered to be generally understood, the interest of investigators shifted to a close study of the mechanisms of personality, and a proliferation of theories ensued. Detailed analyses were undertaken of early etiological factors that affected personality and contributed to the appearance of psychopathology. The new theorists focused, for example, on the ego—on its domain, mechanisms, functions, and its role in object relations.

The most systematic developments in ego psychology were

achieved through the work of Hartmann, Spitz, Mahler, Jacobson, and Erikson, with contributions from Lowenstein, Rappaport, and Kris as well. Heinz Hartmann promoted the new idea of the ego as a conflict-free sphere. According to Hartmann, for example, the ego could actually neutralize the id; the ego was therefore seen by Hartmann as containing energy. Ultimately, the main role of the ego was to adapt in terms of normal developmental achievement. Looking at the arena of ego psychology from a psychoanalytic-cognitive perspective, Hartmann's work is a good example of ego psychology's role in the further explication of adaptation and psychopathology. Some elements of this theory will be presented followed by contributions by other ego psychologists to the understanding of psychopathology and sources of anxiety.

HEINZ HARTMANN

While many followers of Freud deemphasized the role of instincts and focused greater attention on interpersonal and social contributions to the etiology of psychopathology and the development of anxiety, the ego psychologists as a group aimed to preserve Freud's essential biological orientation. Thus, aspects of Freud's theory that ego psychologists both emphasized and reformulated were the role of instincts and the elaboration of the developmental stages of the individual. This reformulation can be seen, for example, in Erikson's scheme of a complex series of developmental stages. Further, Hartmann's focus on the biological underpinnings of psychoanalysis starts with his emphasis on the ego in terms of its adaptational role.

Hartmann emphasized the interplay between individual and environment. In this interplay, he saw the ego as ultimately functioning with its own source of energy, as well as with instinctual energy that has been neutralized. Further, the ego is viewed by Hartmann as virtually preprogrammed for a number of adaptational functions that naturally unfold through development. These include such functions as perception, memory, and thinking. Hartmann emphasized that an average, expectable environment surrounding the infant is necessary for normal development. This environment is chiefly a matter of the child's caretakers and social milieu. Should the child's surroundings become in some way impaired or contaminated, trauma ensues, mobilizing anxiety and creating conflict. This interference with the adaptation process, which involves both the maturing person, through ego development, and the social network surrounding the child, sets the stage for the development of psychopathology.

In emphasizing the importance of the ego, the principle of adaptation, and the conflict-free aspects of normative psychological development, Hartmann restructured the psychoanalytic view of psychopathology. In his view, impediments to this natural growth process alone precipitate psychopathology, and the host of subtle factors affecting development that arise through the child's relationship with its caretakers—that is, through its formative object relations—could be systematically observed and utilized to modify theory.

In Hartmann's integration of pathological and normative functioning, several aspects of psychoanalysis previously identified with psychopathology were broadened. Intellectualization, for example, was seen not only as a characteristic defense mechanism under the control of the ego, but also as a process that could be used by the ego for purposes of analysis and to assist the individual's accommodation to reality. Fantasy, in addition to its role as a regressive defensive operation utilizing primary process thinking, was also seen to serve the ego's adaptational goals when imagery is used for creative purposes, ultimately assisting in realistic problem solving.

Ego Functions

In the system that Hartmann developed, with its emphasis on ego and adaptational functioning and its integration of normal and abnormal accommodation to reality, ego strength and resilience as well as deficiencies were elaborated. Five ego functions were formulated by Hartmann in relation to the ego's role in reality testing.

PRIMARY AUTONOMOUS EGO FUNCTION

The primary autonomous ego function—the most basic function of the ego—involves essential reality contact and the integration of perception, thinking, and feeling. Disruption is reflected by gross and pronounced distortions in the perception and interpretation of reality. A person with this profound disturbance is impaired in the ability to integrate the stream of experience with logical thought processes. Therefore, thought and perception are separated, not only from each other, but from the entire variety of the other ego functions. Alignment of perception, thinking, and feeling is then replaced by compartmentalization and gaps. Such a situation corresponds with the psychopathology of a thinking disorder or a psychotic break from reality. In such psychopathology, the ego resource associated with the primary autonomous ego function is distinctly disorganized; this appears in the manifestations of the various psychoses. In schizophrenia, thought is the most disorganized element, while in manic-depressive psychosis and psychotic depression, disturbances of affect along with delusional thinking predominate.

SECONDARY AUTONOMOUS EGO FUNCTION

The secondary autonomous ego function is the capacity for directed thought. Its impairment is reflected when processes of decompensation and distortions occurring in borderline psychopathology or in thinking are colored by severe crisis, such as those experienced by individuals considered incipiently schizophrenic. When the secondary autonomous ego function is impaired, there is periodic interference in directed thought, causing a disruption in the synthesis of perception, thought, and feeling. Reality testing can become severely strained as the individual's ability to direct his thoughts is impeded, leading to the appearance of primary process thinking. Sporadic anxiety is likely to be experienced with the intrusion of primary process material that periodically erupts at this level of impairment.

Primary and secondary autonomous functions of the ego involve the basic relation to reality and the integration of fundamental ego coherence. Impairments in these functions allow intrusion of primary process thinking and correspond to an assessment of psychotic functioning. Therefore, these ego capacities are utilized as diagnostic criteria in ascertaining the quality of reality testing. Hartmann postulated three additional levels of ego functioning that are applied to an assessment of nonpsychotic functioning. These are the integrative, synthetic, and adaptive functions of the ego.

INTEGRATIVE EGO FUNCTION

The integrative function of the ego regulates anxiety as well as ego processes, energy, and feelings, enabling effective application of resources toward goals. The intactness of the integrative function of the ego indicates that contact with reality is not problematic. Impairment of the integrative function results in distortions and misunderstanding of events. Disturbed integrative capacity undermines the ego operation of defense mechanisms in managing anxiety. Because defensive control over emotions is then unreliable, significant distortions in the understanding and interpretation of events take place, even though primary process material does not break into consciousness. In terms of the diagnosis of psychopathology, the distortions associated with such impairments correspond with personality disorders and neurotic pathology. The disturbances involved may include difficulty regulating anxiety, distorted interpretations that interfere with interpersonal relating, inefficient work patterns, and uncertainty as well as unreliability in mobilizing goal-directed activity. Progress toward mastery and adaptive functioning in any of these areas is weakened because of the energy that must be taken from external goals and invested instead in managing internal preoccupations and conflicts.

SYNTHETIC EGO FUNCTION

The synthetic function of the ego concerns the energy required in attending to detail and managing the ambiguities, inconsistencies, and uncertainties that are faced in the pursuit of goals. When the synthetic ego function is intact, the individual can actively apply resources to tolerate and manage anxieties generated by the usual uncertainties of reality. In psychopathology associated with neurosis and character disorders where this ego function is impaired, the vicissitudes of uncertain external circumstances can only be managed through passivity, fantasy, and regressive responses to pressure. External guidelines may be sought to compensate for the ego structure that is lacking when the synthetic capacity is diminished.

ADAPTIVE EGO FUNCTION

The adaptive function of the ego is fully operative only when all ego functions are unimpaired. Individuals with this intactness have flexible cognitive organization and the ability to apply internal resources and energies inventively. Thinking, feeling, fantasy, and behavior are integrated under the direction of this adaptive functioning, and therefore anxiety is managed constructively. Any impairment in this function will be revealed by anxiety that becomes overwhelming or creates difficulties for the person in sustaining goal direction.

In Hartmann's formulation of these central ego functions, the individual's adaptation to reality is the basic template or standard from which gross disturbance and psychopathology is determined. The intrusion of anxiety and the individual's capacity to manage it or to be overly influenced by it are further contributions to the assessment of pathology or intact adaptational strivings and capacities. A diagnostic hierarchy is connected to these ego functions, permitting categorization of psychosis, prepsychotic or borderline phenomena, disturbances of characterology, and neurotic organization. The fact that the entire spectrum of psychopathology can be addressed through the analysis of ego functioning—in terms of ego strength and ego weakness—fulfills Hartmann's goal in developing an adaptational ego psychology. His goal was to bring ego functioning into a prominent position in psychoanalysis and to broaden Freudian theory so that it would be adaptational and biological, and would apply to both normal and psychopathological findings. From the point of view of diagnostic refinement and finesse and of the spectrum of psychopathology that can be differentiated in terms of adaptational functioning, Hartmann's contribution is a significant milestone; it represents the start of a new tradition of focusing on theories of internal constructs, in contrast to the older tradition of discovering and identifying pathology through diagnosis.

The work of Hartmann enabled further refinements in the understanding of the normal developmental sequence from the point of view of the ego. Margaret Mahler initiated such progress in developmental theory in her conception of the transition of the infant from autism through symbiosis to separation, individuation, and autonomy. Mahler's theory that such individuation leads to the psychological birth of the individual reveals the consistency between Mahler's approach and general ego psychology. In the next section, Mahler's theory of separation-individuation will be presented and its contribution to a more informed understanding of psychotic and borderline psychopathology will be elaborated. In addition, the manner in which Mahler's concept of individuation enriches the understanding of phenomena involved in normal development and experience can also be noted. Mahler's separation-individuation can be considered a by-product of ego psychology's contribution to understanding the general issue of development.

MARGARET MAHLER

Margaret Mahler contributed to the theory of ego psychology by introducing extensive refinements in the understanding of the nuances of the early developmental sequence through which children progress. Mahler started with observations of the nature of the interaction between children and their mothers at different stages of development. From these observations, Mahler theoretically encapsulated the struggle of the child to separate from its mother and gradually assume its individuality and autonomy. Consistent with the ego psychology point of view, a commitment to underlying biological instinct or drive theory was augmented by a theory of the development of ego capacities that Mahler related to the vicissitudes of separation-individuation. Also consistent with the ego psychology perspective, the implications of this separation-individuation sequence were drawn with respect to both normal development and the formation of conflict and psychopathology.

Stages of Development

Through Mahler's observations and original concepts regarding the mother-child dyad, she proposed a theory of ego and personality development covering a sequence of stages. The first of these is the *autistic* stage, which occurs during the first two months or so of life. During this period, the child strives to remain essentially in a state of tensionless balance, since it is unable to discriminate between the mother and itself. Following this stage is a period of symbiosis. During the *symbiotic* phase some separation between self and mother begins to emerge, since presumably there is a sense that needs are gratified by a separate object, which the child however senses as joined to itself. Thus, an interface between two seminal objects, the self and the mother, is the major focus of this phase.

Through this symbiotic connection with the mother, Mahler proposes that the child begins to develop ego functions and the ability to regulate tension. If there is any impairment during the symbiotic phase—whether through a biological deficiency of the child or a deficiency in the diadic relationship—a psychotic reaction can emerge. The psychopathology that can develop, given severe enough impairment in symbiosis, is childhood psychosis. The likelihood of a psychotic reaction is increased if pathology of a physiological or psychological kind was also present during the autistic stage. If there is a failure in the symbiotic experience, the child is then forced to assume some of the functions that would be appropriately managed by the mother. If a lesser degree of inadequacy characterizes the symbiotic phase, instead of psychosis, severe borderline and narcissistic problems involving faulty organization of the ego can be engendered.

More important in the etiology of borderline pathology is the next statge, that of *separation-individuation*. During this period, the child is presumed to begin experiencing itself as an individual with an existence psychologically separate from the mother's. Several complex and subtle subphases during this period include differentiation, practicing, rapprochment, and self-identity. These are all related to the individual's psychological separation from the mother and achievement of a sense of personal identity and object constancy. Object constancy is a concept introduced by Hartmann, and is related to the normal developmental sequence that applies to object relations. When object constancy is achieved, the individual views another person with a consistency that is not affected by fluctuations of needs.

This overview of the sequence of development reveals Mahler's allegiance to the ego psychology perspective. Maturation of the ego is emphasized in the acquisition of potentials for independence, which are based on recognition of separateness and autonomy; these are built, in turn, upon a host of ego strengths. The ego strengths develop from the experience within the separation-individuation sequence. Any interference with the adaptive requirements of the emerging ego during this developmental sequence results in the formation of psychopathology. This psychopathology reflects impairments in the integrity of the ego, such as the distortions and confusions involved in psychosis, and, perhaps more innovatively in connection with current diagnostic concerns, the psychopathology of borderline personality or ego organization.

Instincts and Objects

Mahler's diagnostic clarification of the psychological elements of borderline pathology that have their etiology in the separation-individuation stage is a major contribution. It has advanced the understanding and the treatment of the defective sense of identity, including sexual confusion, and the impaired emotional regulation characteristic of borderline patients, impairments which contribute to the particular interpersonal relationship problems that they display. In Mahler's ego psychology perspective, the dysfunction in emotional regulation relates both to insufficiencies of ego development and to the adaptive necessity in normal maturation to manage the libidinal and aggressive drives. While it is assumed that there is a biologically programmed sequence governed by aggressive and libidinal drives—an assumption that connects Mahler's work to Freudian instinct theory—the unfolding of Mahler's phases is seen as enabling the development of extraordinary ego functions.

In addition, as in the work of another ego psychologist, René Spitz, the relationship with the mother plays an extraordinarily important part for Mahler in the normal unfolding of the developmental sequence. Adaptation between the child and the environment in the person of the mother is crucial, and either biological deficits or psychological impediments can interfere with the adaptational process. As the developing child prolongs its ability to maintain itself with increasing autonomy, the mother must be emotionally available so that the child can return for refueling, comfort, and dependency gratification. The psychologically necessary presence of the mother also calls on her to adapt flexibly to the child's needs. Her shifts must be made in subtle ways as the child masters independence and forms a distinct identity and sense of self, as it achieves psychological intactness and integrity.

In keeping with the approach of ego psychologists, Mahler elaborated a theory of normal development as well as giving detailed attention to anxiety and the psychopathology that may develop. During the separation-individuation phase, when the mother's availability is so important, anxiety and psychopathology can develop from maladaptive pressures in the dyad. For example, if there is premature pressure from the mother for the infant to separate from her, the child becomes anxious about independence and its tendency to merge is strengthened. On the other hand, if the mother interferes with the child's strivings toward independence, the child's sense of self and comfort with autonomy can be impaired. Anxiety involving fear of abandonment as well as preoccupations with merging are psychopathological tendencies accounted for by Mahler's theory. In addition, if the mother is poorly attuned to the child's alternating needs for distance and closeness, separation anxiety, fears about the loss of the object, and predispositions either to become overly dependent or to experience depression may emerge. Another sort of psychopathology traceable to insufficiency in the mother-child dyad is the compensatory but unsatisfying pseudo self-sufficiency of narcissism. In general, the problems that Mahler's theory help account for center on diagnostic issues of dependency and depression and on borderline and narcissistic pathology.

Other ego psychology theorists who have contributed to the revision or expansion of Freudian conceptualizations by developing systems involving adaptation and ego development while specifically retaining basic elements of Freud's instinct theory are René Spitz and Edith Jacobson. Some of their contributions will be noted in the next sections.

RENÉ SPITZ

Just as the work of Mahler emerged from careful observations of the dyadic interaction between infants and their mothers, the work of René Spitz also started with direct observation of young children. Spitz utilized situations in which infants had to be separated from their mothers; his population included children who had to be placed in institutional care. Like Mahler, Spitz studied the infant's reactions to its caretakers at extremely young ages—chiefly during the first year of life—and described various facets of ego development based in large measure on those observations.

For the most part, the institutionalized infants that Spitz studied were physically well cared for. They were fed, cleansed, clothed, and housed in accordance with their biological needs. However, under these circumstances, when factors of extended individual contact and affection were absent, Spitz' findings were quite consistent. Apparently, under conditions in which affectional needs are not adequately fulfilled, normal psychological development does not take place. The child instead becomes listless, apathetic, and depressed, displaying the psychopathology which is diagnostically labeled *anaclytic depression.* This term refers to the type of depressive reaction that occurs when there is an interruption of a necessary early dependency relationship, of which the mother-child bond is typical. In the many cases that Spitz studied, the helplessness and hopelessness associated with this anaclytic reaction could be so severe that some children ultimately died, even though all of their physical needs were attended to. That the absence of an adequately stimulating caretaker could lead to death, even when biological satisfaction was provided, emphasizes the overall finding that the emotional and psychological interplay between caretaker and infant is crucial for psychological development.

The successors to Freud who coalesced as the ego psychology school focused attention on the psychological etiology of psychopathology, as well as on nuances of normal development, in the earliest phases of life. The first year of life that Spitz studied provided him with an opportunity to assess some of the more subtle psychological features associated with infancy. In fact, both Mahler and Spitz drew their observations and theoretical conceptions from birth onwards and considered the many small details in the interplay between child and mother. They correlated with these very early events major psychopathological reactions in the mature individual. These formulations of the early psychological etiology of psychopathology contributed toward illuminating the complexities involved in the manifestations of psychosis, depression, borderline personality organization, and depressive reactions. In addition, separation anxiety occurring in individuals whose pathology is in the neurotic range and merger preoccupations found in a spectrum of reactions also comprised formulations of their psychological etiology.

The ego psychologists who maintained allegiance to the Freudian biological tradition thus introduced a major interest in object relations into their theoretical formulations. These object relations are the aspects of early, significant relationships that are internalized and profoundly affect development and functioning. The ego psychologists' innovative investigations revealed the complexities involved in these internalizations, so that the earliest relationships could be understood as they contributed to the development of psychopathology and disruptive anxiety in later life.

Critical Periods

Spitz's major focus was on the nonbiological components of the oral stage of development, during the first year of life. He noted the occurrence of critical periods during this very early stage, which reflect a fixed program of child development as well as of ego maturation. The sequencing of achievements in ego development is consistent with both the adaptational importance of ego functioning and the consideration of instincts or drives related to psychological development that characterize the ego psychology approach. The developmental phenomena that Spitz associated with critical periods not only require biological satisfactions, but also require proper and sufficient environmental support. This support is in large part the receptive, loving, psychologically nurturant dyadic framework that emanates from the mother in response to the infant. Without the mother's full and adequate response to what is occurring in the child, the child's various ego potentials are not primed properly, and their development is consequently impaired. Among the ego strengths that are critically influenced by the earliest relationship factors are awareness and the development of various sensations—especially the experience of emotions, memory, and object relations. These ego functions affect one another, so that a complex process of development emerges from the interplay between mother and child.

Several aspects of normal development during the first year of life were highlighted by Spitz. For example, at two months of age the child achieves the ability to follow the moving face of the mother, and later, at three months, offers a smiling reaction. These developmental achievements signify the beginnings of object formation and the emergence of a sense of constancy about the object. The gradual achievement of some sense of object constancy, however incomplete, reflects the integration that is taking place in the infant's development of emotions, sensations, cognitions, and memories. The child's integration of experiences of perception, nurturance, and physical comfort in relation to its mother lays the groundwork for the development of object relationships of a meaningful sort. Spitz's coordinated merging of the biological and psychological is similar to the framework developed by Hartmann, and typifies ego psychology.

Later in the first year of life, the phenomenon known as *stranger anxiety* occurs, which signals the synthesis into one specific image of both the good and bad images that have become associated with the mother, based on her gratification or frustration of the child's needs. Theoretically, this joining of the separate images or part objects into one image or object signals the integration of libidinal and aggressive drives. In keeping with Hartmann's ego psychology theorizing, Spitz views the synthesis of the two drives fostered by a predominantly satisfying relationship with the mother as permitting neutralization of energy important for the further development of the infant's ego strengths. When the dyadic relationship does not allow the confluence of drives, pathological development ensues as the resulting deficiency of this neutralized energy impairs adaptive ego development.

An additional aspect of the pronounced stranger anxiety that occurs developmentally in the critical period around eight months of life is the emergence of the infant's capacity to recognize the loss of its mother. The ego's successful integration of memory with emotion corresponds with the central importance of attaining a definite and distinct object. Of course, the achievement of this integration has obvious psychological implications in fostering the development of new ego strengths necessary to help the infant keep the mother close, since anxiety arises in her absence. The infant's communication of this anxiety can draw the responsive mother to it for comforting. Later in the infant's development, when separation anxiety becomes even more pronounced, aspects of the mother are gradually internalized, which helps resolve the separation anxiety, enabling the child to develp the capacity for psychological independence from the environment.

These ego achievements, which stimulate augmentation of ego functioning, are reinforced by the reduction of anxiety. Further, the entire array of skills involved with locomotion and vocalization also represent the expansion of ego development that is fostered by the mother-infant dyad. The crucial ego function of verbal communication through language usage is a further organizer that develops from the mother-child interaction. Thus, in Spitz's work, the ways in which the individual's social character develops depend ultimately on the particulars of the relating factors operating in the complicated mother-child interaction. The etiology of the pathological deficiencies that later emerge when these relating patterns are not learned can also be better understood.

In terms of psychopathology, psychological nurturance and its subtle gratifications—as an integrating component of the exceedingly complex interactions between a child and its mother—has more to do with positive development than does physical nurturance during the first year of life. The work of Spitz reveals that the loss of these psychological gratifications contributes to the etiology of depression, to limitations in the capacities for active mastery as a function of deficiencies in ego development, and to the occurrence of constricted object relations.

Spitz has presented a series of critical periods in early development that are analogous to imprinting in ethology: if the proper response is not elicited in the primed infant and if it is not strengthened in the context of a reciprocating relationship, impairments in psychological development occur that contribute to the formation of psychopathological instead of adaptive functioning.

The relationship between the experience of early nurturance and depression developed into a major variable attracting the attention of several theorists. An important ego psychologist who contributed to the understanding of object relations and depressive phenomena in relation to the experience of anxiety and the crystallization of psychopathology is Edith Jacobson. Her work also focuses on previously neglected phenomena occurring in the infant's earliest relationship and is outlined in the next section.

EDITH JACOBSON

By adhering to an approach in which the operations of libidinal and aggressive instinctual drives are fundamental and in which a specific developmental sequence applies to the vicissitudes of the instincts as well as to psychological growth, Edith Jacobson follows in the tradition of ego psychology. In addition to making an extremely careful theoretical clarifiction of the nature of the drives and their development, she also delineates the special role and importance of inner representations in the developing infant. These inner representations involve images of the self and of the external world based on early experiences with the mother; both self and object representations are considered. In this way, Jacobson illuminates the influence of object relations on development.

This emphasis on object relations includes the relationship to the self. In altering Freud's view of instincts and ego functioning, Jacobson focused on the individual's intrapsychic experience of itself in an innovative theoretical manner. She proposed that through the phenomenon of self-representations, the self can be acted upon by the drives as though the self were an object. Her postulate of the importance of representations of self and objects formed a context for analyzing the development of the experience of self and became a major perspective in understanding normal development and the deviations that result in psychopathology. Jacobson's conceptualizations contributed specifically to the understanding of psychosis, narcissistic phenomena, and borderline psychopathology and depression.

The Psychopathology of Psychosis

Jacobson's concept of self- and object-representations emphasizes psychic images as distinct from the actual objective self or object. These representations originate from impressions of the objects, but allow a distinction to be made between the individual's experience of itself or an object and the actual self or object. The representations of self and object become distinguished from each other in the course of normal development. When this differentiation between self- and object-representations is not sufficiently firm, so that the distinction between self and object is not permanent, or if regressive remerger occurs, the possibility of psychosis exists. Such weaknesses of differentiation and such regressive tendencies occur when there is environmental pressure through external events. Then the weakly differentiated self- and object-representations remerge and distortions inevitably arise, with marked confusion between oneself and others. For Jacobson, these distortions and confusions are the basis of psychosis. Individual identity is lost since there is no longer a distinct self-image that is sharply demarcated from the object world.

The Psychopathology of Narcissism

In brief terms, narcissism refers to the individual's attachment to and interest in itself, in contrast to investment in external objects, that is, other people. The theoretical aspects of narcissism are important in psychopathology because of related problems involving the regulation of self-esteem and the sense of self.

While several ego psychologists restructured Freudian concepts to allow better understanding of narcissistic functioning, Jacobson can be particularly credited with achieving an innovative view of narcissism. Her first step was to emphasize the differentiation between the ego and the self. The ego was retained as the key psychic structure, common to the view of ego psychologists, while the self was postulated to encompass the total person, both in psychological and biological terms. The next and crucial step in her view of narcissism was the addition of the concept of self-representations. Developmentally, as the representations of the self and of objects gradually become distinguished, the mental representations of the self become objects of the drives; the focus of the drives can now be the self. This application of drives to the self presents the phenomenon of narcissism in a more workable form. Much of the current work in the field of clinical and theoretical psychoanalysis by Otto Kernberg and Heinz Kohut derives from Jacobson's reconceptualization of self-representation in relation to drives as the major element in narcissism.

The Psychopathology of Depression

In common with Mahler and Spitz, Jacobson studied the nursing situation in the mother-infant dyad very closely and expanded the appreciation of its influence on the etiology of psychopathology. In this dyad the gratification and frustration of the child leads it to produce both good and bad images of the mother. Jacobson proposed the importance of secondary attitudes toward the object that are then added to these good and bad representations depending on the nature of the dyadic relationship. These additional attitudes include valuing and disappointment, reflecting the real relationship between the infant and caretaker as this relationship influences the intrapsychic world of representational images.

The accumulation of valuing and disappointing experiences has a strong influence on the resiliency of the ego. Therefore, according to Jacobson, at later points of developmental stress, the individual's reaction to a significant loss or disappointment will be based on the nature of the positives and the severity of the disappointments that occurred earlier. The impact of later experience as dependent on the nature of early experience with the mother is central to Jacobson's conception of the etiology of depression. In her view, the severity of the response to an actual loss depends on the ego strength that has developed in relation to the secondary attitudes related to gratification and frustration. Further, if self- and object-representations are not sharply distinguished while disappointing experiences accrue, psychotic depression is the psychopathology that develops.

Jacobson's analysis of the impact of the child's early relationship with its mother on the development of self- and object-representations enables her to discriminate several related forms of psychopathology from one another and to clarify etiological factors contributing to the various diagnoses. Thus, her treatment of the specifics of inner representations is used to differentiate between the etiology of depression, borderline phenomena, and psychoses, as well as to contribute to the understanding of several types of depression. Among the depressive syndromes Jacobson analyzes are the depressive affect experienced as a component of various psychoses, as well as the affect—quite distinguishable from the former—that forms the essence of the disturbance of depression itself, so that it is, in fact, the sole diagnostic entity.

The Role of the Superego

Among Jacobson's contributions are also a number of reconceptualizations concerning superego functioning. For instance, if the secondary attitude of disappointment develops with severity from the earliest periods, devaluation will not only encompass the earliest formation of self, but will establish a basis for extremely harsh superego functioning. The relationship between the psychopathology of depression and the primitively harsh and aggressively critical superego is apparent. In addition to this conceptualization of the etiology of depression, Jacobson's view of the superego also related to her understanding of narcissism and the maintenance of self-esteem. She expanded superego functioning to include a regulatory mechanism. This regulation applies to the integration of morality with ego-oriented activity and is presumably instrumental in the stability of self-esteem. As can be seen, traditional aspects of ego functioning were attributed by Jacobson to the superego, thus expanding its role. In fact, certain defense mechanisms were shifted from the domain of the ego to the superego. For example, in the case of reaction-formation, the anxiety that would accompany aggressive feelings toward an object is controlled by deflecting the aggression to oneself; that is, aggression goes from object to self. In Jacobson's view, this self-devaluing, punitive, defensive outcome of reaction-formation is governed by the superego, which is consistent with her understanding of depression as an outgrowth, in part, of devaluing experiences.

Jacobson's pioneering work on narcissism and on the phenomena of self-experiences relates to recent advances by Kohut and Kernberg with respect to narcissistic and borderline pathology within the context of the broad study of object relations. The work of Kernberg and Kohut may be seen as a link between ego psychology and object relations theory, and will be presented after consideration of the object relations theorists in the following chapter.

SUMMARY OF DIAGNOSTIC FORMULATIONS

The ego psychologists added to Freud's contribution by focusing on ego functions in normal and pathological development. Tracing the development of the understanding of the ego from Freud's original conceptions, the trend that becomes apparent may be characterized as the pairing of an assumed biological underpinning with a new and expanded framework designed to appreciate the vicissitudes of the adaptational role of the ego.

FREUD

Freud first focused on the id as the central source of psychopathology. He later added emphasis to the ego to better understand psychopathology and its management. Repression and anxiety remained central in his formulation of psychopathology and as diagnostic concepts; the ego had a secondary adaptive role. The ego psychologists broadened this view of the function of the ego, elaborating theories of a normal sequence of development and of the ego's contribution to the etiology of psychopathology through its influence on the id.

HARTMANN

Hartmann theorized that when ego functions are compromised, anxiety is mobilized. He was also concerned with concepts of reality testing by the adaptational function of the ego. The ego functions that he described reflect a broad concern with the overall state of normal psychological development as well as with psychopathological manifestations. Table 17.1 shows the five basic ego functions formulated by Hartmann.

MAHLER

Mahler investigated mother-child dyads and formulated a detailed theory of the evolution of the infant from autism to symbiosis to separation and finally individuation. She distilled her data into a template for understanding normal development, psychopathological manifestations, and the adaptational interplay between caretaker and child. Her theory clarified the etiology of psychotic and borderline pathology. Mahler was also centrally concerned with anxiety as a psychopathological concept, as a manifestation of poor adaption in the separation-individuation process, and as instru-

TABLE 17.1: Hartmann's Ego Functions

- Primary Autonomous Ego Function:
    Controls primary process thinking. Impairment associated with psychosis.
- Secondary Autonomous Ego Function:
    Controls secondary process. Impairment can produce a borderline condition or decompensation leading to psychosis.
- Integrative Ego Function:
    Regulates anxiety and the integration of feelings, energy, and ego processes. Impairment releases anxiety and impulse.
- Synthetic Ego Function:
    Regulates goal direction. Impairment results in passivity and excessive use of fantasy.
- Adaptive Ego Function:
    Reflects superior functioning in all spheres. Impairment releases anxiety, interfering with the achievement of both short- and long-term goals.

mental in the formation of ego deficiencies. The types of psycho-pathology that emerge as salient derivatives of early difficulties in transition from stage to stage include features of dependency, separation anxiety, and borderline and narcissistic pathology.

SPITZ

Spitz analyzed psychopathology involving depression as it relates to psychological abandonment and the absence of adequate gratification of affectional needs in the first year of life. The condition resulting from an impoverishment of affectional needs was diagnostically termed *anaclytic depression*. Spitz also utilized the concept of critical periods as opportunities for early developmental accomplishments or the formation of impairments in object relations governing ego maturation.

JACOBSON

Jacobson contributed to further dianostic understanding of psychopathology involved in psychosis, narcissism, and borderline and depressive syndromes. She postulated formulations of self- and object-representations as keys to diagnoses of the nautre and severity of prevailing psychopathology, especially in the currently active area of narcissism. Like Mahler and Spitz, she expanded the knowledge of relatively severe psychopathologies by studying the mother-infant interaction in detail.

Hartmann, Mahler, Spitz, and Jacobson adhered to Freudian tradition insofar as their development of ego psychology was connected to biological aspects of psychology regarding the importance of drives and stable sequences in development. They were also concerned with the assessment of anxiety as the pivotal diagnostic indicator of psychopathology. The ego psychologists clarified concepts such as *stranger anxiety, separation anxiety, individuation, adaptation, object constancy,* and *self- and object-representations*. All of these contributions allowed significant expansion of the domain of the ego in the etiology of psychopathology as well as understanding of normal development. Table 17.2 presents some of the diagnostic references referred to by the ego psychologists.

TABLE 17.2: Diagnostic Syndromes Referred to
by Ego Psychology Theorists

Hartmann
Psychosis
    Incipient schizophrenia
    Schizophrenia
    Manic-depression
    Psychotic depression
    Prepsychotic state
Borderline state
Personality disorders
Neuroses
Character disorders

Mahler
Autism
Symbiosis
Psychosis
Borderline personality
Childhood psychosis
Narcissistic state
Depression
Dependent personality
Separation anxiety

Spitz
Anaclytic depression
Psychosis
Borderline personality

Jacobson
Depression
Psychosis
Psychotic depression
Depressive affect
Narcissism
Borderline state

CHAPTER 18

Object Relations

In the development of psychoanalysis in Great Britain, a group that became known as the object relations school significantly altered Freud's theories by postulating complex internal constructs engendered in early childhood development. Members of this school placed increasing emphasis on the early social environment as a major influence on these internal constructs. This emphasis on the relationships affecting the psychological growth of the infant is similar in certain ways to the increasing environmental emphasis of the ego psychologists in the United States. While Freud had originally emphasized instincts and internal structures that essentially utilized aspects of reality to achieve their own program, his followers placed increasing emphasis on the important contribution to development of people and social forces. This social accentuation, accompanied by a gradual downplaying of the importance of instincts in the individual's development, was a major feature of object relations theory. However, the ground breaker of this school, Melanie Klein, made a strong effort to retain Freud's instinct theory, and even expanded it in some ways.

Klein's approach emphasized the importance of the development of a complex fantasy life, involving conflicts between internal objects, in the etiology of psychopathology. While her theories gave limited attention to actual early relationships, intense focus was placed on inner objects and inner object relationships that resulted from the fantasy representations of early vicissitudes of the instincts. Since people are referred to as objects in psychoanalytic theory, and since relationships—real and fantasized—are the focus of development, anxiety, and psychopathology in Kleinian theory, her work and that of her followers is known as the object relations school; Klein and the theorists she decisively influenced form this school on the basis of the emphasis they place on inner object relations.

MELANIE KLEIN

The basic effort of Melanie Klein was to combine Freudian instinct theory with the internal object relations that she postulated as a primary and intensely conflict-ridden part of psychological development. Thus, in Klein's thinking, the child's anxiety is mobilized not only in connection with instinctual drives, but more importantly in connection with the nature of the relationships obtaining among the child's naturally developing internal object relations, and with the interplay between these fantasies and the activity of the child's caretakers. In this chapter, the Kleinian foundation for object relations theory will be presented, followed by the work of other object relations theorists who departed further from Freud as well as from Klein.

The development of Klein's theory occurred in stages, in such a way that she emphasized different coping mechanisms for anxiety and different highlights in the child's development at different points. In this overview of Klein's object relations theory, a composite picture will be presented of her major contributions to anxiety regulation and psychopathology.

Three major innovations stand out in Klein's conceptual approach. First, there is her emphasis on aggression as an instinct, emphatically following Freud's proposal of a death instinct in his work *Beyond the Pleasure Principle* (1920); second, there is her elevation of the importance of relationships as an inherent part of the program of both alleged instincts—the libidinal and the aggressive; and, third, there is her condensation of the developmental stages of the infant, in such a way that momentous conflicts are considered to be undergone at extremely early ages.

Primitive Defenses and Positions

In object relations theory, two primitive defense mechanisms that predate repression are considered highly significant in the child's effort to manage anxiety. The emphasis placed on these defenses is comparable to that which Freud placed on repression, and these primitive mechanisms are considered by object relations theorists to account for psychopathology based on preoedipal stages of development.

The first defense is that of *splitting*. Because the emerging infant is unable to integrate feelings of frustration and pleasure or hate and love in response to the disturbing and satisfying activities of the mothering figure, these intense and widely manifested emotions are kept separate from each other. Thus, an image of the *good mother* based on gratifying experiences is developed, separate from the image of the *bad mother* which is formed from frustrating experiences. Later, even when the potential for integration is present, if massive anxiety and fear would be mobilized by the acknowledgement of such contradictory feelings, splitting is still maintained as a primitive defense mechanism. An important aspect of splitting is that the mothering relationship and subsequent relationships patterned after it are split by the child so that these relationships are experienced as fragmented rather than unified.

Paralleling the split in the infant's experience with its caretaker, two separate aspects of the self or ego also begin to emerge—a *bad self* and a *good self*—based respectively on the accumulation of frustrating and gratifying experiences that cannot be securely integrated without mobilizing highly threatening and fragmenting anxiety. This recognition of the importance of the divisions emanating from the defense of splitting has paved the way for a more advanced understanding of the pathological mechanisms involved in borderline conditions. In borderline personality pathology, fragmentation of the self, the predominance of fearful and limited interpersonal relationships, and poorly regulated aggression are among the major ingredients. In addition, consistent with the major defense utilized in borderline conditions, the splitting of good and bad aspects of people is habitually relied upon. In this way contradictions that produce anxiety are avoided, but so is the possibility of integrating the different aspects of objects.

The second primitive defense mechanism brought to prominence by Klein and her followers is *projective identification;* like splitting, it is associated with extremely early periods of development and predates the possibility of repression. In the early experience of the infant, it is naturally confused as to which sensations and images are exclusively its own and which come from the outside. The unpleasant intensity of aggressive feelings following frustration are particularly prone to be projected onto the outside caretaker and the infant's surroundings. When this projective identification takes place, a reaction of persecutory anxiety is experienced. This sense of external threat occurs because the child now fears destruction, loss of security, and retaliation from the aggressive feelings that have been projected to the outside.

The experience of persecutory anxiety, emanating from the infant's own projected anger, culminates in the formation of a developmental position. This position was first called the *paranoid position* by Klein, and was later expanded to the *paranoid-schizoid position* under the influence of one of Klein's followers, W. R. D. Fairbairn.

When the caretaking relationship does not enable adequate resolution of persecutory anxiety, paranoid fears and schizoid distancing mechanisms are mobilized, which are associated with psychopathology involving autistic and paranoid phenomena and interpersonal withdrawal. Such features operate in pathological experience, for example, in the form of isolation and withdrawal, governed by fears of destruction.

The primitive defense mechanism of projective identification is consistent with the view of ego psychologists such as Mahler that a developmental stage of symbiosis occurs in early infancy. In this stage, the child experiences such closeness with its mother that the two of them are not differentiated by the child, and the source and location of the child's experience cannot be attributed exclusively to one or the other. Klein's emphasis on aggression and the threatening aspects of the aggression that promote its projection led her to formulate projective identification as a defense and to designate a developmental stage related to this aggression in early infancy. Failure to resolve aspects of the paranoid position that characterizes this stage serves as a basis for later surfacing of paranoid psychopathology.

In Klein's developmental theory, a later stage of development centers on what is known as *the depressive position*. This occurs, again, quite early in life and is particularly associated with the frustration and anxiety experienced at the time the infant is weaned. In Klein's conceptualization, this important weaning experience engenders intense aggression toward the objects the infant associates with the source of frustration. According to Klein, the destructive aggression is sensed by the infant as so powerful and uncontrollable that a reactive fear ensues, based on the fantasy that the caretaking object, the source of supplies, and everything associated with these nurturing supplies could be destroyed.

In contrast with the paranoid-persecutory anxiety, an anxiety that the self could be attacked from the outside, the depressive position centers on the fear that the infant's own aggression could destroy the important and necessary external objects. A grave sense of depression is engendered by fears and preoccupations involving the possibility that these objects could be lost, and that depletion of the self would then inexorably follow. The experience of guilt also accompanies the infant's fear that its own aggression could destroy loved objects. The components of anxiety and guilt involved in these depressive phenomena are managed by fantasies of reparation and restoration, through efforts related to the libidinal instinct that inherently seeks to maintain and enhance the object of affection.

As can be seen from this encapsulation of aspects of Klein's theory, an inner world of varied and turbulant objects is considered contral in the child's functioning. These objects are created in several ways: by the program of the drives themselves; by the need to externally focus the death instinct, requiring the creation of fantasies of objects; and by the need to create objects to which the various sensations that are experienced can be attached. The objects, which are for the most part in Klein's view natural extensions of the instincts, are then affected by internalizations of experience with caretaking figures and are driven by libidinal and aggressive motivating instincts. The psychosexual sequence of stages through which the instincts unfold in Freudian and ego psychological theory is greatly condensed in Klein's object relations theory, so that these stages overlap with early periods of infancy. In addition, the sequence of stages is replaced by a series of early positions through which the developing infant experiences typical conflicts. These positions involve the defenses and emotions generated by conflicts involving the internal object relations and their projected representations.

The Etiology of Psychopathology

One of the unique facets of the Kleinian proposals is the particular emphasis placed on the powerful emotions of greed and envy. On the libidinal side, greed represents an outgrowth of the limitless search for positive nurturing stimulation; on the aggressive side, envy is the particular emotion that predominates when restrictions in the supply or source of nurturance and affection are noted. The development of excessive greed stimulates manic searching, which can crystallize in psychopathology in which mood elevation and application of persistent energy toward acquisition and affection predominate. On the other hand, excessive envy following the frustration of nurturance and affection leads to psychopathology in which chronic anger or depressive symptomatology predominates. In the context of this anger or depression, a series of bodily complaints may also symbolically express frustration at the experience of insufficient supplies.

As can be noted from this consideration of some of the important aspects of Kleinian theory as they relate to the experience of anxiety and the formation of psychopathology, emotions are seen as vividly and persistently experienced. There is considerable range and variety to these emotions, growing out of the basic libidinal and aggressive instincts. Most importantly, the instinctual impulses necessarily relate to an object such as the mother or father, or to a part object, such as the good or bad aspect of an object not consistently integrated into a whole. Therefore, in Klein's view, the infant is always involved in intense personal relationships, whether the feeling is aggressive or loving.

In the aggressive experience, an inborn sensitivity to the consequences of destruction initiates efforts at restoration through loving. The anxieties the infant experiences within the context of these overwhelming instincts give rise to fears about people and about destruction as well as to preoccupations with maintaining necessary sources. The early salience of feelings of love and hate within this framework led Klein to a reinterpretation of the Oedipus complex. She viewed this complex as a triangular constellation occurring with great intensity extremely early in life and fused with oral interests. This condensation of oedipal dynamics into the earliest stage of development reflects another significant feature of the object relations school. The importance of a relatively long, fixed, instinctually programmed series of developmental phases anchored in the oral, anal, and phallic stages and culminating in a final stage emphasizing an oedipal triangle has been abandoned. Instead, all phases occur simultaneously throughout the earliest period of life.

In spite of Klein's emphasis on the emotions of aggression and affection, the relinquishing of instinctually programmed stages of sexual development in favor of conflicts involving internalized objects ultimately weakens the importance of instinctual drives in her theory. Instead, the objects and the conflicts between them in the infant's early object world and the anxiety and defenses mobilized by these inner conflicts become crucial for Klein's conception of the etiology and development of the various forms of psychopathology. Object relations theorists following Klein were even more thoroughgoing in their emphasis on internal objects in emotional conflict and their minimization of the importance of the instinctual developmental sequence on the formation of psychopathology. The conception of psychopathology and its development through object relations held by Fairbairn will be presented next.

W. R. D. FAIRBAIRN

Although W. R. D. Fairbairn was influenced by Melanie Klein's work, his understanding of object relations was significantly different. He also revised central aspects of Freud's theories involving instinct, drives, and libido as they relate to development, psychopathology, and motivation. In Fairbairn's view, since people inevitably direct their energy and attachment toward relationships with other people—that is, toward objects—there is no need to view this energy as related to instincts conforming to a fixed developmental sequence. This minimization of the role of instincts is further supported by Fairbairn's view that psychological relationships are the key to the etiology of psychopathology. As a consequence of this minimization of instinct, for Fairbairn there is no longer a structural need to separate ego from id. The distinction between these psychological agencies is dismissed by Fairbairn, because in his view the motivation to develop relationships begins at birth, and this motivation is the adaptive principle that must be considered in order to understand and diagnose psychopathology.

In the process of development, the central issue is the emerging individual's patterns of relating, which are learned through the long period of dependency to which humans are subject. Consequently, psychopathology does not result from conflicts between biological instincts requiring pleasure and tension reduction that are opposed by social and reality considerations impeding gratification. Instead, the etiology of psychopathology is wholly based in Fairbairn's theory on disturbances in relating, which derive from early and persistent impairments in the relationships between the child and its caretakers. Thus, the essential groundwork for psychopathology is seen as the child's early interactions with its mother and the nature of the intimacy and mutual interplay that occurs. Curative conceptions then center on amplifying the ability to initiate and sustain deeper relationships, rather than on conflict resolution.

Theory of Psychopathology

In Fairbairn's noninstinctual approach, object relations form the context which determines development and which ideally permits adequate maturation. The child depends on the maternal object for a long period of time, however, and imperfections in the quality of this object can arise when it is excessively absent, depriving, or unreliable in its relating. In Fairbairn's view, these conditions force the child to form internal objects designed to take the place of the disappointing or deficient external caretaking object. The extent of the interference in the child's relationship with its mother determines the investment in creating internal objects to replace the impaired object. Therefore, the focus of psychopathology for Fairbairn is the relationship between the self and the internal compensatory pathological objects.

When the child's efforts to sustain external relating are interfered with, the frustration involved in this interruption of the natural proclivity for relating produces the reaction of aggression. Thus, aggression also derives from inadequacies and impairments in early relationships. The child's development of compensatory internal objects and its persistent attachment to them restricts development, maturation, and the achievement of independence, and limits the ability for full independent relating. Then, when adulthood is reached, satisfying interpersonal relationships are constricted, and the ego or self experiences fragmentation due to its pathological internal objects.

The Development of Internal Objects

According to Fairbairn, the internal compensatory objects develop in a specific manner. The child's relationship with its mother has several important aspects, grouped under gratifying and frustrating qualities. These different aspects of the relationship become internalized as an idealized object, an exciting object, and a rejecting object. Such internalizations become the inner object relations that split the ego or self from within. By splitting the ego and by maintaining attachments to portions of the split ego, these inner object relations limit the ability to achieve gratifying actual relationships.

Under these pathological conditions, because of the fragmentation engendered by internal objects, the individual cannot maintain mutually satisfying experiences with people. The essence of the individual's psychopathology involves clinging to unfulfilling interpersonal patterns based on relating deficiencies. These interpersonal patterns derive from internalized pathological object relations that have become a template for subsequently attempted interpersonal relationships. The only alternative available is abandoning the internal objects that were originally established to compensate for deficiencies in maternal care. However, the possibility of abandoning internal objects arouses a fear of being alone, a sense of basic anxiety and terror that motivates continued attachment to unfulfilling relationships in which the pathological internal objects can be projected.

The Developmental Sequence of Psychopathology

In his theorizing, Fairbairn distinguished between two levels of psychopathology. The first of these involves psychopathology deriving from the child's total dependence on the parent. When there is impairment of this naturally occurring dependency, the child senses that its love is not appreciated and returned by its mother. This sense of maternal deprivation and rejection is interpreted as devaluation, and the child draws the conclusion that it is itself impaired. Thus, from the child's point of view, its own flaws cause the parent to avoid relating. From the interpretations made by the child, an orientation diagnosed as schizoid evolves. This schizoid diagnosis involves avoidance of relationships, based on the person's sense that its affection is flawed.

The second level of psychopathology theorized by Fairbairn concerns the child's aggressive reactions. If there are impairments in the child's involvement with its mother causing frustration that promotes its aggressive responses, then the child believes that its own hostility and destructiveness is the cause of the difficulty. The child's belief regarding its own hostility then leads to a diagnostic state of depression. Reactions of frustration to impaired dependency and fears of the consequences of aggression mobilize anxiety, which is ultimately managed by depressive pathology.

In Fairbairn's later theorizing he emphasized the importance of schizoid phenomena and regarded depressive manifestations as special instances of the schizoid orientation. This theoretical arrangement underscores the schizoid quality of emptiness in psychopathology and regards the emptiness as the outcome of withdrawal from people. This withdrawal from people, motivated by anxiety, insures the individual's contact with inner objects that cannot be abandoned because of fear of still further depression. The defective qualities of the inner objects are also sought in the pathological relationships that are pursued with people. As a result, unfulfilling interpersonal contacts are maintained and repeated, based on attachments to deficient inner objects.

In highlighting Fairbairn's theoretical views, it may be said that in his conception, psychopathology derives almost entirely from problematic interactions with the mothering figure at the early dependency stage of development. The substitute internal objects that develop from maternal deprivations provide a singular focus for understanding the etiology of anxiety and psychopathology. Therefore, the range of psychopathology that is considered is based upon a rather limited range of the infant's experience. Harry Guntrip, who both followed and revised elements of Fairbairn's theory, will be considered next, as another representative of the object relations school.

HARRY GUNTRIP

In Fairbairn's theory a central position was ascribed to the development of compensatory internal objects. These objects become substitutes for real interpersonal relating, and it is this substitution that can produce a fragmentation of the ego. In extending Fairbairn's theory, Harry Guntrip proposed the likelihood that some of the internal objects become further withdrawn, leading the person to experience further regression and possibly despair in the form of hopelessness. This regressive phenomenon is regarded by

Guntrip as extremely important in psychopathology because it leads to the depletion of the personality. The result is the appearance of severe isolation and passivity. In addition, for Guntrip, psychopathology involves an experience of intense anxiety as well as a sense of vulnerability. Both of these internal experiences are governed by a fundamental fear of complete abandonment and aloneness. Disturbed relationships with people result and are maintained in an effort to prevent further regression.

The inexorable tendency toward schizoid withdrawal in psychopathology and the effort to limit this withdrawal through pathological attachments to people and inner objects is the basic phenomenon Guntrip highlights and analyzes in disturbed individuals. He conceives of the disturbed individual's withdrawal and retreat from people as essentially an attempt to return to the womb; the pathological attachments that are developed serve to protect against this regression.

Guntrip's view of flight as the typical maneuver in pathological functioning is connected with the disturbed individual's maintenance of characteristic impaired interpersonal relationships that serve as defenses against further regression. The threat of experiencing regression culminating in a state of objectlessness—that is, a state in which no object relations exist, either internal or external—is the gravest and most persistent anxiety. The importance of this anxiety is signified by the numerous pathological defensive efforts engaged in by disturbed individuals.

Consistent with his view that the fear of a loss of relating underlies psychopathology, Guntrip's conception of treatment is built on relationship factors. His approach to resolving psychopathology involves weakening the dysfunctional attachments that have been defensively developed and working toward replacing them by a caring relationship with the analyst. It is presumed that this will enable integrated maturation and development.

For Fairbairn, the need for objects was the major consideration in evaluating psychopathology. For Guntrip, the main phenomenon in psychopathology is withdrawal, with the effort to maintain disturbed relationships serving as a protective defense. An anxious, terrified, yet passive state is the core of psychopathology for Guntrip, while for Fairbairn, psychopathology involves an active state in which the individual tenaciously clings to compensatory internal objects which perpetuate poor object relations.

Both Fairbairn and Guntrip imply that the development of self-awareness is intrinsically dependent upon the vicissitudes of object relations, either in terms of the need for objects used in a compensatory manner, or the anxiety regarding loss of contact with objects. Another theorist concerned with the issue of self-awareness, or more specifically, self-identity, was D. W. Winnicott, who focused on the essence of the separate self.

D. W. WINNICOTT

The contributions of D. W. Winnicott combined elements of Freudian and Kleinian thought but largely focused on the development of the self, with a concentration on the self's evolution from the mother-infant relationship. Winnicott devised a theory of development different from both Klein's and Freud's; his essential concern was the paradox that development strives toward individuation, yet with retention of relationships to other people. In other words we become separate, yet need not relinquish our ties.

The Development of the Self

In Winnicott's theory, the first steps toward selfhood emanate from the infant's dependence on its mother for the organization of experience. The mother first provides a secure environment into which the infant can comfortably fit. Winnicott calls this the *holding environment*. Within the holding environment, as the infant experiences needs, the closeness and rapport between the infant and its mother allows the mother to provide the need-satisfier that the child imagines in a hallucinatory manner. The repetition of such experiences promotes a sense of omnipotence in the child. For Winnicott the development of this sense of omnipotence is the foundation for the emergence of a sound sense of self. In this process the mother's attunement to the child is the key factor. As in the theoretical conceptions of Sullivan and Kohut, the mother's failure to anticipate and mirror the child's needs and to provide precise need-satisfiers interferes with the development of self by diminishing the infant's belief in itself and its powers.

The mother's attunement and response to the child's needs for activity such as play, affection, stimulation, and engagement are important, but equally crucial is the mother's not putting demands on the infant when it is not experiencing needs. In fact, a second aspect of the development of the self depends on the mother's ability not to be intrusive when the infant is peaceful within the holding environment and not hallucinating specific satisfactions of needs. For the infant to be secure with itself requires the mother's mirroring of the state in which needs do not press for overt satisfaction.

In the next phase, the mother's gradual reduction in the precision with which she matches the infant's needs allows the child to relate increasingly to objective conditions. In this way the child becomes gradually involved in the processes of reality outside of the mother and can absorb what the mother cannot do. This gradual exposure to frustrations in the objective world and imperfections in the mother's satisfying of the child's needs leads to the establishment of separateness. When this process of separation is managed at an appropriate pace, with sufficient gradualness, differentiation and a more behaviorally active interactional style replaces the child's earlier behavioral passivity.

The Etiology of Psychopathology

In accordance with the developmental theory that Winnicott proposed, two types of deficiencies introduce pathology into the child's development. One type of dysfunction arises from the mother's difficulty in meeting the infant's needs in terms of its imagined satisfactions. The second type of dysfunction stems from the mother's interference in the child's quiet periods. These dysfunctional experiences can introduce fear and trauma into the child's sense of existence. The anxiety that these dysfunctions can evoke Winnicott characterizes as *annihilation anxiety*. In the first case, in which the mother fails to satisfy the child's needs, the child experiences a deflection of its own wishes. In the second case, in which the child's relaxation is intruded upon, the child begins to mold itself to the provider rather than developing and securing its own self. Thus, impairments in the child's development and the etiology of psychopathology are linked to parental dysfunctions, reflected in mothering that is destructively inconsistent with the child's psychological needs.

THE FALSE SELF

The psychopathology that develops from interference with the child's quiet, need-free stages is characterized by fragmentation. As the child responds to external pressure, loss of peacefulness with its own self and loss of self-acceptance occur. This happens because what is offered is inconsistent with the child's own state. The child's psychological fragmentation is viewed by Winnicott as a split between a compliant false self and a true self that becomes detached and weakened; as a result of this split, the true self is held in abeyance. The child who relies upon a false self is seen as avoiding risks, interactions, and encounters. At the same time, the false self comes to represent the mother's wishes concerning what the child should be.

Correlated with the true self is the developing child's potential to function authentically and spontaneously, to feel secure and to appreciate other people while retaining individuality. On the other hand, from the development of the false self derives a compliant pattern, in which emphasis is on consistently adapting to others.

TRANSITION FROM SUBJECTIVE TO OBJECTIVE

At first, the child's experience of itself as central is based on its subjective view of its powers, inflated by its mother's empathic responsiveness. As a result of development, the child needs to adopt a more realistic conception of the nature of the objective world and the existence of separate, independent people. To construct this bridge, Winnicott introduced the idea of *transitional objects* or transitional phenomena. The concept of transitional objects is one of Winnicott's best-known contributions and refers to such items as stuffed animals and blankets that the child utilizes as symbols. These symbols reflect the metamorphosis leading from hallucinatory omnipotence to objective reality. The child's investment in transitional symbols enables the process leading from the importance of the self, with its subjective experience, to the acceptance of the independent, objective existence of people. Transitional objects are crucial for this transition because they relate both to the personal world in a special, subjective way and to the objective world in which they have no extraordinary meaning.

Since transitional phenomena lie between the subjective and objective domains of experience, the child's relationship to transitional objects helps it make a gradual transition toward understanding objective reality and mastering it. In an important theoretical point, Winnicott also states that the child's play activities and fantasies can be engaged in by adults and still retain importance as transitional phenomena.

In conditions of pathology, the distinction between subjective and objective reality remains unclear; there is a failure to accomplish the transition to managing objective reality. Even in the absence of pathology, however, there always remain elements of anxiety deriving from conflicts between subjective needs and objective, external reality. In addition, anxiety regarding the safety of the true self is central for all people, regardless of pathology. In fact, in Winnicott's view, anxiety regarding exposure of the true self within the context of interpersonal relations is the deepest fear that people have. The extent of this anxiety is such that a degree of isolation is required to help regulate it. In instances of psychopathology, the quality of this isolation and its duration become extreme. This symptomatology reflects the underlying problem: certainty regarding the self has not been established. Disturbed patterns in the child's early relationship with its mother is the context in which a secure and distinct self was not achieved.

As in the views of other object relations theorists, instincts, drive reduction, and instinctual frustration versus satisfaction have little importance in Winnicott's conception. Instead, early relationships are the fulcrum for development and the key to the etiology of pathology. Winnicott's view of early relationships is characterized by his regard for parental pathology as it bears on the relationship with the child. He sees such pathology as threatening the greatest interference in the child's development of itself.

Because Winnicott considers limitations in the relating capacities of parents instrumental in the development of pathology, his recommendations for treatment emphasize relationship factors. One such recommendation involves an analytic situation in which corrections can be introduced into the relationship by the analyst to compensate for failures in what the parent provided, thereby rekindling the developmental process. Although Winnicott made an effort to retain much of Freud's terminology and traditions, clearly object relations are for him the central phenomena in the development of anxiety, pathology, and the consolidation of security regarding the self.

Diagnostic Nomenclautre

In Winnicott's conceptualization of the diagnosis of psychopathology, he originally proposed three distinctions. The first category was that of *pre-self disorders*. These include psychotic, schizoid, and borderline conditions in which the establishment and utilization of a false self predominate. Such disorders derive from incomplete or faulty early object relations, through which the development of the true self has been compromised in a major way. Winnicott's second category was that of *depressive disorders*. In these, the focus of the patient's pathology is the realm of subjective experience. Winnicott regarded the impairment of subjective experience as corresponding to conflicts between love and hate involving mood disturbances. The third category in Winnicott's diagnostic scheme was *whole person disorders*. In this category Winnicott placed neurotic patients, esentially comprising what in the Freudian tradition would be considered oedipal-type conflicts.

In Winnicott's later writing, he revised his diagnostic system, basing it on the false self. In this scheme, *psychosis* is regarded as reflecting the disintegration of the false self. In the next category, known as *nearly healthy*, the false self is utilized at times as a buffer between the true self and external reality. The final category involves the *neuroses*. These, however, Winnicott now equates with what he views as ordinary difficulties of living; they are inseparable from normalcy.

This discussion of Winnicott emphasizes his reliance on object relations theory. In the next chapter contrasts between object relations and ego psychology will be presented, along with the combinations that seem to have been devised by Kohut and Kernberg.

SUMMARY OF DIAGNOSTIC FORMULATIONS

The object relations school, influenced largely by Melanie Klein, is concerned with the etiology of psychopathology from efforts to manage anxiety that is generated from early relating with caretakers as well as from the complex fantasies, intense feelings, and rich inner life that absorb the developing infant. Anxiety is the vehicle that telegraphs both attendant coping demands and/or psychopathology, and it offers a path to the understanding of psychopathology. The members of this school have elaborated varying theories of child development and need systems and have emphasized different concepts of disturbance in parent-child interactions that are internalized as object relations contributing to dysfunction.

MELANIE KLEIN

Complex operations of projection and introjection were described by Klein in connection with libidinal and aggressive instincts. In the child's effort to manage anxiety, she emphasized the primitive defenses of splitting, which illuminates borderline functioning, and projective identification, which clarifies paranoid and schizoid pathology, persecutory anxiety and withdrawal. Expanding the dynamics of the interaction of these defenses with the emotion of aggression, Klein established the paranoid position, the paranoid-schizoid position, and the depressive position as developmental steps that can contribute to the genesis of psychopathology. Although focusing on libidinal and aggressive instincts, which generate elaborate fantasies involving object relations, her theoretical formulations are also necessarily invested with the profound importance of interpersonal relatedness and its internalization. Emotions of greed and envy were emphasized by Klein and related to manic disturbances on the one hand, and to pathology involving anger and depression on the other.

FAIRBAIRN

Minimizing instinctual and structural concepts, Fairbairn relied wholly on relationship impairments involved in the dependency of the child on its mother in his understanding of psychopathology. He focused on the compensatory value of internal objects that substitute for caretaking deficiencies and understood pathological development through an analysis of the attraction of these internal objects. In addition, he focused on faulty early mother-child interactions, which he viewed as resulting in a schizoid orientation in the child. For Fairbairn, a diagnostic state deriving from later impairment was that of depression. Anxiety, in his view, is mobilized by frustration and aggression, and related to unmet dependency needs. Withdrawal to internalizations relieves anxiety and the terror of being alone. He considered pathological relationships with people to develop as reflections of the deficiencies of the compensatory internalizations that also substitute for relationships.

GUNTRIP

Regression played a major role in the understanding of internal objects in the theory of Guntrip. Personality features that derived from regression could include passivity, isolation, and depletion. Intense anxiety was also considered a main psychopathological manifestation that stimulates pathological attachments to people and internal objects to reduce anxiety about further regression. Schizoid character configurations were emphasized in Guntrip's view, with withdrawal as a major diagnostic feature. The possibility of entirely losing objects through severe regression was seen as arousing the gravest personal anxiety.

WINNICOTT

Winnicott emphasized the development of the separate self that maintains relating potentials, and connected disturbances of self-identity to the formation of psychopathology, illuminating the development of psychosis. He described the necessity for the mother to offer the child a holding environment to promote a sense of omnipotence that is the foundation of a sound sense of self. Difficulties that arise from interference with child's needs are seen to produce annihilation anxiety as well as a compliant, false self, in contrast to fostering the true self that is necessary for authenticity and the ability to relate to others while maintaining a secure individuality. Winnicott introduced the concept of transitional objects, which reflect and enable the gradual working through and transformation of the child's experience from those governed by subjective hallucinatory omnipotence to objective reality. He proposed pre-self disorders—psychotic, schizoid, and borderline—that involve reliance on the false self which itself disintegrates in psychosis; depressive disorders, which consist of affective disturbances, and whole person disorders, which includes neurotic pathology. He also proposed nearly healthy states. His focus on concepts of health suggests that object relations psychology can be seen as representing a move toward the creation of what might be called the psychology of healthy development.

Taken together, the work of Klein, Fairbairn, Guntrip, and Winnicott comprises an approach to the understanding of development that relies on internal phenomena corresponding with early relationships. The role of instinct in the developmental process is largely minimized as internal object relations and the ensuing interpersonal capacities become the focus for the generation of anxiety and the etiology of psychopathology. At this point in the history of psychopathology, it again becomes clear that anxiety plays a major role both in the etiology of psychopathological processes and as a key to their diagnosis. In addition, the manifestations and consequences of anxiety in relation to psychopathology strongly stimulate investigators to understand its morphology. Table 18.1 presents some of the diagnostic syndromes focused upon by these object relations investigators.

TABLE 18.1: Diagnostic Syndromes Referred to by Object
Relations Theorists

Melanie Klein
Paranoid position
Paranoid-schizoid position
Depressive position
Autistic behavior
Manic mood elevation (based on greed)
Chronic depression or anger (based on envy)

Fairbairn
Schizoid orientation
Depression

Guntrip
Schizoid withdrawal

Winnicott
Early diagnostic classification:
Pre-self disorders
Psychotic
Schizoid
Borderline

TABLE 18.1, *continued*

        Depressive disorders
          Affective disturbances
        Whole person disorders
          Neurosis
    Later diagnostic classification:
      False self
      Psychosis (disintegration of false self)
      Nearly healthy (partial use of false self)
      Neurosis (healthy self associated with "normalcy")

CHAPTER 19

Object Relations and Ego Psychology: Comparisons and Combinations

Many similarities can be noted between the theory of object relations represented by Klein and her followers and the ego psychology approach previously described. In both theoretical contexts, primary importance for the vicissitudes of development is placed on the relationship factors between the infant at early ages and its caretakers that are not limited to the biological needs for nurturance. Various interpersonal factors at the earliest stage of life are regarded as fundamental to the advent of anxiety, and thus as forerunners of psychopathological developments.

The central role given to the process of internalization represents another similarity between the contexts of object relations theory and ego psychology. Significant elements of the relationship that develops between the caretaker and child based on early impressions become internalized as object representations. One internalized representation develops based on the caretaker, while another representation develops based on the self. These images of the external object and the self are thus formed in a parallel fashion. The structure of this formation of self and object can contribute to healthy maturation or, in contrast, to the etiology of psychopathology.

Further, both images—the self image and the object image—contain different aspects. One aspect of each image has developed in relation to gratifying experiences (the good self and the good object), while another aspect of each image has developed in relation to frustrating experiences (the bad self and the bad object). These good and bad aspects of each image were originally separate part self and part object images. Central to the etiology and understanding of psychopathology in both object relations theory and ego psychology are the various ways in which the good and bad images of self and the other are related, split, become integrated or fused, and how they may redifferentiate and become projected and introjected. Thus, many of the processes intertwining the self and the other are shared by object relations theory and ego psychology theory.

A major distinction between object relations theory and ego psychology is that object relations theory eliminates the fixed, lengthy developmental sequence based on inevitable vicissitudes of the instincts that is prominent in ego psychology. Thus, one of the basic distinctions between ego psychology and object relations theory involves the conception and role of instincts. While Klein's object relations theory does include emphasis on instincts, nevertheless in her view the child's relationship to objects is ultimately more fundamental in the etiology of anxiety and psychopathology. The importance of object relations—even when conceptualized as a function of instincts—was Klein's most significant contribution, and the one most developed by her followers. In contrast with the emphasis object relations theory places on early relationships, ego psychology theorists retain a fixed program of instinctual development. For such theorists, an important part of understanding anxiety and psychopathology is based on considerations regarding the nature of the instincts and their long-term development.

Several psychoanalytic theorists have evaluated anxiety, disturbed interpersonal relationships, problems with self-esteem, the development of independence, and other psychopathological manifestations by drawing on both object relations theory and ego psychology. Prominent among these are Heinz Kohut and Otto Kernberg. Contributions to the diagnosis and etiology of psychopathology of these investigators will be considered in the following presentation.

HEINZ KOHUT

In his early work, Kohut aimed to create a special combination of conventional Freudian instinct theory and his own conception of the development of the self. Thus, he proposed a separate component of psychological development to account for relationship factors as they affect the formation of the self, but he joined this conceptualization regarding self formation to the traditional developmental sequences of instinct theory. The original part of Kohut's theory, which concerns the relationship between the parents and the child, presumably accounts for the formation of the self.

Like several other theorists who focused on problems of the self that emerge from early parent-child interactions, Kohut aimed at understanding and explaining more severe pathology. His conception represents an effort to define and present a treatment for the narcissistic personality disorder. Kohut's approach has become known as *self psychology* because of its emphasis on the etiology of self-esteem and the development of a stable sense of self. Although Kohut's viewpoint regarding the evolution of the self reflects the internalization of object relations, instinctual drive theory is retained in much of his writing, with his new contribution complementing this drive theory.

In Kohut's self theory, the self is given prominence as a structural entity in its own right. As such, the self functions along with the id, ego, and superego in the individual's psychological development. This self develops from interpersonal interactions and connects the person with objects. Along with Kohut's addition of the self to the psychological apparatus, he attributes a variety of component functions to the self, such as integration, consistency, and strength; these accrue to the self only gradually, through an advantageous relationship with caretakers.

The Development of the Self

The fragility of the early self requires that caretakers provide it with stability; these caretakers are thus not psychologically separated from the early self. Consequently, these supporting figures are defined as self-objects. The interaction between the child and the self-object allows for the sharing of feelings until the self of the developing child can take over the functions of the self-objects. It is by reacting sensitively—with empathy—to the needs of the infant that the self-objects enable the strengthening of the child's own self into an independent existence. As part of this process, the emerging self seeks to secure admiration from the supporting self-objects. This will create a sense of grandiosity and omnipotence, considered by Kohut an aspect of normal development. In addition, an idealization of one parent is created, with which the child can then psychologically join. Thus, admiration or mirroring of the child's perfection by the self-object, and the child's merger or twinship with the idealized self-object, form elements based on relationship factors around which the self can gradually form.

As a result of gradual disappointments in the relationship between the child and its self-objects, the normal and desired internalization of this relationship occurs, through a process called *transmuting internalization*. According to Kohut, the process of transmuting internalization enables the child to build its own system of internalizations as part of a strong self. This enabling process can best occur when disappointments in the caretaking sphere— a natural occurrence of relationships—are small enough and well-enough distributed over time so that they are manageable. Such conditions allow more realistic, positive identification to occur and lead ultimately to a strengthened and independent self. In a sense, Kohut's transmuting internalization process is analogous to Winnicott's concept of transitional objects, in that each of these mechanisms or processes provides a bridge for the child's further maturation.

Two aspects of the self and self-object relationship are involved in the development of the self: a striving to achieve goals, to accomplish; and the development of idealistic beliefs. The presence of these elements reflects a positive transmuting internalization process. Deficiencies in the development of these final elements of the self result in an inadequate sense of self-worth—the clinical problem of self-absorption or narcissism that Kohut's system seeks to illuminate.

The Etiology of Self Pathology

In Kohut's theoretical conception, narcissistic pathology develops when parents are persistently insufficient in their functioning as self-objects. Their sustained inadequacies of empathy prevent the development of structure through transmuting internalization, because the parental and interactional failures are not gradual, are too intense, and are not sufficiently relieved by success. These severe limitations of empathy are presumably experienced by the child as an attack on the integrity of the self.

Under the conditions of inadequate empathy and insufficient internalization, the self-objects that the child needs for development are not available. Then the child's self can become disorganized and can decompose into pathological aggressive and sexualized patterns. The nature of the disturbed patterns that appear relates to whatever family and parental pathological behaviors exist. Thus, because of Kohut's focus on the development of the self, in his view the early relationships of the child assume more importance in the child's development than instinctual programming.

Narcissistic Pathology and Treatment

The component of psychopathology that Kohut's theory focuses on involves efforts to cope with a deficient sense of self. Such coping draws on various means of compensation. For example, the individual with a narcissistic deficiency may seek praise, admiration, and recognition of specialness to an unusual degree. Acute reactive anger and deflation are experienced when others fail to meet expectations and demands. This acute sensitivity and a severe sense of vulnerability regarding self-esteem and the integrity of the self are basic to narcissistic pathology.

In treatment, Kohut recommends that the analyst be intensely committed to making up for the original empathic failures in development. This effort at repair allows for transmuting internalization through the course of therapy, which provides growth of the self. The traditional objective analyst, who interprets conflicts between drives and defenses against these drives, is replaced by the empathic analyst, who repairs the arrest in the development of the self.

Kohut retains a connection to ego psychology theory. For example, he indicates that the sequence of development related to drives in psychosexual terms can proceed provided the self becomes adequately structured—meaning that the self is correctly processed in terms of internalization mechanisms. Conflicts between drive satisfaction and defenses can then occur as later parts of development. Accordingly, Kohut proposes separate lines of development for the emergence of the self on the one hand, and for conflict associated with psychosexual development on the other— an interface between the development of the self and the drive theory of ego psychology.

In Kohut's later view, the role of drive and conflict is increasingly demoted, as secondary to self psychology. In this theoretical change, the typical neurotic strategies of individuals in conflict are conceived of as by-products of pathology of the self. When there are defects in the structure of the self so that the self has not become cohesive, instinctual manifestations can then arise. Thus, diagnostically speaking, neurosis and conflict is derivative of pathological self-development, or narcissism.

Kohut's earlier work retains a concern with the struggle among instincts, guilt, and conflict, seeing this struggle as an important aspect of human experience. He conceives of drive theory and self psychology as revealing different portions of the complexity of psychological functioning. However, increasing emphasis is later placed on the primacy of the evolution of self-cohesion and stability; conflict becomes secondary, largely viewed as a derivative of faulty self-development.

Kohut's presentation of an approach to the understanding and treatment of a severe sector of psychopathology—that of narcissism—is among his major contributions. He offers an elaborate theory to account for the variety of self-esteem problems. This narcissistic pathology involves disturbances in the sense of self, difficulty regulating self-esteem, and persistent sensitivity, reactive anger, and deflation. His theory promotes understanding of the degree to which narcissism is prevalant and problematic and enables a more secure diagnosis of this complex disturbance. Further, his theory reveals the infantile roots of dysfunctions involved when a stable sense of self-esteem cannot be maintained.

Another contribution of Kohut is his revision of the concepts of idealization and grandiosity. His theory focuses on these important phenomena as normal developmental processes with a natural place both in child development and in the analytic situation. This revised view of idealization and grandiosity allows an alternative to the view that they are defensive positions that must be treated as pathological. Kohut's alternative is to encourage and accept the development of infantile idealization and grandiosity in order to repair an arrest in healthy narcissistic development. In fact, Ko-

hut's writings about aspects of narcissism as healthy and important even in adulthood have created a new understanding of
narcissism.

Another of Kohut's important contributions has been his central
focus on the experience of self in subjective terms, and how this
experience is influenced by early relationships during development. His emphasis on the importance of a corrective emotional
experience in treatment is a further contribution; the role of such
an experience had been previously touched on by many psychoanalytic theorists, but is now made central. An empathic relationship
as a framework for treatment is viewed as more important than
interpretation itself, presumably, according to Kohut, allowing for
greater choice and flexibility in psychoanalytic therapy.

Perhaps one of the weaknesses in Kohut's theory regarding the
etiology of psychopathology is his attempt—which has intensified
over time—to relate the entire range of pathology essentially to
one factor. His view that parental deficiencies in the promotion of
the child's idealization and grandiosity through empathy ultimately account for most of the domain of psychopathology seems
strained. It seems clear that there may be many other potential
deficiencies in the parent-child relationship that also contribute to
the etiology of disturbance. Kohut's later theorizing offers little
acknowledgment, however, of any other components, as he strives
to make the narcissistic factors predominant in all sorts of disorders. Consistent with his goal of subsuming a wide spectrum of
pathology within the narcissistic framework, there is little differentiation between the variety of pathologies encountered in analytic work that are compatible with a varied, differentiated nomenclature. Therefore, his theory may have most value when it is
restricted to accounting for pathology in the narcissistic sector of
personality functioning. Within such a restriction, Kohut's original
intention of bringing together elements of classical psychoanalysis,
ego psychology, and object relations theory in the form of self psychology is accomplished. In this mixture of two lines of development, of classical instinct theory and object relations theory,
even though the combination is not perfect, quite different sorts
of psychopathology can be etiologically and symptomatically
differentiated.

Another theorist addressing relatively severe psychopathology
from a perspective that seeks to combine elements of psychoanal-

ysis, ego psychology, and object relations theory is Otto Kernberg. In the following section, the work of Kernberg will be set forth.

OTTO KERNBERG

Kernberg combines extensive elements of Freudian and ego psychological theory with those of object relations theory in order to develop a means of understanding the diagnosis, etiology, and treatment of relatively severe pathology. His approach relies on classical analytic constructs such as drives, the structural theory encompassing the agencies of the ego, id, and superego, and Freud's metapsychology. From ego psychology, Kernberg retains an emphasis on the importance of a maturational sequence, neutralized drive energy, and the development of self- and object-images as representational phenomena. From object relations theory, Kernberg retains an emphasis on the development of images of the self and object from nuances of the infant's relationship with its mother, and on the imprint this forms, which strongly affects later relationships as well as self-regulation. His focus on the internalizations of the infant's early relationship with its mother and the influence of these internalizations on later relationships, on psychopathology, anxiety, and on the utilization of particular levels of defense mechanisms is a distinct theoretical amalgamation of object relations theory within an ego psychology framework.

The Diagnostic Framework and Accompanying Defense Mechanisms

The scope and application of Kernberg's theory encompasses the relatively severe pathology occurring in narcissistic and borderline disorders. He classifies such disturbances as at the lower end of the severity dimension of character disorders. A major consistency that appears with the types of patients Kernberg's theory addresses—a consistency that is a reflection of his theoretical focus itself—is the clinical presence of various primitive defense mechanisms in patients. He offers detailed analyses of these mechanisms, as they appear in the treatment situation and as they embody relatively primitive developmental and dysfunctional elements of the particular psychopathology his theory considers.

The primitive defenses characteristically used by the patients that Kernberg's theory addresses include splitting, projective identification, devaluation, and idealization. Reliance on such primitive defenses reflects chaotic, fluid qualities in ego functioning among these patients, as well as early relationship disturbances which cannot be integrated into more mature interpersonal patterns.

For Kernberg, the gradual development of more mature relating patterns that assimilate earlier ones is known as *metabolism*. Metabolism, a process of more mature development, enables formation of an adaptive structuring of psychological functioning. The persistence of nonmetabolized, early, primitive relationships and psychic structures typifies the character disorders from which Kernberg's theory derives. Such persons persist, for example, in repeating behavior that reflects archaic psychological functioning. This repetition or acting-out reflects the problem of inadequate development, in which the individual cannot integrate and organize experience more adaptively. When cognitive capacities and ego maturation are underdeveloped, then the contrasting emotions accompanying experience—good or bad affects—become the organizers of experience. The reliance on emotional organizers creates the circumstance by which emotion of one affective type can be kept separate from its opposite type for defensive purposes. In the severe disturbances that Kernberg's theory focuses on, this defensive splitting is sustained as a pathological state.

Developmental Theory

In Kernberg's theory, the major experience that leads to the development of permanent psychic structure evolves through metabolization of the experiences which arise from the relationship between the infant and its mother. The relationship factors in maturation involve several elements that combine to form an internalization system. The first element of this system of internalization consists of a representation of the image of the self; the second element consists of a representation of the image of the object in the relationship; and the final element of the internalization system is an organizing affect—the emotional quality that is present during the mother-child involvement.

These three elements of internalization generate three internalization systems or mechanisms that occur in the normal developmental sequence. The first, *introjection*, is a primitive internalization system. This primitive level of internalization assimilates representations of the self and object that can be considered to be relatively undifferentiated. These primitive introjects are organized by the influence of extremely intense affect, and are therefore limited in their flexibility and functional potential.

The second mechanism of internalization is known as *identification*. Identification occurs when relatively specific roles of the people involved in the relationship—that is, the self and object— are understood, are not threatening, and are accepted. Identification typically proceeds within interactions in which the self and object are synergistic and thus offer each other a sense of mutuality and completeness. The emotional context that organizes this level of internalization is that of smooth and unobtrusive affect.

The final form of internalization, called *ego identity*, is an advanced and most sophisticated level of internalization. Ego identity is based on a stable view of objects along with an integrated experience of the self. One of the major functions of ego identity is the amalgamation of previous internalizations, which are sorted according to common affective qualities. Thus, in Kernberg's formulation, object relationships, and especially the mechanisms of their formation, are exceedingly prominent. Kernberg's view of drives is also distinctive, in that the drives are actually triggered by the affective quality of the interaction. Therefore, for Kernberg, the drives reflect the quality of interaction more than they do innate biological dispositions.

The Distinction Between Normal and Abnormal Development

Kernberg utilizes his conception of drive and internalization process to account for the greater number of negative than of positive introjects found in the psychopathology within the borderline diagnostic range. This predominance of negative introjects in borderline conditions is attributed to the probability that more frustrations than gratifications were experienced in early relationships, or to the postulate that aggressive drive has an inborn extra prominence.

In addition to the developmental sequence involving the internalization systems of introjection, identification, and ego identity, alterations as a function of more mature development also occur in several aspects of psychological functioning. These changes affect the nature of internal objects, the feelings promoting interpersonal relating, the ego, superego, and id structures of the mental apparatus, and the type of defense mechanisms most basically employed. As development proceeds, for example, the primitive mechanism of splitting with respect to good and bad parts of self- and object-representations recedes. With this reduced reliance on the defense of splitting, the good and bad aspects of the self-representation combine, as do the good and bad aspects of object-representations. Developmentally, this maturational combination allows for relating to proceed at higher levels, which can now encompass motivation based on factors that include more social considerations and the influence of an emerging conscience. These motivations involve emotions such as concern for others and guilt.

The development of an ego ideal occurs as part of this maturational process. The ego ideal acts both as a guide for behavior and as an integrator of the world of inner object representation. The effect of the ego ideal on inner object relations is to encourage their alignment with reality. As the integration between inner objects and external reality occurs, the higher-order defense mechanism of repression can be utilized in place of the less needed defense of splitting. The main purpose of repression occurs when primitive internalizations are incompatible with a more mature level of ego development: repression is then instituted in order to expel the immature internalizations and organizations to the unconscious. For Kernberg, it is at this point, the reliance upon repression, that the id appears as a structure in the mental apparatus. Thus, Kernberg postulates that the birth of the id follows the development of the ego as a higher-level structure that functions in an integrated manner with reality. When this normal maturational sequence cannot occur because of the inability for the good and bad aspects of self- and object-representations to merge, splitting is retained to separate positive and negative experiences relating to the self or objects, and higher-level functioning cannot evolve.

The pathological functioning that Kernberg describes in relation to splitting and the retention of primitive object relations is then sustained in the borderline personality organization.

Kernberg's Use of Ego Psychology and Object Relations

In spirit, Kernberg seeks to combine object relations with concepts of ego psychology. His theory relates to many ego psychology constructs—especially those of Hartmann and Jacobson. For example, Kernberg employs Hartmann's idea of autonomous ego functioning and his neutralized drive terminology, as well as relying strongly on Jacobson's representational world. Nevertheless, there are many differences in Kernberg's use of these ideas that reveal important influences of object relations theory. For example, in Hartmann's theory, neutralized drive energy can be invested in object relations. Kernberg reverses this: favorable object relations allow the neutralization of drive energy, promoting repression, development, and ego maturation. Further, Kernberg ultimately concludes that the motivational aspects of the drives—libido and aggression—develop from the accumulation of good and bad experiences. This concept of motivation is therefore dependent on internalized object relations, rather than on preexisting instinctual components.

With regard to the structure of the psychic apparatus, the id is no longer viewed as the unconscious source of drives that are biological givens and as a repository of abandoned object relations governed by the primary process. Instead, for Kernberg, the id only becomes a psychic structure after the establishment of repression, and it is characterized by the primary process because of the primitive quality of self- and object-representations that are internalized. Further, as stated above, the ego becomes a structure before the id. Thus, Kernberg's psychic structures appear to incorporate object relationships more than they do biological instincts. Last, in Kernberg's approach, psychosexual and aggressive conflicts are no longer the key to individual development and the etiology of psychopathology. Instead, early object relations, organized according to good or bad affective qualities, are the cornerstones of the development of pathology.

SUMMARY OF DIAGNOSTIC FORMULATIONS

The focus on early relationship factors in the context of instinctual drives harmonizes developments in object relations theory and ego psychology. In object relations theory, however, instinctual vicissitudes are minimized with regard to biological implications and programs, while in ego psychology relationships are focused by instinctual needs. Heinz Kohut and Otto Kernberg have utilized and generated conceptions of psychopathology that reflect elements of both object relations theory and ego psychology.

KOHUT

Narcissistic pathology is stressed by Kohut within a theoretical framework referred to as self psychology. The self becomes a separate, viable psychic structure following its own developmental line. Early experience of grandiosity and omnipotence reflects healthy caregiver-child relationships, involving adequate empathy from the caregiver, or self-object. Self-object idealization is also important, leading to a coalescing and cohesion of self. Kohut proposes the concept of transmuting internalization, through which cohesion and structuring of the self gradually occur. Deficiencies in the structuring of the self can result in a variety of narcissistic pathologies involving faulty regulation of self-esteem. Instinct theory is largely eclipsed by emphasis on the importance of object relations in development, even though Freudian and ego psychology frameworks are employed in various stages of theory.

KERNBERG

Although Kernberg utilizes Freudian metapsychology, the importance of internalized interpersonal experience aligns his theory with object relations, within an ego psychology framework. Narcissistic and borderline conditions and concepts of splitting, devaluation, idealization, and projective identification are central concerns for Kernberg. He proposes that in borderline and narcissistic conditions, metabolism—a form of maturing by assimilating earlier relating patterns—is not sufficiently developed. Emotions and acting-out then dominate the personality. Mother-child contact is the matrix from which the nature or the success of maturation is determined. Kernberg proposes introjection, identification, and ego identity as three basic kinds of internalization during normal development. Kernberg's psychic apparatus also permits object relations paradigms to take precedence over drive theory.

Table 19.1 presents some of the diagnostic syndromes focused on by Kohut and Kernberg.

TABLE 19.1: Diagnostic Syndromes Referred to by
Kohut and Kernberg

Kohut
Narcissistic personality disorder
The clinical problem of narcissism associated with other disorders
Neurotic pathology as derivative of narcissistic pathology

Kernberg
Character disorder
Narcissistic pathology
Borderline pathology
Neurosis

Conclusion

This survey of historical developments since antiquity has revealed two major orientations that recurrently, in one form or another, have been used to account for the nature of personality functioning and pathological deviations: the biological-organic approach, and the introspective or psychological approach.

The first, the biological, organic, or neurological conception, seeks to explain psychological functioning on the basis of the physical, physiological, and material structures of the individual. The precursors to this view start as early as the Hippocratic theory of humors and include even earlier concepts of visitations and intrusions by supernatural beings. This point of view suggests the utilization of physical agents, chemical admixtures, and, more recently, biological treatments to modify pathogenic substances within the body. This physical approach is strongly represented in the contemporary field in psychiatric methods associated with hospital settings, in laboratory studies of psychopathological phenomena, and in brain research with direct pharmacological implications.

The biological approaches to the understanding and treatment of emotional disorder seem to have substantial value in relieving the anguish of extreme crises, terrifying anxiety, and some chronic psychotic conditions. However, the philosophical implications regarding the material nature of psychopathology, and the reliance on such physical control mechanisms as, for example, chemical agents, can interfere with the understanding to be gained through the examination of interpersonal conflict and through an emphasis on the importance of insight and personal struggle with regard to psychological conflict. On the other hand, however, claims are also made that psychotherapy itself can obstruct successful alleviation of a disorder by its tendency to disallow any physical explanations for the etiology of psychopathology.

The conceptualization of emotional disturbance in material terms has been throughout history, as it remains currently, associated with an essentially medical view of psychopathology. This medical view has been applied in a wide variety of approaches to treatment. At times—during Greek antiquity, for example—treatment has consisted of an attempt to rebalance the patient's inner humors. Later, the Romans, and even investigators in the early part of the twentieth century, used cold and hot baths as a treatment. In the eighteenth century, a typical control mechanism and so-called treatment for a variety of bizarre behaviors was to imprison and chain the sufferer. As recently as the 1950s, many thousands of patients were lobotomized, inducing in each one a permanent condition usually referred to as the vegetable state. Even as this page is being written, there are places in the world where another bizarre application of the physical approach to treatment is being made: the use of pharmacology to control a person's political orientation and preferences. Most of these methods are now judged to have been primitive and irrelevant at best, and at worst, quite cruel.

In contemporary society, the biological approach continues to exert enormous influence on treatment methodology. This approach largely advocates the application of psychotropic and other varieties of drugs that affect emotion and thinking; lithium is used to manage manic-depressive psychosis, thorazine to manage schizophrenia, and elavil to manage depressive reactions, just to name a few. In addition, the new information and ferment derived from brain research promises further to fuel the philosophy of the biological model, the approaches to treatment that derive from this philosophy, and the development of pure description as the essence of diagnostic nosologies.

This nonintrospective approach has also influenced treatment methodologies which do not involve biological treatment, but are nevertheless philosophically compatible with the biological model. An example of such methodologies is behavior therapy. An element of external control and the imposition of structure rather than the use of dialogue and introspection characterize this mode of treatment; in this way, behavior therapy becomes aligned with the medical model.

In many cases, these contemporary approaches to the treatment of psychopathology yield positive results. For example, elavil does alleviate neurotic depression; thorazine does seem to reduce bizarre schizophrenic symptoms; electric shock does seem to alleviate psychotic depression. Yet, it should also be noted that hot and cold baths did occasionally alleviate bizarre symptoms, and at times the rebalancing of humors, which required doctor-patient interaction, was similarly effective; physical restraints did quiet patients, and lobotomies did cure excess aggression. The point is that in the management of people, desired results can be obtained from a wide variety of methods—some humane, others cruel. What is noteworthy, however, is that a gradient of control exists in such treatment applications, ranging from total control over a person, as in the inexcusable permanence of lobotomies and damage to the brain by pharmacological treatment in the service of political persuasion and torture, to temporary control, as in the administration of mild tranquilizers. This physical approach to treatment reflects the nonintrospective pragmatic tradition that has existed throughout the history of psychopathology. In this physical tradition, the authority of the practitioner controls and structures the diagnosis and treatment with respect to a passive, compliant, or even unwilling role for the patient.

The second major trend throughout the history of the development of the understanding of personality dysfunctions and their treatment is represented by the introspective tradition. Also emanating from antiquity in the soul-searching dialogues of Plato and Socrates and in the Greek tragedians' investigation of guilt and interpersonal conflict, this introspective-dynamic approach reached its full flowering two thousand years later, in Freud's investigation of intrapsychic conflict and personality development. What distinguishes this introspective point of view is the consideration of emotional distress and psychopathology as essentially psychological matters that are not material in any practical sense, but are instead related to intangible inner conflicts, patterns of living, and interpersonal strains. Within this second tradition, the essence of treatment and the alleviation of symptoms is the progress the individual makes in improving his own stance and adjustment through the assistance of a therapeutic ally who verbally interacts with him within a helping relationship.

Since Freud, there has been a ferment in theory and technique largely concerned with the issue of control, with allowing the patient to be as free as possible from the control of the therapist. In addition, introspective methods have also been increasingly applied to more severe pathologies. Such a development addresses a basic, underlying philosophical problem: are the resources to ameliorate an individual's disturbance present within the individual? Or does the individual lack sufficient capacity for self-adjustment? And if the resources for change are available within the individual, can they be activated for the purposes of such growth? Each of the two traditions described provides an answer. The biological tradition seems to view the issue as being relatively unimportant, so that this tradition, since it avoids offering the opportunity for introspection, becomes self-generating in terms of its own development. The introspective, psychogenic tradition answers resoundingly in the affirmative, that the resources for change do exist in the individual and that treatment technologies can be developed to foster emotional and psychological change even without imposing control over the individual—or especially without the imposition of control.

At certain points in the history of the study of personality and psychopathology, the two traditions described here have intersected in a way that helped create the precursors to current nosologies such as *DSM-III* and *DSM-III-R*, leading to *DSM-IV*. Typologies, for example, originate out of each tradition, and their formation seems to have created a mechanism for blending the disparate biological and psychogenic philosophies.

These typologies, even those created by investigators from the introspective tradition, contain an implicit assumption that all people fall into a limited and specified number of categories; therefore, an oblique sense is generated that there is either some biological basis for this arrangement, or that culture is arranged in such a way that only a few kinds of personalities can emerge and that this arrangement is perhaps immutable. This confluence of the philosophical underpinnings of both the biological and psychogenic tradition provided the *DSM-I, II, III,* and *III-R* nosologies with their historical imperative—that is, their context as descriptive structures. On the other hand, the psychoanalytic, psychodynamic, and newer theories—especially those of the ego, self, and object relations psychologies—provide a compelling counterpoint to pure description in the domain of diagnosis and psychopathology. These newer approaches to the understanding of personality create a coexisting imperative that calls for the development of a theoretical underpinning to all diagnostic nosology and to the understanding of psychopathology and personality.

In volume 2, *The Diagnostic Primer,* the implications of this debate of description versus theory will become evident, and wherever possible, theoretical formulations will be brought to bear on the differential diagnostic problem.

REFERENCES AND SUGGESTED READINGS

Historical Roots of Psychopathology and Diagnosis

The following readings include analyses of psychopathology and diagnosis from antiquity through the Middle Ages, the Renaissance, and the modern world, including the Age of Enlightenment of the eighteenth century and the nineteenth century up to the appearance of Sigmund Freud.

Ackerknect, E. H. 1959. *A Short History of Psychiatry*. New York and London: Hafner.

Alexander, F. G. and S. T. Selesnick. 1966. *The History of Psychiatry: An Evaluation of Psychiatric Thought from Prehistoric Times to the Present*. New York: Harper and Row.

Altschule, M. 1957. *Roots of Modern Psychiatry*. New York: Grune and Stratton.

Barbu, Z. 1960. *The Emergence of Personality in the Greek World: Problems of Historical Psychology*. New York: Grove Press.

Dodds, E. R. 1964. *The Greeks and the Irrational*. Los Angeles: University of California Press.

Foucault, M. 1965. *Madness and Civilization: A History of Insanity in the Age of Reason*. New York: Pantheon Books.

Gladston, I., ed. 1967. *Historic Derivations of Modern Psychiatry*. New York: McGraw-Hill.

Gold, H. R. 1957. *Psychiatry and the Talmud*. Vol. 1, no. 1. New York: Jewish Heritage.

Homer. 1931. *The Iliad*. Cambridge, Mass.: Harvard University Press, Loeb Classical Library vols. 1–4.

Homer. 1931. *The Odyssey*. Cambridge Mass.: Harvard University Press, Loeb Classical Library vols. 1–4.

Howells, J. G., ed. 1975. *World History of Psychiatry*. New York: Bruner/Mazel.

Lain-Entralgo, P. 1970. *The Therapy of the Word in Classical Antiquity*. New Haven: Yale University Press.

Murphy, G. 1949. *Historical Introduction to Modern Psychology*. New York: Harcourt, Brace.

Robinson, T. M. 1970. *Plato's Psychology*. Toronto: University of Toronto Press.

Simon, B. 1978. *Mind and Madness in Ancient Greece: The Classical Roots of Modern Psychiatry*. Ithaca, N.Y.: Cornell University Press.

Zilboorg, G. 1935. *The Medical Man and the Witch During the Renaissance*. Baltimore: Johns Hopkins University Press.

Zilboorg, G., with G. W. Henry. 1941. *A History of Medical Psychology*. New York: Norton.

Pre-Freudian Roots, Freud, and Followers of Freud

The following readings include studies of the pre-Freudian origins of the idea of the unconscious and psychoanalysis, works by Freud, and references to investigators who were either colleagues of Freud or early rivals whose own approaches were nevertheless strongly influenced by Freud's dynamic emphasis.

Adler, A. 1951. *The Practice and Theory of Individual Psychology*. New York: Humanities Press.

Adler, A. 1956. *The Individual Psychology of Alfred Adler*. New York: Basic Books.

Arlow, J. and C. Brenner. 1964. *Psychoanalytic Concepts and the Structural Theory*. New York: International Universities Press.

Chapman, A. H. 1976. *Harry Stack Sullivan: The Man and His Work*. New York: Putnam.

Chertok, L. and R. de Saussure. 1971. *The Therapeutic Revolution: From Mesmer to Freud*. New York: Bruner/Mazel.

Ellenberger, H. F. 1970. *The Discovery of the Unconscious: The History and Evolution of Dynamic Psychiatry*. New York: Basic Books.

Erikson, E. 1963. *Childhood and Society*. 2d. ed. New York: Norton.

Freud, Anna. 1966. *The Ego and the Mechanisms of Defense*. In *The Writings of Anna Freud*, vol. 2. New York: International Universities Press.

Freud, Sigmund. *The Standard Edition of the Complete Psychological Works of Sigmund Freud*. 24 vols. James Strachey, ed. London: Hogarth Press, 1953–1974.

    1900. *The Interpretation of Dreams*. Vols. 4 and 5.

    1905. *Three Essays on the Theory of Sexuality*. Vol. 7.

    1920. *Beyond the Pleasure Principle*. Vol. 18.

    1923. *The Ego and the Id*. Vol. 19.

    1926. *The Problem of Anxiety*. Vol. 20.

Horney, K. 1939. *New Ways in Psychoanalysis*. New York: Norton.

Horney, K. 1950. *Neurosis and Human Growth*. New York: Norton.

Jung, C. G. 1960. *The Psychogenesis of Mental Disease*. In *Collected Works*, vol. 3. New York: Pantheon Books.

Riese, W. 1958. *The Pre-Freudian Origins of Psychoanalysis*. In J. Masserman, ed., *Science and Psychoanalysis*. New York: Grune and Stratton.

Sullivan, H. S. 1953. *The Interpersonal Theory of Psychiatry*. New York: Norton.

Whyte, L. L. 1960. *The Unconscious Before Freud*. New York: Basic Books.

Diagnostics

The following readings include accounts of historical conceptions of schizophrenia and hysteria as well as of diagnosis and diagnostic nomenclature.

Arieti, S. 1955. *Interpretation of Schizophrenia*. New York: Brunner.
Bleuler, E. 1912. *Dementia Praecox or the Group of Schizophrenias*. New York: International Universities Press, 1950.
Breuer, J. and S. Freud. 1895. *Studies on Hysteria*. In *The Standard Edition of the Complete Psychological Works of Sigmund Freud*, vol. 2. James Strachey, ed. London: Hogarth Press, 1955.
Diagnostic and Statistical Manual of Mental Disorders. 1980. 3d ed. Washington, D.C.: American Psychiatric Association.
Diagnostic and Statistical Manual of Mental Disorders. 1987. Rev. 3d ed. Washington, D.C.: American Psychiatric Association.
Kraepelin, E. 1962. *One Hundred Years of Psychiatry*. New York: Citadel Press.
Rorschach, H. 1949. *Psychodiagnostics*. New York: Grune and Stratton.
Sheldon, W. H. 1940. *Varieties of Human Physique*. New York: Harper.
Sullivan, H. S. 1962. *Schizophrenia as a Human Process*. New York: Norton.
Veith, I. 1965. *Hysteria: The History of a Disease*. Chicago: University of Chicago Press.

Personality, Ego Psychology, and Object Relations

The following readings concern the shaping of personality, largely in the form of ego psychology perspectives and object relations theory.

Ausubel, D. P. and D. Kirk. 1977. *Ego Psychology and Mental Disorder: A Developmental Approach to Psychopathology*. New York: Grune and Stratton.
Barron, F. 1979. *The Shaping of Personality: Conflict, Choice, and Growth*. New York: Harper and Row.
Blanck, Gertrude and R. Blanck. 1974. *Ego Psychology: Theory and Practice*. New York: Columbia University Press.
Blanck, Gertrude and R. Blanck. 1979. *Ego Psychology II: Psychoanalytic Developmental Psychology*. New York: Columbia University Press.
Fairbairn, W. R. D. 1952. *An Object-Relations Theory of the Personality*. New York: Basic Books.
Greenberg, J. R. and S. A. Mitchell. 1983. *Object Relations in Psychoanalytic Theory*. Cambridge: Harvard University Press.
Guntrip, H. 1971. *Psychoanalytic Theory, Therapy, and the Self*. New York: Basic Books.
Hall, C. S. and G. Lindzey, eds. 1970. *Theories of Personality*. 2d ed. New York: Wiley.
Hartmann, H. 1958. *Ego Psychology and the Problem of Adaptation*. New York: International Universities Press.
Hartmann, H. 1964. *Essays on Ego Psychology*. New York: International Universities Press.
Jacobson, Edith. 1964. *The Self and the Object World*. New York: International Universities Press.
Jacobson, Edith. 1971. *Depression: Comparative Studies of Normal, Neurotic, and Psychotic Conditions*. New York: International Universities Press.
Kernberg, O. 1975. *Borderline Conditions and Pathological Narcissism*. New York: Jason Aronson.

Kernberg, O. 1976. *Object Relations Theory and Clinical Psychoanalysis.* New York: Jason Aronson.

Klein, M. 1964. *Contributions to Psychoanalysis, 1921–1945.* New York: McGraw-Hill.

Kohut, H. 1971. *The Analysis of the Self.* New York: International Universities Press.

Kohut, H. 1977. *The Restoration of the Self.* New York: International Universities Press.

Mahler, Margaret. 1968. *On Human Symbiosis and the Vicissitudes of Individuation.* New York: International Universities Press.

Mahler, Margaret, F. Pine, and A. Bergman. 1975. *The Psychological Birth of the Human Infant: Symbiosis and Individuation.* New York: Basic Books.

Schultz, D. 1976. *Theories of Personality.* Monterey, Calif.: Brooks-Cole.

Segal, H. 1964. *Introduction to the Work of Melanie Klein.* New York: Basic Books.

Shapiro, D. 1965. *Neurotic Styles.* New York: Basic Books.

Spitz, R. 1959. *A Genetic Field Theory of Ego Formation.* New York: International Universities Press.

Spitz, R. A. 1965. *The First Year of Life.* New York: International Universities Press.

Winnicott, D. W. 1958. *Through Paediatrics to Psychoanalysis.* London: Hogarth Press.

Winnicott, D. W. 1965. *The Maturational Process and the Facilitating Environment.* New York: International Universities Press.

Index

Aberrant behavior, 3, 8, 12, 75; attribution to external agents, 3-4, 5, 6, 7, 12; diagnosis as code for, 16; first classification of, 16-17; in Hippocrates, 11-12; inferential constructs in, 11, 12; in Plato, 23-25; possibility of change in, 21-22; psychosomatic sector of, 34

Abnormal psychology, 16, 21, 22, 86

Abreaction, 26, 107, 115

Acting-out, 6, 184, 234, 238; anxiety in, 37

Acute conditions, 76-77

Adaptation, 37, 38, 185, 194, 204; anxiety and, 163; in ego development, 183, 186-91, 196, 203; in Freud's typology, 145; reason as key element in, 70; role of ego in, 185-86; role of mother in, 193

Adaptive ego function, 189-90

Adaptive striving (concept), 169-70

Adaptive theory (Freud), 119-20

Adjustment (concept), 36-37, 38

Adler, Alfred, 163, 166-72, 176, 177

Affect(s), 84, 85, 98, 128; in Aristotle, 27-28; in depression, 201; disturbances of, 84, 188; dynamic framework for, 103-04; good/bad, 234; in hysteria, 132; organizing, 235

Aggression, 89, 117, 133, 237; in anal types, 141, 142; deflected toward self, 202; impaired interpersonal relations and, 213,

214-15, 222; in infancy, 208-10; as instinct, 207

Aggressive drives, 184, 193, 197, 207, 210-11, 222, 236; development of, 198

Alienation, 153, 155

Altruism, 153-56, 162

Anaclytic depression, 195, 204

Anal: anal aggressive type, 142; anal expulsive type, 142; anal retentive type, 142, 154; anal stage, 116, 158, 211

Anesthesias, 114

Anesthetic temperament, 135

Anger, 27, 89, 211; as basic emotion, 16; and illness, 34; reactive, 230, 231; suppression of, 6

Ambivalence, 70, 128

Animal magnetism theory, 73-74

"Anna O." (patient), 115

Annihilation anxiety, 218, 223

Anthony, St., 44

Antiquity, 52, 226, 243; preservation of psychological writings of, 48-50; psychopathology in, 3-10; Roman civilization in, 31, 36; typologies in, 125-26

Anxiety, 25, 67, 69, 72, 103-04, 143, 145, 202, 227; in Adler, 167, 172; basic, 150, 151, 214; in developmental stage crises, 162; in ego psychology, 203-04; in Epicurianism and Stoicism, 36-37, 38, 39; as essential phenomenon in understanding personality and